THE PENTAGON UNDERGROUND

THE PENTAGON UNDERGROUND

DINA RASOR

Times
BOOKS

To Thomas, my parents, and the Bon

Copyright © 1985 by Dina Rasor
All rights reserved under International and
Pan-American Copyright Conventions. Published in the
United States by Times Books, a division of Random
House, Inc., New York, and simultaneously in Canada
by Random House of Canada Limited, Toronto.

Library of Congress Cataloging in Publication Data
Rasor, Dina, 1956–
    The Pentagon underground.
    Includes index.
    1. United States—Armed Forces—Procurement.
2. Whistle blowing—United States.   3. Rasor, Dina,
1956–   .   4. Project on Military Procurement (U.S.)
I. Title.
UC263.R37   1985   355.6'212'0973   85-40262
ISBN 0-8129-1249-7

Grateful acknowledgment is made to the following for
permission to reprint previously published material:
The Boston Globe: "Lockheed's Battle for a Plane: An Inside
View," by Fred Kaplan, June 22, 1982. Reprinted courtesy
of *The Boston Globe.*
Chicago Sun-Times: "Army Tests 5 M-1 Tanks-All Flunk,"
article by Bruce Ingersoll. © News Group Chicago, Inc.,
1985. Reprinted with permission of the *Chicago Sun-Times.*
Conservative Digest: "One Man's Battle with the U.S. Army,"
by Donna Martin. Reprinted from *Conservative Digest,*
November 1983.
Knight-Ridder Newspapers: "Despite Law, Air Force
Lobbying for Lockheed Jet," by Frank Greve, Knight-Ridder
Newspapers.
St. Louis Post-Dispatch: "GAO: Pentagon's Lobbying on Jet
Illegal," by Bob Adams, copyright 1982, *St. Louis Post-
Dispatch.* Reprinted with permission.
The Washington Monthly: "The Flying Lazarus," by Fred Kaplan,
February 1983. Reprinted from *The Washington Monthly.*

Manufactured in the United States of America
9 8 7 6 5 4 3 2
First Edition

ACKNOWLEDGMENTS

THIS BOOK and the organization that inspired it, the Project on Military Procurement, would not have been possible without the unfailing help of many individuals. Obviously, I cannot name the individuals in the Pentagon underground, who, at great personal risk, guided me through so many investigations. However, I want them to know the depths of my appreciation.

The Project staff helped to greatly expand the scope of the organization and were a great help in assisting me with the many factual details of this book. Donna Martin, Paul Hoven, Joseph Burniece, and Marsha Cunningham of the staff deserve the credit of babysitting me through my various crises in writing this book.

The board of directors of the Project's parent organization, the Fund for Constitutional Government, has helped the Project survive and expand and was tolerant of our nonideological approach. Special thanks goes to board members Anne Zill, Stewart Mott, and Nancy Ramsey for their support.

My thanks also goes to my book agent, Andrew Wylie, for convincing me that I should write this book and to my book

editor at Times Books, Elisabeth Scharlatt, for patiently explaining all the steps in book writing and assuring me that I was capable of doing it. A special thanks goes to my friend Alfred Johnson for helping me survive the last minute fact-checking for the book and for being a friend during that period. Ernest Fitzgerald deserves much of the credit for keeping Washington and the Pentagon from overwhelming me and for teaching me, with a wonderful sense of humor, how the system works.

I want to thank my parents, Ned and Genevieve Rasor, for teaching me to try and to take chances and for giving me the emotional and financial backup to make me not afraid to try to achieve my goals.

Much of the credit of the success of the Project and the completion of this book goes to my husband, Thom Lawson, who not only supported my decision to start the Project and write this book but also put aside his own career plans during the hard times to work long and hard for the Project for free until funding was secured. His level-headed advice has kept me steady during the great ups and downs of the last five years. The Project and his wife owe him a great deal.

Dina Rasor
June 1985

CONTENTS

PREFACE

I had to be persuaded to write this book for several reasons. First, I felt that there had already been some excellent scholarly books written on the subject of military reform, and I did not think I could do a better job. Second, many people wanted me to write a book about myself. Because I have been trained as a journalist, I was uncomfortable about bringing myself and my experiences into anything I would write about the Pentagon underground. Finally, I was persuaded that I could write a book to help the average person understand what was going on in the Pentagon and could also give the Pentagon underground the recognition it so richly deserves.

Five years ago I knew nothing about the Pentagon or military life. In fact, I learned about the order of military rank by watching *M*A*S*H* reruns. Then, little by little, with the guidance of the underground, I came to understand why the Pentagon establishment and the Congress were not providing us with an effective defense program. I want to take the readers through the process of my education and let them experience the skepticism and then the outrage I felt as this story was laid out to me by the underground. The first four chapters take the reader through that process, and the last five chapters explain, through examples, why the system acts the way it does with the press, Congress, and the public.

I also want to give readers a peek at the people in the underground—and show their courage, patriotism, honesty, and even some of their faults. If this story of what is wrong with our nation's defense makes an impact on the citizens of this country, credit must go to the foresight and courage of the underground. These people, after spending most of their military careers trying to work within the system, decided that they had to go outside the system in order to save it. These members of the underground are the real heroes in this story. I happened to be at the right place at the right time.

Conversations presented are based on my notes at the time. Whenever possible I reviewed my memory with those who were present with me when the conversations took place and also with those with whom I had related conversations shortly after they occurred. Though I don't claim they are verbatim, I vouch for their essential accuracy.

It is my hope that I've made clear the story behind the stories of overpriced spare parts and the weapons systems that don't work. I believe that if we understand the system that produces these problems, we, as Americans, can work together to convince the Pentagon and the Congress that we want a national defense that will work for the soldiers at a reasonable price, a price that will not unnecessarily add to our national debt.

The
Pentagon
Underground

1.

BREAKTHROUGH

IN THE LATE AFTERNOON of February 17, 1981, there was a knock at the door of my office, a one-room cubicle on Capitol Hill. As I threaded my way around my cluttered desk to answer it, the door swung open on a lanky man with piercing eyes.

"May I help you?" I asked.

"Are you Dina Rasor?" he said softly.

"Yes," I replied and offered him a seat.

"I understand you're investigating the M-1 tank," he said, once again so softly that I strained to hear him. "We have some test results that you might be interested in."

I assumed any weapon test results would be classified. This character's probably from the Pentagon and is trying to plant a classified document on me, I thought. "Who are you?" I asked.

He mumbled his name, which meant nothing to me, and launched into a rambling explanation of the M-1 and its many technical failures. He was shifting in his seat and darting his eyes back and forth. This guy is a real cloak-and-dagger type, I thought.

Finally, after mumbling some vague answers to my questions about where this document came from and whether or not it was classified, he volunteered a name. "You should call this guy," he said, "and he will give you the document." Then he rose dramatically and declared that if the document was released, it would mean the end of the M-1 program. With that he was gone.

The name he gave me was familiar. A journalist I knew to be reliable had told me that this man—I'll call him Smith—would be a good person to contact concerning technical questions on the M-1, but had not said anything about any documents. I had not contacted Smith because I did not have any technical data and was concentrating on the cost-overrun problem of the M-1. I was extremely suspicious of the man who had just left my office, and I had second thoughts about Smith if he was working with him.

I called Ernest Fitzgerald, the famous whistle-blower in the Department of Defense (DOD) and one of the people who had convinced me to start an organization to expose Pentagon fraud and waste—the Project on Military Procurement. He had never heard of the man who had just left, but he had heard of Smith. "I hear he's a good guy," he said. Fitzgerald told me what little he knew about this man, and we ended the conversation.

Well, I thought, it's about time I check out this lead, even though his name was given to me this time by a suspicious source. I dialed the number. Smith did not seem surprised to hear from me. However, when I asked him for a copy of the M-1 test results there was a long pause, and I grew uncomfortable. "I'll give you the title and serial numbers of the report, but I won't give you the report," he said.

"Is it classified?" I asked.

"No," Smith replied, "it's labeled 'For official use only,'[1] but it's not classified." He assured me that there were no criminal sanctions for receiving the material.

Next he read me the title of the report: "Customer Test of

Fort Knox XM-1 Extended FSED Durability/Reliability Test, Phase II and Final Report, 18 April 1980. U.S. Army, Armor and Engineer Board, Fort Knox, Kentucky, TRADOC Trms No. 9-000158."[2]

Smith told me to call him again if I had any questions about the test results. I sat back and reread the report title: it sounded hopelessly complicated. What was I getting myself into?

In the course of the next three weeks, I made dozens of phone calls to the Army, to no avail. The bureaucrats I reached either proclaimed ignorance of the existence of the report or told me that it was classified. That left me with no other alternative than to use the Freedom of Information Act. I filed the requests, but I knew from experience that it would take months to process and receive an answer and then I probably would be turned down anyway.

On March 11, I contacted Smith again and explained the situation. He was not surprised by my call. "Come over to my office and I'll show you the report," he said.

After a short subway ride I walked across to a gleaming office building in the heart of downtown Washington. I entered and headed for the nearest restroom. I looked up in the mirror and my heart fell. What am I doing here? I thought. This guy is going to laugh at me. I look like a high school girl even though I'm a few days from my twenty-fifth birthday. I puffed up my hair, added some more makeup, then reexamined myself. That adds about a year, I thought dryly.

The secretary at the front desk led me through a maze of hallways to a small and cluttered room. There sat my source, an average-looking middle-aged man with graying temples. He smirked when he saw me and led me back to a conference room. (Later, when I asked Smith what he had thought when we met, he replied that I'd seemed a little "green" to be in the weapons business.) In the center of an otherwise bare wood table lay the test report I had tried so hard to get. Smith marched quickly to the far end of the room, motioned for me to sit down, looked me directly in the eyes, and said, "Let's talk tanks."

I reached into my bag for a pad and pen. I knew nothing about tanks and had never seen one outside the movies, but the thick report on the table intrigued me, and I settled down to listen. Several times in the course of Smith's three-hour lecture, my eyes glazed over as he dove deeper into the technical issues of what a tank must do in battle and how the Army's new tank, the M-1, failed to meet even the minimum standards of battlefield survivability, given its dismal performance in the most recent operational tests. Smith saw my predicament and carefully explained the M-1's faults in terms that I could understand. I left the session armed with the rest report, a pile of notes, and a glimmer of understanding of the strategy and goals of tank warfare.

I asked my new source about the mysterious character who had shown up in my office and freely given me Smith's name. He made a face and advised me to steer clear of this character. I later found out that Smith was willing to see me on the advice of a friendly journalist.

The next day, as I began to read the test results, I realized that I should not have been so worried about understanding the technical details. The disastrous history of the design and procurement of the M-1 became clear even to me. Although I didn't understand the jargon of the report and didn't have enough knowledge of the details of tank warfare to confirm what Smith had claimed, I found a section about the serious and frequent failures of the engine, transmission, and final drive of the tank. No one could reasonably dispute the vital necessity of a reliable drive system, yet the executive summary of the second operational test (OT II) barely mentioned the problem. I later found out that most decision-makers in the Pentagon and in Congress rarely look at the details of weapon tests; they base their decision on whether to go ahead with full production of a weapon on executive summaries of the tests.

Even more astonishing than the terrible performance of the engine and the power train was the apparent cheating by the Army on the M-1 test. The total mileage racked up by three tanks in the test was 16,070.4 miles. During the testing period 1007 "maintenance actions" were recorded. Taken in raw form, this meant that the tanks had a problem approximately every 16 miles. Of course, it was reasonable to assume that at least some of those maintenance actions, which can be as minor as changing a light bulb, represented trivial problems that would not seriously hamper a tank's performance in combat.

The Army, however, took this logic far beyond any reasonable threshold of credibility. In interpreting the raw data from the test results Smith gave me, it appeared that the Army's scoring conference,[3] a group of senior officers and civilians from various commands, had thrown out 836 of the 1007 maintenance actions. This gave the tank only 171 "chargeable" or "recorded" maintenance failures of the 1007 failures actually noted—or 93.97 mean miles between failures.

When I saw these numbers in the test documents, I thought that perhaps the scoring conference knew something about the tank that I didn't. But as I flipped through the computer printout of the failure log that was kept during the testing of the tank, I noticed that the operational test director (the field officer directing the tank test) had also noted which tank failures required *immediate* maintenance in order to prevent much worse trouble. Luckily, he had recorded the numbers, and with the help of my newly found source, I counted up the test director's score and discovered that the tank actually failed seriously every 34 miles—against the Army's own requirement that the tank go 101 miles between failures at this stage of development.

Another statistic that came out of this operational test was the serious rate of failure of the tank's power train—the engine, the transmission, and the final drive. The power train is the most important part of any land vehicle, whether it is a car, a tractor, or a tank. And when there is a power-train failure in a tank during a battle, the crew stands a good chance of being killed. There will be no tow truck to pull them out during the heat of the battle.

Yet the M-1 had failed miserably to meet the Army's own requirement for the power train.[4] The Army had set up the requirement that 50 percent of the M-1 tanks had to go 4000 miles without requiring a power-train overhaul (that is, replacing or rebuilding the engine, transmission, and final drive). The rate that the M-1 had achieved during this operational test was only 22 percent according to the Army's own scoring, less than half of the requirement. It was easy to check this rate for accuracy, because the major engine, transmission, and final-drive failures were listed in the back of the report in the computer failure log.

Although these statistics were some of the most damning in the OT II test results, they were by no means the only problems with the tank. Many other failures of design and equipment, which may seem trivial compared to the power-train failures, were also reported in the test results. These failures, which could also prove to be fatal on the battlefield, included:[5]

—There was leaking flammable hydraulic fluid in the crew compartment of the tank. Fire inside a tank is one of the disasters most feared by tankers.

—The design of the mounted tank commander's machine gun made firing it with any control or accuracy almost impossible.

—The tank's treads had a very short life span. They were supposed to last 2000 miles, but were lasting only around 850 miles during the test.

—Bad ventilation inside the tank allowed personnel heater fumes and excessive heat to accumulate in the crew compartment of the tank.

—Dust filters for the gas turbine engine had to be taken out and cleaned every 75 to 100 miles of operation in a dusty environment. Tanks often operate under dusty conditions. Consider the risk a soldier would have to take to get out and clean the dust filters in a hostile zone. An ABC news program had pointed out this failure of the M-1 about a year earlier, but the Army claimed that the problem had been corrected.

—Because of the tank design, the driver of the M-1 tank could not see 27 feet of ground immediately in front of the tank. This blind spot could be fatal to him and could mean destruction of the tank if he could not see to avoid a land mine or a sudden deep ditch.

—Although the M-1 tank holds 500 gallons of fuel, it was able to go only 250 miles on a tank of diesel fuel in normal use (instead of the 275 miles required by the Army at that point in the test), and only 130 miles under combat conditions. The average speed during the test was only 10 miles an hour (the top speed is around 40 miles an hour) and the tank averaged only approximately 4 gallons to the mile. (NOTE: Read that again; it was 4 *gallons* to go one mile, not 4 miles to the gallon.) Refueling is obviously hazardous on a battlefield, and there are historical examples of tank wars won or lost on the amount of fuel available to each side.

—The test crew complained of getting injured while the tank was moving because there were not enough hand grips to hold on to. I found this an incredible oversight for a tank costing almost $3 million.

I could not figure out if stupidity, incompetence, or corruption had allowed a tank like this to be at such an advanced stage of development without fixing or redesigning its glaring errors. I had learned from Smith that the first operational test (OT I) had also gone badly.[6] In OT I, the M-1 was tested side by side with the M-60, the Army's then current tank. The M-1 averaged 77 mean miles between failures as opposed to 493 for the M-60. Although the M-60 was a mature design, this large discrepancy should have set off alarms in the M-1 tank program office. On top of that, the main portion of the OT II test results I had received was actually an extension of the original OT II tests: its purpose was to prove that the tank had improved over the original OT I and II test results.

The Army had known about the bad news in the OT II extended test for about a year, but it had still allowed the tank to go into limited production. At this point in the spring of 1981, the M-1 was entering its final testing stage, and the decision of whether or not to move to full production was only a few months away. If the decision was affirmative, the tanks would be deployed in Europe to be ready for a possible war.[7]

My sources maintained that the Army could not hope to have these serious problems fixed so soon, especially since many of them stemmed from major design flaws. It became apparent from the documentation that the Army had sidestepped any checks and balances that would prevent this inadequate tank from being deployed. I told myself that this charade could not continue and that public inspection of this program was necessary to prevent such an unreliable tank from being placed in the hands of the soldiers.

As I began receiving more documents from the M-1 network of sources, I found that gathering this information was going to be much easier than disseminating it. I had just started to work with several reporters on the cost aspects of weapon scandals. Since my main sources and experts on the tank from inside the military system could not go public for fear of losing their jobs, it soon became apparent that I would have to be the "front" for them; I would have to explain this test report and other M-1 documents to reporters, who would then inform the American public. The only way I could pull it off was to go carefully over and memorize every detail of the Army's documents, and more importantly, confirm with an independent source the facts presented by the Army's tests and by my expert.

Although Smith was reluctant to go into the details of where he was getting his information and documents, his wide range of information and varied documents suggested that he was representing a group inside the Pentagon who were alarmed about the state of affairs of the M-1 and were willing to take a measurable risk to get this information out. I realized that some of these sources might have been involved directly in the M-1 program because of the depth of detail Smith had on the subject. I decided that if I was going to be the front for this group, who risked their careers to get these results to me, I would not probe Smith on the details of his network. I was not sure how the Army and the Department of Defense were going to react when we released this information, but if there was a big investigation of my sources I wanted to be able to say honestly that I did not know where my source, who of course would remain anonymous, got the information.

I also realized I had to be careful not to state as fact anything that was not backed up by documentation, even if several sources confirmed the facts. I could not pretend to the press and the public that I was a tank expert without being laughed out of the room. My role as a front for those who could not speak publicly would not be easy.

For the next three weeks, I threw myself into learning every aspect of tanks and every detail that could be gleaned from OT II, since I wanted to be sure I could hold my own in any spontaneous debate on the M-1. I knew that the Army would immediately use any mistake I made to question my credibility, even though my facts came from their own documents. I met with Smith regularly to be sure I understood the implications behind each of the disconcerting failures of the M-1. The task was made more complicated as the weeks went by, and I began to look at congressional testimony and reports that showed numerous production problems at the Chrysler tank plant which resulted in severe quality-control problems and a significantly reduced delivery schedule. I was amassing so much evidence that the entire M-1 program was in deep trouble that it was hard to decide what to emphasize.[8] I began to reel from the number of tank facts that I was memorizing.

To my surprise, I found that understanding tank warfare and what makes a good tank does not require detailed technical knowledge as much as simple logic and common sense. For example, any tank that can go only 34 miles between serious failures can turn its crew into sitting ducks in a combat situation. So in combat, our soldiers' lives would be endangered not only by the enemy but also by the poor quality of the M-1.

It was upsetting to me that most of us assume that our weapons perform as well as the various advertisements by defense companies claim and as the DOD promises to Congress. Yet if this is not true, we, as well as the soldiers, have a false sense of confidence in our ability to defend ourselves. It was hard for me to accept that the Army bureaucracy would allow a faulty weapon to go through the system, but that seemed to be exactly what they were doing.

I decided that the lives of combat soldiers could be most affected by technical failures, and the easiest technical failure for the public and the Congress to understand was the unreliability of the power train. After about three weeks of review and study, we were ready to approach the press. Because of the technical complexity of the information we had gathered, I knew that we would not have successful coverage with the traditional Washington-style press conference or press release. Instead, Smith and I picked several reporters whom we felt would do the necessary background work in this complex story. Bruce Ingersoll and Patrick Oster of the *Chicago Sun-Times* and Stephen Webbe of *The Christian Science Monitor* were particularly interested in this type of information, and learned the intricacies and the implications of the data on the tank. In addition, one source, who also had a copy of the OT II, had independently given it to *The Wall Street Journal,* whose reporter Walter Mossberg was persuaded to work with us because of the solid backup of our sources.

Each of the reporters had met with my sources and agreed that everything they said would be off the record. I asked the reporters to name my organization, the Project on Military Procurement, as the source of the documentation and to quote me freely on anything I had to say about the OT II test results. I was very careful to point out that I did not have the expertise my sources had to verify the detailed battlefield complaints, but that I had checked most of the M-1's glaring errors with separate sources. Besides, the Army's own test documents told the main story.

At this time we had also obtained an analysis on the M-1 production and other problems by Charles Murphy, a staff aide of Representative Jack Edwards (R-Alabama). In a report on February 23, 1981, Murphy outlined a dramatic drop in the production of the M-1 because of poor quality control and the inability of the company that supplied the engines for the tank to Chrysler to deliver the engines on time. Perhaps the most important statistic from this report was that the previous reliability figure that 22 percent of the tanks would go 4000 miles without a power-train overhaul in OT II had slipped to 19 percent during the first part of the third operational test of the M-1 (OT III). I was relieved to see that current data on the M-1 backed up the results of OT II, since OT II's test report was now a year old. The third operational test was going on at the time and we were not expecting to get any of the results until the end of the summer. At the same time, I was disturbed to see that the reliability of the tank continued to diminish as we got closer to the full production decision.

On Monday, April 20, 1981, *The Wall Street Journal* ran Mossberg's story on the front page with the headline: ROUGH RIDING: COSTLY NEW M-1 FAILS MORE ARMY TESTS; PRICE KEEPS INCREASING. On Wednesday of that week, before the

Army had a chance to catch its breath, *The Christian Science Monitor* published its story saying: "While publicly lavishing superlatives on its new XM-1 tank last year, the U.S. Army knew privately that a host of problems threatened its combat effectiveness." The *Chicago Sun-Times* finished out the week with a long piece on Sunday featuring other independent sources that backed up what the test results had revealed and presented other complaints I was not aware of.

I, of course, was very satisfied with the stories and with the role that the Project on Military Procurement had played, but I was also in shock. I had not expected so much publicity in such a short time and in such large media outlets. My sources were pleased to be able to tell their stories without being identified. They had not worked very successfully with most reporters in the past.

Although the Army had dealt with negative reports on the tank before, they were obviously unprepared for this degree of negative publicity from three major newspapers. Before the *Chicago Sun-Times* story appeared on Sunday, the Army came out with a five-and-a-half-page rebuttal dated Saturday, April 25.[9] It came in a very thick press packet that had a positive article about the M-1 in the Pentagon's newspaper for the troops, *SSAM* (Soldier, Sailor, Airman, Marine). The article, entitled I RIDE THE XM-1: A TALE OF MUD AND DUST, was written by one of their staff writers who had gone out in the field to ride in the M-1. My sources also noted with great amusement that the other articles in the press packet were from such newspapers as the *Temple Telegram* and the *Killeen Daily Journal,* near Fort Hood, Texas, where the M-1 was being tested. I found it hard to believe that the Army press relations office was so unsophisticated as to believe that these positive articles on the M-1, which were based mainly on Army handouts, would sway any journalist when compared with the facts backed up by their own test results in *The Wall Street Journal,* the *Chicago Sun-Times,* and *The Christian Science Monitor.*

The five-and-a-half-page point-by-point rebuttal to what the Army called allegations by *The Wall Street Journal, The Christian Science Monitor,* and the Project on Military Procurement either downplayed the importance of the test results by maintaining that the purpose of the extended OT II test was "to demonstrate whether the fixes worked to mission-reliability and power train durability during the DT [development or engineering]/OT II" or claimed that the reporters and the Project on Military Procurement misunderstood what the test results meant. The Army also claimed that the M-1 was showing better results in the 4000-mile durability test and that the M-1 had reached a 54 percent requirement in the Fort Knox OT II test.[10] Then they proceeded to contradict themselves in the next sentence by saying they did not believe the M-1 would meet the Army's requirement that 50 percent of the tanks could go 4000 miles without a power-train overhaul.

I knew they were not telling the truth about this important requirement because the Charles Murphy report said the success rate was 19 percent in the first part of OT III. The Army made many claims in this rebuttal about the improvement of the M-1 and threw around a lot of conflicting data, but never produced any actual test documents to rebut their own OT II test document that I had released. So it was not the Army's word against the Project on Military Procurement's analysis, but rather their word against their own documents. The Army did not convince many journalists, and I immediately realized that working with the press using the Army's own documents was much more powerful than having one of my experts argue with their experts. By using the Pentagon's own documents against themselves, we prevented the Pentagon from claiming that the source of the information was faulty or incompetent. I decided to continue to push them on the issues that I knew had solid documentation—the dismal reliability and maintainability of the M-1.

In the rebuttal, the Army pulled another trick or mistake that

I knew I could not leave unchallenged. One of my sources (whom I had met through Smith) had prepared a detailed briefing on the results of the OT II test and other information that he had discovered. His briefing showed that the M-1 would not work as well in true tank battlefield situations. He had given the briefing to interested members of Congress—some of which I had arranged. Although I had confidence in the briefing because of this man's very good credentials in this subject area, I was careful to note to any member of the Congress or press that this was his work and although it had great merit, it was not a Project on Military Procurement briefing.

However, in its rebuttal, the Army characterized this briefing as one "prepared by the Project on Military Procurement." I knew that if I let this go, the Army would try to hurt my credibility by claiming that I (then the only person on the staff of the Project) was trying to pass myself off as an expert. So I called the Army press office and was transferred to a Lt. Colonel Highlender, who did not sound happy to hear from me. I explained to him that the briefing was not a Project on Military Procurement briefing and that it was prepared by an individual outside my organization. I then asked him if he would make that correction to the members of the press who had received the rebuttal package.

He claimed that the title page of the briefing was on a piece of stationery from the Project on Military Procurement; therefore it was the Project's briefing. He said he had received the briefing charts from the Army congressional liaison office. I was immediately miffed that it appeared that one of the congressional staffers whom we had briefed in confidence had given the briefing to the Army. But then I became more concerned that perhaps someone had gotten a piece of my stationery out of my office. I politely told him that there was some kind of mistake, and the stationery was not connected to the briefing. I reiterated that it was not a Project briefing.

He then suggested that someone on my staff must have prepared the briefing without my knowledge. I told him that I was aware who had prepared the briefing and I *knew* that no one on my staff had prepared the briefing. I was not about to let him know that the organization that was giving him so much trouble consisted of just one twenty-five-year-old woman.

He then outright refused to acknowledge or correct their mistake to reporters, even if they asked him. At this point I began to get angry. He then asked me how I had received the Army rebuttal package. When I refused to tell him, he said that he knew I had gotten it from ————. I sat in stunned silence. The reporter who had given me a copy of the rebuttal had found it lying around the press room. I suspected that the Army might have wiretapped my phone, since that was the only way I had communicated with this reporter.

"The only way you could've known how I got that rebuttal was if you tapped my phone," I said.

"Think what you want," he said and hung up.

I called the reporter who had given me the press package and pressed him on the details of how he got it, if anyone had seen him pick it up, and if he had told anyone he'd given me the package. He assured me that no one could have known how I'd gotten it unless they had heard our phone conversation. We were both apprehensive about Lt. Colonel Highlender's knowledge of our activity and agreed to be more careful.

My sources had warned me in the past that the military was not above tapping my phone, but I had ruled out that possibility because I had not done anything illegal or anything that would threaten the security of the country. I believed that any wiretap, especially in this post-Watergate era, would have to be justified in those terms. My sources thought such an attitude very naïve, and for the first time I thought they might be right. The thought of possibly being bugged was unnerving to me. Although I could not prove that my phone had been tapped, I would now have to assume so for the protection of my sources.

As for my phone conversation with Lt. Colonel Highlender,

I was angry at the way I had been treated. I decided to go over his head to complain. I eventually reached the head of the Army public affairs office, Major General Sullivan. He listened to my complaints about Lt. Colonel Highlender and the characterization by the Army of this tank briefing as a Project on Military Procurement staff paper, but he seemed annoyed to have been brought into this conflict. Although he would not promise to change the Army's position on the briefing, he acted as though it would no longer be characterized to reporters in that manner. At that point I realized that that was the best I could hope for and ended the conversation. But the next time I had to deal with Lt. Colonel Highlender on questions about the M-1, he was much more polite and cooperative.

The day after *The Wall Street Journal* article, I received a call from NBC reporter Gene Pell, who asked if I would be interviewed for a story he was doing on the M-1 for the *Today* show. When I agreed he said he would be right over with the cameras. I was so stunned and nervous that I barely remember saying yes. Although I had been trained as a journalist and had worked in television news I suddenly realized that it was one thing to be a faceless quote in the newspaper and another to be on camera. When Pell arrived he walked into my little office and asked with surprise, "Are you Dina Rasor?" I meekly said yes and he began to interview me without the cameras. As we went over some of the technical details of the M-1 test, I lost my nervousness as I began to dive into all the numbers of the test and what they meant. Pell seemed satisfied with my explanations and knowledge and told the cameramen to set up. He then conducted a short ten-minute interview in which I started out well. Then I began to stumble when I looked into the lifeless eye of the camera. For the first time in my short experience in journalism, I began to see what it was like to be on the other side of an interview. I disliked feeling that I didn't have control over the situation and I now can sympathize more with public officials who face this dilemma every day.

Gene Pell did a short M-1 story on the *Today* show a few days later. I barely remember what I said because I was so shocked by my appearance. Although I spoke with confidence and authority, I looked like a vulnerable, timid, and washed-out young girl. I was forced to acknowledge that if I ever had to go on television again, my days of casual dress and little makeup were over. I did not like the thought of changing myself, but I knew I had to if I wanted to be convincing.

Seeing myself quoted so authoritatively in major newspapers and on television had a disconcerting effect on me. Though I was confident of the facts as we had presented them, I realized that I had taken another serious step into controversy. By volunteering to be a front for these sources, I became the main target for the wrath of the U.S. Army. I was not sure that I was up to the task, and my insecurity was heightened when I heard rumors that some congressional staff members and Army personnel considered me a joke and a fluke. Clearly, I had set myself up for some severe ridicule if we could be proven wrong. I should have realized that it would be tough on me personally to take on the Pentagon, but I was too naïve. Despite these fears I was ready to take the next step—turning our information and the Army's test results over to the U.S. Congress.

Every year the House and Senate Appropriations committees have a "public witness day" on which any group can testify on their concerns. I had requested and received permission from the Senate Appropriations Committee to testify on any subject I wished. I reduced the large volume of material on the M-1, much of which I had received after the three press reports, into a thirteen-page document that had to be checked and rechecked up to the day I testified in order to incorporate all the facts on the M-1.

Although I had received the OT II test results from my sources, I had also filed several Freedom of Information requests with the Army, asking for this test and other recent documents. The Army sent me a ravaged version of OT II which had practically all the information taken out except the height, weight, and training background of the crew that had tested the M-1. But through this process I managed to learn about a 1979 logistics report[11] on the M-1 that had been prepared by the U.S. Army Logistics Evaluation Agency, a group that would later be responsible for maintaining the M-1. This was one of their first evaluations on how hard that task would be.

After the three stories on the M-1 appeared in the newspapers, I received a call from a member of that agency who told me that they were reviewing the document to see what they would release to me. He seemed to know who I was and was far more friendly that anyone else from the Army I had spoken to before. Still, remembering what I had received on the OT II test from the Army, I was not very optimistic.

To my total surprise, that agency sent me the *entire* document with no deletions. Once my sources and I examined it we realized we had a real find. This agency was very concerned about the reliability of the tank and the increased maintenance problems they were facing because of it. One trouble was with the tank's instrument panel, which was supposed to warn of problems. The report stated: "Of the 23 warning lights on the driver's instrument panel, 11 lit up at various times during the test when no malfunction could be found, or failed to light when a malfunction existed."[12] This would be similar to the problem you'd have if the oil light in your car lit up if there was no problem and you had to stop for fear that your engine would freeze up, or worse, if the oil light did not light up at all and you continued to drive and severely damaged the engine. That would be annoying and potentially dangerous to you, but imagine how serious a problem it would be if your life depended on keeping that vehicle working.

The Army logistics report also suggested that more fuel tankers and pumps would have to be added to tank battalions to accommodate the increased fuel the M-1 would need. Remember, during the OT II test, the M-1 averaged over 4 *gallons to the mile*, about twice the amount consumed by the M-60 tank the M-1 was replacing. Besides being an additional logistics burden during a war when you can ill afford it, imagine how difficult it is to fuel a tank in a hostile area; it should therefore have to be done as few times as possible.

But the worst news was that the bad reliability figures from the OT II test were confirmed in this report, which put the problem in perspective to the performance of past tanks. The Army's logistics report explained that preliminary estimates of the personnel needed to support the M-1 were based on experience with the M-60 A1 (the earliest model of the M-60) and a belief that the M-1 would perform well in its reliability tests. In fact, the actual reliability testing indicated that the M-1 "requires an unscheduled maintenance action about seven times more frequently than the [M-60 A1]."[13]

On top of that, the report was concerned that after approximately the same number of test miles (over 20,000), the M-1 accumulated about three and a half times the number of performance reports as the M-60 A2. This meant that this model of the M-60 could travel a little less than twice as far between unscheduled maintenance actions as the M-1. Expectations that the M-1's performance would improve between testing and production were not high because the M-60 A2 improved only 2 percent between service tests and tests performed by the troops. To understand the seriousness of how poorly the M-1 was doing in comparison to the M-60 at the same stage of development, it should be noted that all 750 M-60 A-2s were recalled from Europe after they were deployed, in part because of maintainability and reliability problems.

I incorporated this new information into my testimony before the Senate committee, and felt that with this new report and inside knowledge of a new unreleased General Accounting

Office (GAO) report, which backed up OT II, I was on solid ground.[14]

On the morning I testified, I wound my hair into a tight and severe bun, and donned a navy blue suit with a white blouse. When I emerged from the bedroom, my husband, Thom, laughed and teased me about my "Tricia Nixon" look. My testimony had turned into a real family affair. It happened that my father, my brother-in-law, and his wife were visiting me in Washington, and they all wanted to come along. I agreed reluctantly, so with this entourage in tow, I headed for the Senate hearing room. When my sister-in-law and I stepped into the restroom for a last-minute check, she remarked that she would be terrified if she had to testify and did not understand how I could go through with it.

Little did she know: I was afraid to my core as I stepped into the hearing room. At the table reserved for the press, there were only a few reporters. However, I was surprised to see Gene Pell of NBC there with his camera crew. A smattering of people were in the audience, most waiting to testify. The two senators present, Warren Rudman (R-New Hampshire) and the chairman of the committee, Ted Stevens (R-Alaska), looked bored as they listened to a seemingly unending line of witnesses filing past them in the course of an hour. Each witness had ten minutes to summarize his statement. A Jesuit priest from Georgetown University asked for more funding for the campus ROTC program. A man representing a nonprofit world council was trying to convince the senators to only "Buy American" in defense.

Even I was bored by the time Senator Stevens called my name. As I approached the witness table, I desperately searched for a way to catch the senators' attention and still appear credible. I sat down in the witness chair. Senator Stevens looked up, half smiled when he saw me, and asked me to keep my statement to ten minutes.

Breakthrough

After a few preliminary statements about the goals o.
organization, I stated that one of the first weapons the Pr̶o
had looked at was the M-1 tank. "I want to make it very clear,"
I said in a forceful voice, "that *tanks are important.*" I banged
my fist loudly on the table for each of the last three words. "The
U.S. Army must buy tanks. We must have tanks that work. They
are very crucial weapons. This is potentially a $20 billion pro-
gram and it is not a matter to be taken lightly.[15]"

The senators, the press, and the audience all looked up in
surprise, but they could not have been more startled than I was
at the intensity of my opening statement and the sound of my
fist banging the table. I launched into the rest of my statement,
detailing the failures of the M-1, and the inconsistent statements the Army made to the press and Congress to cover up
a pitiful performance. When I came up for air, I realized that
twenty minutes had slipped by and Senator Stevens had not
interrupted me. I felt that was a good sign. I finished quickly
and braced myself for some rough questioning and possibly for
ridicule. Surprisingly, none came from Chairman Stevens. In
fact he stated: "We have some real difficulties with the tank.
There is no question about that." He made a few comments
about the rise in the cost of the tank and then turned the
questioning over to Senator Rudman.

Senator Rudman also assured me that the committee was
going to take a close look at the tank as it made its way through
the testing cycle. By this time, the NBC camera was rolling and
Senator Rudman began to make a speech about the effectiveness of the newest set of initiatives to come out of the Pentagon
that were designated to clean up the procurement process. He
asked me if I was familiar with them. I said yes, but I did not
tell him that my sources had informed me that the initiatives
were considered a joke in the bureaucracy and only good for
public relations to get the Congress off the Pentagon's back.

Then he asked me if I knew about the Nunn Amendment,
which he had cosponsored that year, to clean up the Pentagon's

reporting system to the Congress. Again, I answered yes without telling him that one of my sources had written the amendment and offered it to certain members of Congress. He probably doesn't even realize it was written by someone in the underground, I thought smugly. Senator Rudman's questioning was beginning to sound like a campaign speech, and I am sure that the rolling camera was egging him on.

I responded by concluding that general reforms were useful but the bureaucracy would sit up and take notice if you cracked down on one weapon system as an example and that the M-1 would be a good place to start. To my surprise, Senator Stevens basically agreed with me.

Senator Rudman responded by saying: "In addition to looking at the raw data rather than quantified results, several of us, including this senator, intend to observe firsthand some of the latest rounds of tests of the tank on the site. I think you will find many people do have a deep interest in following this."

As he was giving me this mildly condescending assurance, my mind drifted back to something Ernest Fitzgerald had told me about such events that senators attend to review military equipment. "Don't let the members of Congress fool you with their 'kick the tire' syndrome," Ernie remarked. "They go down to the base, kick the tires, and come back and vote billions of dollars for weapon boondoggles."

Before I could stop myself and realize that I was close to trampling on senatorial dignity, I found myself repeating that wise observation to Senator Rudman. I winced after I said it and laughter swept the room. My comment had come out rather sarcastic and insulting. I was surprised to see that Senator Stevens was also laughing. Senator Rudman was not and told me that he had spent some time in tanks and knew what he was talking about. I could not wait to get out of that room.

Afraid that I did not serve well the people in the Pentagon that I was representing, I resolved that I would learn to be more diplomatic in the future. Unfortunately, that was by no means my last experience with such a problem.

About a week later I was surprised to receive a call from Dwight Dyer, Senator Stevens's chief staff aide on the committee. "How would you like to go down to Fort Hood and kick the tires with us?" he joked.

"Are you serious?" I replied. He assured me that the senator had specifically requested that I go along on the trip. We both agreed that I should take a commercial plane to Fort Hood instead of riding along with the senator in a military transport plane. I felt it was important for me not to accept any favors from the military or the Senate that might be used to question my objectivity.

I was flattered and excited by the invitation, and my sources thought it was an extraordinary opportunity to see if the Army had fixed some of the faults in the M-1. Then I realized that I had no idea exactly where in Texas Fort Hood was, so I called the Army's public affairs office in the Pentagon. The man who answered the phone did not identify himself, but by the tone of his voice I suspected that I had once again reached Lt. Colonel Highlender. I identified myself and, after explaining that I had been invited to Fort Hood, asked for the nearest commercial airport.

"I don't know," he replied in a strained voice. I asked him if anyone in public affairs knew. Once again he said no. Exasperated, I asked him if anyone else in the Pentagon could help me discover where the Army's largest base was located. The answer was no. I asked him how else I could get this information, and finally he gave me a phone number at Fort Hood and abruptly hung up. I called the number, once again identified myself and my organization to the man who answered, and asked where the airport was located. "Just a minute," he replied and after a few minutes of muffled sound, he came back on and stated that he was not authorized to give out that information.

After arguing with him for a few fruitless minutes, I hung up.

I called Dwight Dyer to inform him that I could not go with the senators. When he asked why, I replied sarcastically that the Army did not know where Fort Hood was located, and I recounted my experiences of the past half hour.

Now it was his turn to be angry. "They can't treat you like that!" he exclaimed. "You're the guest of a U.S. senator!" He told me he would take care of the problem.

Within twenty minutes I received a call from a person in the Army public relations office. He asked me how the Army could assist me with my trip, and if the Army could make my hotel reservation or send a staff car in the morning to take me to the base.

"No," I replied emphatically, "just simply tell me where the nearest airport is to Fort Hood." He finally let the secret out of the bag. It was Killeen, Texas.

In preparation for the trip to Fort Hood, I once again threw myself into absorbing the most recent tank data. I was looking forward to translating the data and briefings into hands-on experience, and I was hoping to confront the Army straight on with their inconsistencies, especially in front of the senators.

I arrived in Killeen, Texas, on July 12, 1981, the night before we were supposed to tour the base. As I unpacked my clothes in my room at the Holiday Inn, I went over in my mind what my role was on the tour the next day. I knew that it was important for me to point out the tank's problems, but I did not want to be too pushy, especial since Senator Rudman was to be with the group. I had caused enough trouble when I'd testified. I resolved not to hesitate in pointing out blatant mistruths, but I did not want to appear to be a spoiler.

The next morning I took a cab to the base. I was ushered into a waiting room across from a long counter where a group of enlisted men and junior officers were bustling about. The senators had not yet arrived and there was a flurry of activity. I could see that the visit had top priority.

One lieutenant was trying to make me comfortable and asked if I wanted a cup of coffee. The rest of the crew eyed me as if I were a creature from another planet. They had probably been briefed about me and warned not to talk to me because they would shift their gaze quickly away when I looked at them. Only the lieutenant ventured a conversation with me. In the middle of a conversation about my trip and the Texas landscape, a phone next to us rang. The lieutenant leapt to answer it and after a few minutes said, "I would like to help you, Joe, but I'll be up to my ass in senators in a few minutes." He seemed to enjoy telling the listener of his important assignment.

Three senators arrived with four staff aides from the committee and a small group of legislative liaison officers from the Army. Senators Stevens and Rudman said hello and introduced me to Senator Mark Andrews (R-North Dakota) and the rest of the staff. Dwight Dyer winked at me and I was relieved that there was someone with whom I felt comfortable. Then I was introduced to Lt. Colonel Dick Ladd, a tall, gangly man from the Army legislative liaison staff. In a soft, easygoing manner he explained to me that he would be my escort to try to answer any questions I might have.

We were all ushered into a large auditorium where we met the base commander and saw a short slide show on the history of Fort Hood. Senator Stevens grew restless. "I want to see the tanks," he complained. Immediately the presentation ended and about a dozen men began to engage in rapid activity to move us on out.

We walked out of the building and met Major General Richard Lawrence, who was in charge of running the third operational test (OT III) that was currently in progress at Fort Hood. I had to smile because he was dressed in full battle fatigues, down to a service revolver and two stars on his helmet. I was used to seeing generals in the Pentagon in their dress uniforms and I felt that we were going out to play GI Joe. I also discovered that the general was rather deaf and almost had to be shouted at. I deduced that this was from spending so much time around loud tank guns. He eyed me warily, but politely said hello while touching the rim of his helmet in respect.

We were led to a helicopter pad where several UH-1 helicopters were to take us to the tank area. I was thrilled because I had never ridden in a helicopter. We got into the helicopters and before I knew it Lt. Colonel Dick Ladd had wedged himself between me and a staff aide and asked me if I had any questions about helicopters. I realized it would be hard for me to spend much time one-on-one with anyone from the committee as long as Dick Ladd was "helping" me. The problem was that he was just so nice about isolating me that it was hard to get angry.

A group of soldiers met us at the tank area out in the middle of a Texas sagebrush field with only a few trees. The ground was sticky from an overnight rain. Although it was still morning, the hot sun began to burn its way through my hair and the sweat trickled down my back.

By this time I began to get a little rattled and felt I was losing my equilibrium. As the only female in the group, it seemed to me everyone tensed up when I came near. I could also tell that most of them, including some of the congressional aides, thought I was a spoiler. The soldiers and officers eyed me with curiosity and I began to feel somewhat like a sideshow freak. I could tell that I had invaded male territory and everyone was unsure of the situation. I'm usually able to ignore the uneasiness of being the only female in a group, but this time I was in totally unfamiliar territory. I felt myself growing timid and reluctant to raise any fuss. I was surprised at myself for being intimidated. It was not like me.

A soldier ordered both the M-1 and M-60 tanks to roll up for our inspection. I had seen the M-1 before at a display at Aberdeen Proving Ground in Maryland, but this was the first time I was allowed to get close to it. As they rolled up I asked the ever-present Dick Ladd what kind of demonstration we were going to see.

"Don't you know?" he said. "You are going to drive them and fire their guns."

I was stunned. I had no idea that we were actually going to operate the tanks. I grew very excited at the prospect because I would get the opportunity to check out some of the crew members' complaints that were in OT II.

We split up into groups, and I was paired with Shawn O'Keefe from the committee staff. We were going to drive both tanks and compare their gun stabilization systems, but only fire the M-1 later on the shooting range. Through each stage of the test drive, I wanted to try to compare the tanks as evenly as possible. I knew more about the exact faults of the M-1 because I had read its test results more thoroughly. But I had an open mind to see if some of the design faults were also in the older M-60. Just outside the tanks you could see clearly that the M-1 was more complicated than the M-60, partially because of the outward sensors placed all over the M-1.

As we went through the exercises I compared the tank in these main areas:

Driving

I drove the M-60 first. The driver's seat on the tank is in a small cavity outside the turret in the front of the tank. I slid into the seat while a soldier leaned over to explain how to start the tank. No problem for me: the tank started up with a pull starter very similar to my former 1960 British sports car.

I put on a helmet that was connected by an intercom to the tank commander inside the tank and he gave me instructions on where to go. I pushed the accelerator and the tank immediately jumped to life, which surprised me because it had a diesel engine. The M-60 responded quickly to the accelerator pedal, but in the long run after you got started the tank was certainly underpowered. The M-60 maneuvers sharply and drives like an older car that handles well, but it has a tight suspension that makes the riding rough. Occasionally the tank commander would remind me that there were people in the crew compartment of the tank. I could tell where the tank was and where it was going at all times. I did a few driving experiments based on suggestions that a source had told me were important mobility factors in a battlefield situation.

On the way back, while we were going cross-country in the tank, I asked the commander if he wanted me to drive to the left or the right of a tree we were rapidly approaching.

"Drive over it," he responded casually.

"What?" I cried. "You have got to be kidding!"

He assured me that it was all right and I steered the M-60 straight for a tree that was at least eight inches in diameter. I braced myself for the impact, but none came as the tank went smoothly over the tree with barely a hitch.

I could see a big difference between driving the M-60 and the M-1. When it was my turn to go in the M-1, the crew eyed me with suspicion. Climbing into the driver's seat in the M-1 was similar to climbing into the seat of a luxury car. There were all kinds of lights and switches but surprisingly few gauges. The seat was tilted so that the driver was slung low and my knees were parallel with my shoulders. I was surprised that there was less room in the driver's seat than in the M-60, and then I noticed that some of the M-1 drivers were small men.

I had seen pictures of the M-1's rather complicated instrument panel before and I knew some of its faults. So I began to test the tank commander as he explained how to turn the tank on. The process is much more complicated than for the M-60 because the M-1 has a gas turbine engine similar to a jet engine. A certain order has to be followed to turn the tank on and off so that the engine would not burn itself up. I knew from OT II that the crew had complained that it was too easy to accidentally hit the master power switch that would immediately shut off the engine and cause considerable damage.[16] I decided to check with the tank commander who was briefing me to see if that really was a problem.

"What happens if I need to turn the engine off?" I asked. "Should I just hit this switch?" I said, pointing to the master control switch.

"No, don't do that!" he exclaimed and then showed me how the tank had to be turned off in a specific sequence. I observed that I thought this was a problem because the crew had complained about it in OT II. He grew defensive and said that hitting the master switch would not really cause that much trouble.

The tank was running by this time so I put my hand on the switch and said with a grin, "Well, if this isn't going to cause any major damage, let me try it and we'll see."

"Jesus!" he answered, "don't do that or I'll get my butt kicked and we won't go anywhere in this tank." He grabbed my hand and after a tense moment we both laughed. He knew I had caught him, and he took it quite well.

Later, when I had the chance to think about it, I was concerned that this sophisticated tank had to be turned on and off in a precise way. I wondered if a soldier running up to start the tank under fire would remember all the steps and not hit the master control switch during a battle. The last I heard, the Army had put a shield over the switch, but that does not address the problem of starting and stopping this tank in chaotic combat situations. In every new device or system, I tried to put myself on a battlefield to see if the procedure was simple enough to remember under adverse conditions. My sources had trained me well and, for the first time, I really understood the importance of having experienced combat soldiers, as well as scientists and theorists, design equipment for the battlefield. Everything should be designed for a worst case scenario.

Luckily, Dick Ladd did not go with me on the M-1 ride. I eased the transmission in the M-1 into high gear and pressed hard on the accelerator pedal. The gas engine paused a few moments and jumped into action like a coiled spring. As we drove over the first hill and away from the prying eyes of Major General Lawrence, the crew began to relax. The ride was very smooth—similar to a large Buick—and the steering had a floaty feel. I knew that the Army had designed the M-1 with a very loose and springy suspension, but I also knew that this loose suspension had a tendency to throw its track.[17] I kept turning the tank swiftly and sharply from side to side to see how it reacted to sudden movement and once again it reacted like a Buick with power steering. The tank commander called me over the intercom to warn me that I was tossing people around in the back and I might throw a track. I had done the same tests in the M-60 and the tank commander never said anything about losing a track. Overall, the M-60 crew was willing to take more risks with its older tank than the crew of the newer M-1, giving me the impression that the M-60 was more rugged.

On the way back, I drove the M-1 on a flat dirt road and pushed the accelerator all the way down to see how fast the tank could go. The Army had claimed that the top speed of the M-1 was 45 miles per hour, but I could never get this tank to go faster than about 36 miles per hour.

When the Army does a side-by-side comparison of the M-1 and the M-60 for the public and the Congress, they usually race the two tanks on a flat drag strip. The M-1 with its 1500-horsepower engine leaves the 750-horsepower M-60 eating its dust. But my sources point out that wars are not fought on drag strips and the most important speed of a tank is the first 50-foot jump, to get out of the way of incoming fire such as missiles. They told me that a diesel engine can make that jump quickly, even though its overall speed after that is slow, and although the M-1 gas turbine engine may have more horsepower than the M-60, a gas turbine must wind up a few vital seconds before it makes its jump. Their observations certainly appeared to be true with my short test of the M-1 and M-60. As I mentioned before, the M-60 jumped immediately when I floored the accelerator and although the M-1 did have a lot of pull when I floored the accelerator there was a definite hesitation while the turbine wound up. That simple difference in the engine design could mean life or death on the battlefield because tanks have to try to get out of the way of large armed fire. Although we briefed two of the senators who were on the trip about this problem, I didn't think they would consider it important enough to test. I wished I had gone along with one of them to point out this vital difference.

When I was driving the M-1, I noticed that something was rubbing over the top of my helmet and occasionally my neck would get wrenched by something pulling at the top of my head. After a few times I figured out that the gun turret of the tank was rubbing my head and I was surprised and concerned. I quickly learned to scrunch down in the seat to avoid it, but this interfered with my driving and made my back ache. Then I remembered that in OT II the drivers had complained of back injuries while driving.[18] Perhaps this was the reason. I also knew from the tests that driving the tank with the hatch closed could be dangerous, to say the least. I later had a crew member close the hatch while I was in the driver's seat. In order to fit, I had to dig my chin into my chest and put myself in an almost impossible driving position. I now knew why the crew had small drivers for the M-1. My head banged against the turret in the M-1 and I am only 5 feet 6 inches tall. An average-sized man might have a hard time preventing the turret from even knocking him out.

Gun Stabilization System (Aiming the Gun)

When it came my turn to aim the gun using the stabilization device in the M-1 and M-60, I tried to determine if the idea of stabilizing the turret in order to have the gun point level while the tank was moving up and down was realistic. I knew from various media accounts that in the past, during important M-1 tank trials, U.S. gunners had succeeded best by turning the stabilization off, and as a result, a switch was installed so they could. I knew that the stabilization in the M-60 was not as "advanced" and the Army was claiming that the new stabilization ability of the M-1 made it superior to other tanks.

I personally found the stabilization device in the M-60 and the M-1 disorienting and confusing to the gunner. Although I did not have experience in this area, I found that when I had the device turned on and the gun aimed at a target, it was impossible to tell which way the tank was heading and whether the gun was facing the front or the rear of the tank. I tried to imagine the confusion that this would cause during the chaos of a battle, and I could see why a capable gunner in a contest would be more confident of winning the shooting match by turning off the switch and just eyeballing the target. Although the crew members tried very hard to show me the difference between the stabilization system of the M-60 and the M-1, I honestly could not see an improvement.

Inside the Tank

As you can well imagine, the inside of a tank is very important to the effectiveness of the crew. The OT II test had many complaints by the crew about the interior of the tank, so I was interested to see if the M-60 tank was any better and if the M-1 continued to have the problems that the testing crew had complained about.

Since I had never been in a tank before, I had nothing with which to compare the M-60 when I first climbed in. However, it didn't take long to see that being inside a tank can be claustrophobic. There is very little room for the three men (the driver is on the outside) and little padding to protect them from bumping sharp corners while the tank is moving.

But the M-60 seemed to be well ventilated and as comfortable inside as you could expect a tank to be. I do not remember having difficulty holding on while the tank was moving and I seemed to be able to maneuver around the rest of the crew. I noticed that the M-60 had its ammunition stored directly in the back and was within easy reach. I winced when I noticed that there was no protection between the crew and the ammunition. This has been a deadly problem in past wars when a fire or explosion has set off the tank's own ammunition. In the design of the M-1 ammunition bay, in some respects, however, the cure turned out to be even more potentially dangerous.

By the time I climbed inside the M-1, the hot Texas sun was becoming unbearable, so the intense heat may have colored my opinion of the inside of the tank. Although the M-1 is a bigger and heavier tank on the outside than the M-60, the inside is surprisingly smaller. My sources claim that is due to all the computer equipment inside the tank and the extra spaced armor on the front of the tank. The inside of the tank was stifling and hot, at least 100 degrees F. The gas turbine engine put a tremendous amount of heat and fumes out the back. The small ventilation fan was desperately trying to circulate the air but instead seemed to be pulling in more exhaust than fresh air. After about twenty minutes in the tank, I began to get light-headed from either the heat or exhaust, or both. The crew was also sweating heavily. I realized that fighting in a tank in a desert must be hell. I used the gun stabilization equipment and after that I began to go around the tank and ask questions.

The ammunition was stored in an armored box that would explode upward outside the tank if a shell hit it. For the crew to gain access to the ammunition, though, they had to push a button and open two heavily armored doors. The problem with this system was that if the hydraulic system failed, which is not an unusual occurrence, the crew would have a hard time getting to the ammunition. Also, the doors operate much like an elevator door by opening a few seconds and then closing. The crew in OT II complained that one could get fingers caught and broken in the doors when they closed.[19] I asked one of the crew members if he could open the doors if the hydraulics failed. "Sure!" he replied and proceeded to show me the manual override of the doors. Grunting and putting all his strength, he slowly wound the doors open. I noted that this procedure would not be realistic during a battle and to my surprise one of the crew members agreed. Another crew member showed me that his hand could stop the armored doors from sliding shut, but admitted that he would not dare to use his hand to stop the door, for the last eight inches it was possible to catch his fingers.

My sources claimed that in the heat of battle, a crew would not risk being unable to reach their ammunition and would just leave the doors open, thus negating the whole concept of the ammunition box. When I mentioned this problem to various congressional staff members, they responded that some protection is better than none.

But I knew from sources and articles in the weapons magazine[20] that the British and the Israelis have found a simpler, less expensive, and more effective way to sovle this problem on their new tanks. Both use the concept of a double-walled bathtub type of container to hold the ammunition. Inside the two walls, the British fill the space with water and the Israelis go one better by filling the space with a fire extinguishing liquid. Then when a shell penetrates the ammunition box, it is flooded with liquid that kills the blast and extinguishes any resultant fire. Because tank ammunition is waterproof, the crew will still have access to their ammunition to retaliate. Unfortunately the Army was not interested in the bathtub concept and at times grew hostile when the matter was brought up. Institutional pride of their own design had overridden good sense. This was not the last time I would encounter this bias.

At one point, I asked an M-1 crew member to show me how the loader's machine gun on top of the tank could be loosened and swung from side to side to a C-shaped ring. I knew that in

OT II the crew had complained of levers and knobs breaking off due to inferior metal, and that the clamp holding down the loader's machine gun while the tank was moving was especially vulnerable.[21] After looking at the machine gun and swinging it from side to side, I asked the crew member to cinch it tight again because we were on the way back to the main group. True to form, the clamp broke when he tried to tighten it. The metal was very malleable and twisted off when he tightened it. I was the one to suffer the consequences, however, because I rode back in the loader's hatch. Besides insufficient handles to hold on to, the machine gun was shifting wildly from side to side as I rode in the hatch. I was lucky to stay in the tank and not go flying out onto the Texas countryside. I knew from OT II that crew members had been worried about being thrown from the tank for lack of handles, and I could now see that was a legitimate concern. It was frightening.

Once we returned from driving and aiming the guns from the two tanks we settled down to eat lunch out in the field, Army style. I had my first taste of C rations and found them better than I'd expected. We ate in a command post area marked off by camouflage nets and Army tents. Once again, I sensed the uneasiness of some of the men at my being there. Dick Ladd sat by my side and the tank crew members who had been so friendly when we were out in the field grew distant and wary.

After lunch we went out to the firing range. I went with the same crew as I did before and they resumed their friendliness. They seemed excited to see how I would do firing the gun. The gun on the M-1 tank has a complicated and advanced laser range finder that shoots a laser out to the target, and sends the information back to a computer that adjusts the gun, taking into account environmental factors such as wind, bias, and temperature. The Army claimed that this feature made the tank one of the most advanced in the world. Although I was not aware of it at the time, a month earlier six NATO countries had staged a "tank Olympics" in West Germany. The Americans' performance was feared by competitors because their M-60 A3 was outfitted with a thermal imaging device and a laser range finder similar to the new equipment in the M-1. The British also entered their tank with a laser range finder.

None of these advanced devices was included on the German-made Leopard IA4 and IA3 entered by the West Germans and the Belgians. The West Germans, who have won these contests in the past, said they placed emphasis on training and tactics—and they won again in this contest, with the Belgians second and Americans third. As *Defense Week* reported: "The competition is a test of marksmanship, yet the laser rangefinder in the U.S. and British tanks seemed to help them little. 'The optical range finder is better,' asserts a German tank commander."[22] The optical range finder is a simpler telescopic device that enhances eyesight.

When we pulled up to the firing range, I was the only one in my tank to fire the gun. The crew told me that I was allowed to fire three shells at outline cutouts of tanks in the distance. The loader pulled out one of the massive 105-millimeter shells and loaded the gun. The tank was cramped and hot when I took my place in the gunner's seat. The tank commander showed me how to put my hands on the gun control handles, called the cadillacs. He then proceeded to open a computer right above me and show me how they programmed in the temperature outside the tank, the wind speed, and other environmental factors. He did it so nonchalantly that I wondered if he ever thought about whether he would remember all these details when someone was firing at him. I also wondered if the computer could not be programmed in an emergency, it would hurt the accuracy of the gun. One of the reasons temperature is important is because the gun of the tank droops slightly under certain temperatures and the computer adjusts the gun angle. But if you have an optical range finder where you use the boresight of the gun, the human eye automatically adjusts the gun. The West Germans won the tank contest by using the quickest adjusting gunsight computer, the human eye.

I began to look through the gunsight, when there was a tremendous explosion that shook my whole body. I leapt back in alarm and exclaimed that I had accidentally fired the gun. The crew laughed and told me that the gun of the tank next to me had been fired. I then realized that firing the gun was going to be a jarring and somewhat terrifying experience.

The heat and the noise had rattled me but I was determined to test the gun. The tank commander showed me how to aim the gun, push the button to send out the laser to the target and back to the computer, and then fire. In the first shot, I followed the instructions and aimed the gun, "lased" the target, and fired. The breech of this enormous gun was only three feet to the right of my knees and when I pushed the fire button, I was thrown back in my seat as an enormous explosion rocked the tank. I had never felt anything like it and it set my gut churning. The breech of the gun expelled a red hot shell casing next to me, and if I'd had my arm near there it could easily have been cut off. It took me a moment to recover, but the tank commander was excitedly reporting that I had hit the target square.

On the next shot, I did not lase the gun when the commander told me but just used the optical sight to aim the gun and fired. This time I braced myself and did not get thrown so far. To my amazement, I hit the target straight on again. To be fair, I used the laser range finder on the third shot and hit the target again. The crew was very excited and asked me if I'd had a lot of target practice. At that moment I realized that this was the first gun of any type I had ever fired. Later, it became a standard joke among my friends that the only gun I have ever fired is a 105-millimeter cannon.

The tank commander wanted me to fire one more shell and the loader had loaded the shell. By this time, the senators and I had hit most of the targets. The tank commander suggested that I try to take off the ledge of a nearby cliff. I thought he was joking, but he told me that it would take better marksmanship than the targets. I decided to try it.

I aimed the gun without the help of the laser range finder and actually took off the side of a cliff. It was only then that I really understood the tremendous destructive power of this machine. When we returned to the main tank area, my crew bragged to the other tank crews that I had hit every shot. I did not tell anyone there that I had used their prized laser system in only two of my four successful shots. Since I did not have *any* experience in firing guns, I was not convinced that this very expensive and delicate computer system would make that much difference in a war.

All I knew was that I was feeling rather shell-shocked from the noise of the tank guns and the intense heat. I was bruised from being tossed around the tank during the firing of the gun. My big toe was bleeding because the loader had accidentally dropped one of the shells on my foot. I was convinced from my short experience in the tank that being in a tank battle would be pure hell. One of the staff aides came up to me afterward and said, "Wasn't that fun?" All I could answer was that I imagined being in a tank with all the noise and heat, knowing people were firing back at you, would be a terrible experience. I guess he had thought about the tank not as a war machine but as a toy, because he gave me a dirty look and walked away.

After the firing range we went to see a demonstration by a nervous enlisted man of how the test equipment on the M-1 worked. He was not very convincing. Although none of us had enough knowledge to tell if the numbers on the equipment were correct, you could tell by this man's look of dismay that the equipment was not working correctly. He said nothing and the group said nothing as we shuffled on to the next display.

We went by some test equipment next to which was a row of approximately twenty large looseleaf binders. I mustered the courage to ask what the binders were for. The soldier who was leading us said they were the instruction manual for the tank. There had been reports that the instruction manual had to be rewritten because it was too complicated.[23] When I mentioned in disgust the potential problems of a tank so complicated to fix and operate that it needed a set of instructions large enough to fill up a whole jeep, several of the senators and staff aides eyed the binders with curiosity. Major General Lawrence gave me a pained look and hustled the group forward.

We came to a tank maintenance area in which enlisted men were examining some of the components of the M-1 with the housing off the equipment. I was amazed at the rows and rows of electronic circuit boards in the equipment of the tank and wondered how these delicate silicon chips and wires could be protected in a bouncing and overheated tank. A man in a maintenance trailer showed us some test equipment. He wore a blue jumpsuit, not an Army uniform, and I suspected he worked for the contractor of the tank, Chrysler. The M-1 was in the middle of its third *operational* test (OT III)—that is, a test conducted with average tank crews and average Army mechanics to simulate a war situation as closely as possible—so no contractors should have been allowed to work on maintaining the tank. After all, there would be no contractor mechanic in a war zone to help take care of the tank during a conflict. *Major General Lawrence later insisted to Congress that no contractor personnel were involved at direct support levels during OT III.* I could have kicked myself for not asking the man whom he worked for, but I felt the pressure from the officers in the group to move on.

We reached an area where an M-1 and an M-60 were sitting side by side, their engines pulled out. They were showing us that the M-1 engine and power pack was one unit and easier to pull out and change than the M-60. They'd better be able to pull it out and change it easily because of its horrible failure rate, I thought. When an officer mentioned that it took only a half hour to change the engine, I asked him how long it took the engine to cool down before they could touch it. I knew that the gas turbine engine of the M-1 got a lot hotter than the diesel engine of the M-60 and it would take a very long time before the engine was cool enough to remove. In fact, the mechanics had to use asbestos mittens[24] that reached to their elbows to check the oil in the tank. No one answered my question, everyone grew uncomfortable, and we moved on.

Finally, we moved to an area to view a videotape of the M-1 being hit with shells, surviving the hits, and being driven off. This was one of the Army's biggest selling points for the M-1, but I had heard rumors that Russian shells could penetrate the M-1 secret and highly vaulted "Chobham" armor. The tapes jerked so much, apparently due to editing, that it was hard to follow what was happening.

During this video show I sat next to Major General Lawrence for the first time. I was so frustrated by the tape that I asked what shells were fired at the tank.

"They were Russian shells," he replied.

"What size?" I asked.

"105 and 120 millimeter," he answered.

I was so shocked that I didn't know what to say, and I looked around to the senators and the staff aides for a reaction. There was none. Even a greenhorn to the tank business should know that the Russians do not use 105- and 120-millimeter tank shells. Typically they use 115- and 125-millimeter shells. Major General Lawrence should have known that. If 105 and 120 shells were fired at the tank, they would most likely be ours or from our allies. Though I contemplated blowing the whistle on him in front of the senators, I was reluctant to confront him on his own turf. I whispered to Dwight Dyer that the Russians did not have 105- and 120-millimeter shells and that he should tell Senator Stevens. He nodded his head as we moved on to our final briefing.

The final briefing was rather anticlimactic compared to the noise, heat, and exhaustion of the mock battlefield. It was held in the quiet confines of the base commander's conference room, with cleanly dressed sergeants ferrying drinks back and forth for us. Everyone was weary from the experience and the conversation rambled on for a few minutes. I felt I was expected to make some statement about the tank. After making a rather feeble attempt to discuss the laser range finder, I decided that this was not the time or the place to reveal to the senators that I had used the range finder only twice to hit all the targets. Even so, the conversation turned to the problems of the tank. I was beginning to listen passively when Senator Rudman said something that caused me to sit upright in horror.

He began with the remark that he had received a briefing from my so-called Mr. Jones, and he used the source's full name. I lost the rest of the remark as I hurriedly examined the military men around me taking notes. I had arranged for Senators Stevens and Rudman to hear a briefing on the M-1 from one of my sources under the strict agreement that he would remain anonymous. And here was Senator Rudman blurting out his name to this group of high-ranking officers. I was furious because I knew that this information would undoubtedly make its way back to the Pentagon and make life miserable for my source. I do not know if the senator had made a mistake or purposely revealed the name, but I found it inexcusable. I realized that I had to be more careful around members of Congress.

Although this slip by Senator Rudman did not end up causing the source any undue trouble, it made me painfully aware that the careers of at least ten men rest on my shoulders every time I go out in public and that my burden in this job is to make sure that they are not discovered. This responsibility weighs heavily on me because of the trust that these men have given to me. I became extremely cautious.

The big day was suddenly over. We said our good-byes and were presented with honorary memberships in the First Cavalry Division at the base and a cap with the M-1 emblem on it.

I was numb with fatigue during the hot cab ride back to the Holiday Inn in Killeen. The motel room was dark and cool because the shades had been drawn and I collapsed on the bed as the thoughts and impressions of the day swirled around in my head. I had learned a lot—mostly that the concerns my sources had brought me based on the Army's test results were justified. I had a very small but significant taste of how horrible the battlefield must be and how the best-laid plans would vanish during the intense emotional reaction to the noise, heat, confusion, and fear. But I also realized that I could not have learned about the tank in one day by going out and kicking the tires. The test results had given me a solid base of knowledge on the M-1; without it I'm sure the whiz-bang technology might have overwhelmed some of my common sense.

As I lay there in the cool refuge of the motel room, I was grateful that I would probably never have to see a battlefield. While my intestines were still churning from the noise of the tank cannons, I began to think about the guys I had met in the tank crew who would have to go out in a tank that had serious engine and transmission problems. I fished out my honorary membership certificate. I had to smile when I read the inscription: "Be it known on this day, Ms. Dina Rasor is declared an honorary member of the First Cavalry Division *in recognition of outstanding effort in support of the Division.*" A nice public relations touch.

Major General Lawrence had signed the certificate, but I'm sure he didn't think of my activities with M-1 as "outstanding effort in support of the Division." I did not think my activities of the day fit that description because I had been too intimidated and meek. But after I met the men who would be asked to risk their lives in that tank in a war, I felt that if I could, through public exposure, force the Army to fix just some of the glaring faults of the M-1 before it reached the battlefield, I would be supporting that division. My determination to continue the fight with the Army to get that tank either canceled or fixed was renewed.

For the next few months, I concentrated on keeping the pressure on the Army concerning the failures of the M-1. I began to receive more and more documents from the "underground" as we began to call it. The Project was beginning to become more than an idle curiosity to the Army and the rest of the DOD. My sources warned me that the Pentagon was more and more interested in flushing out my sources and trying to find out my true motives for releasing this material. I did not see any overt activity in this area but my sources told me to be careful. I still believe that at that time I was just a gnat buzzing at the Pentagon's ear.

On November 10, 1981, in the late afternoon, a man appeared at the door of my office.[25] I was on the telephone and motioned for him to take a seat in front of me. I quickly ended my conversation and smiled across at him. The man was tall and heavyset, with a pale, putty-like complexion and heavily greased hair that was combed straight back. This physical appearance contrasted markedly with his dark Brooks Brothers suit and V-necked sweater.

He leaned forward and opened both hands toward me. "Are you Dina Rasor?" he croaked in a thick, heavily accented voice. "My name is Boris. I am from Soviet military attaché."

I was dumbfounded. I could not decide whether to laugh or be concerned. I tried to regain my wits as I fumbled for a pencil. "Do you have a last name, Boris?" I asked. He gave me his last name, Tatarintev, and his phone number. I took them down carefully. At this point I was convinced that he was part of some U.S. intelligence ploy to discover my sources and see if I could be caught cooperating with the Soviets. "Well, what do you want?" I asked, glancing up into his small brown eyes.

He began a long, disjointed monologue: he knew that we had

information about important U.S. weapon systems and that he would like me to give him all the information I had. Figuring that he was part of the CIA or DIA (Defense Intelligence Agency), I looked at him squarely and told him that my organization was interested in exposing problems in our weapons to force our military to make *better* weapons so that they would be more effective against Soviet weapons.

He appeared surprised at my remarks and pondered that point for a moment. Then he started a political conversation with me, asking whether I felt that the United States was truly a democracy. I argued that my type of investigative organization, dedicated to making the Pentagon work better, would not be tolerated by most countries in the world—and especially not by his country. He countered that President Reagan had forced the AWACS aircraft sale to Saudi Arabia through the Congress. I was fast getting tired of this discussion, so I sarcastically remarked that we were able to get rid of presidents by election or resignation, while his country has a tradition of eliminating leaders who have fallen from grace. This remark did not deter him from boring into me.

"If I have question on particular American weapon, will you show me what is wrong with it?" he asked.

"No," I replied.

"Why not?"

"Because you are not an American taxpayer," I replied smugly. It was getting hard for me to take him seriously. I thought he was acting like a clown so I couldn't believe that he was really a Soviet.

Undaunted, he asked again if I would cooperate with the Soviets. Again I told him no, and anyway I did not have anything classified. He then surprised me with another question. "Do you have perhaps direct line to Caspar Weinberger?" I burst out laughing and said no. "Why then you do not want to cooperate with us?" he asked. I tried to define the meaning of loyal opposition to him but failed.

He had been in my office for more than fifteen minutes. I stood up from my chair to signal the end of our conversation and told him firmly that I would not help him. He rallied one more time and asked me if I was interested in Soviet weapons. I replied that I was, but only to defeat them. He offered me a chance to visit the Soviet embassy to look at their weapons in exchange for the information they wanted on U.S. systems.

At that point, I asked him to leave and he did so reluctantly. I immediately tried to call Ernest Fitzgerald, but he had left his office and was on his way home. I called another source at home and asked him where I should report this incident. He told me to call the FBI and the CIA because if it were one of those two agencies trying to frame me, it was unlikely the other one would cooperate with them. So I reported the incident to both agencies and set up an appointment with an FBI agent several days later.

When I arrived at work the next day, I was still convinced that Boris had been sent by one of the U.S. intelligence agencies to check up on my loyalty. I had kept the slip of paper with his name and phone number, so I decided to do some sleuthing on my own before I spoke to the FBI agent. I opened the Washington, D.C., phone book and looked for the number of the Soviet military attaché: it matched the number Boris had given me. I dialed that number and asked for Boris Tatarintev; I was shocked when I was connected and recognized his voice. I hung up abruptly and sat back against the wall in disbelief . . . he really was a Soviet agent! I raced back through our conversation —I am sure I wouldn't have been so flip if I'd thought he was a Soviet agent.

The FBI agent arrived a few days later and presented his card. It read simply: Fred Ross—FBI. (NOTE: His name has been changed at his request to protect his ability to investigate.) He was a young, clean-cut man who could have passed for an extra on any cop show; he just seemed almost too All-American.

I underestimated Fred. He proved to be a crack interrogator

and was able to help me reconstruct just about everything Boris had said to me. Apparently Ross had been following Boris around for quite a while; he told me that Boris had never been quite this bold, and that in the past he had always offered money for information. Ross finished his note-taking and looked up. "Dina," he said, "you were a good American for reporting this."

I had to smile, and I replied that I liked to think so. He followed up by pointing out that I would be a *better* American if I would contact Boris, take him up on his offer to go to the Soviet embassy and look at their weapon books, and report this information to the FBI. It took me a minute to realize what he was asking me to do. He was actually asking me to spy on the Soviets. I politely refused. He appeared mildly disappointed and left. I was quite rattled because he told me, in the course of the interview, that Boris was with the GRU, which is part of the Soviet intelligence agency. I realized that Boris was no diplomat but a member of a very dangerous organization.

I busied myself with other activities for the rest of the day. Later, walking in the supermarket with my husband, Thom, I was struck by the realization of what I was doing. My sources and I had embarked on a mission to expose Pentagon waste and produce better weapons for our soldiers. Along the way, I had picked up a Soviet agent, mumbling strangers, and hostile military men. My sources had warned me about what could happen, but I had brushed them off as unnecessarily paranoid. Now my knees grew weak as I wheeled my grocery cart to the checkout line. Little did I know that I had experienced only a taste of things to come.

2.

BACKGROUND

IF A FORTUNE-TELLER had told me that three years after I graduated from college I would be a focal point in the struggle to make better weapons for less money, I would have laughed. There was certainly nothing in my past to suggest I would land in this position. I have always had a fascination for history and politics, so it was natural that I enrolled in college as a political science major. During college I participated in two student internships that placed me in a California state legislator's office and with a national lobbying group in Washington, D.C. Both of those experiences left me with a distaste for partisan politics. Although I believed that politicians could accomplish great things, the taint of sliminess that is necessary to succeed in politics made me uncomfortable.

I developed an interest in journalism during my junior year at the University of California at Berkeley. I realize now that I had a very idealistic view of the press. As a teenager during the Watergate scandal, I came to view the press as the defenders of truth, justice, and the American Way. I believed that it was the duty of the journalist to question the status quo and force the nation's politicians to follow a high moral standard. During my last six months of college I worked part-time for KCBS radio in San Francisco as an off-air reporter and put together a documentary on city politics and its effect on the San Francisco waterfront. I liked the journalist's role of a detached observer and it came to me easily. By the time I graduated from college in June 1978, I knew I wanted to continue in journalism, though not by covering city politics.

My main interest was in national politics, but my journalism advisors had drilled into me that I had to start at a small paper or broadcast station in "outer Podunk," and after ten or so years I could gradually work my way into national politics in a Washington, D.C., media outlet. I did not like the advice. Being a rather impatient person, I do a job poorly when I feel that I am just putting in my time. I had a burning desire to go to Washington and cover national politics.

However, I had recently become engaged, and my fiancé was finishing his master's degree in forestry in Oregon, so I considered looking for a radio news job there. My fiancé, Thom, knew that my real ambition was to test the waters in Washington and urged me to try for a job there. He agreed to follow me to Washington after he received his degree and stay for a year. My parents gave me enough money to fly to Washington and stay for two weeks. I decided to try to land a job there, and if I couldn't do it in the two weeks, find a news job in Oregon.

I knew my best chance was in radio because I had some experience in that area. By using every scheme to get in to see the news director of the local and national radio stations, I managed to get a few interviews but had no success in getting any job offers. My second to last day was one of those notorious steamy Washington days in August. I trudged down the sidewalk in my standard "interview" suit while the perspiration rolled down my back. A blast of cold air chilled me as I stepped into the reception area of the ABC News Bureau in downtown Washington. As usual, a door with a security buzzer separated me from the news director. I explained to the receptionist my intentions and she agreed to take my résumé. I pushed hard to see the news director of radio but to no avail. Behind the reception desk was a smart-looking middle-aged woman who had heard my conversation with the receptionist.[1] Motioning for me to go through the buzzer door and then meeting me on the other side, she introduced herself and escorted me to the assistant news director of national news radio, who was looking for a desk assistant to the editor and was very encouraging after my interview. He was on his way to Camp David, Maryland, where President Carter was holding his historic summit meeting, but promised to let me know about the job when he returned to Washington. I went back to California with great anticipation and watched the progress of the Camp David accords very carefully. I wanted Carter, Sadat, and Begin to settle their differences and come to an agreement quickly so I could get a job.

The assistant news director returned shortly after the agreement and offered me a job for four days a week. I quickly accepted because I had already arranged to work as a stringer for Associated Press Radio for $10 a story. With that as a backup, I felt I could survive on the $7000 a year from ABC. I think that at that time I would have taken any salary to end up in Washington rather than "outer Podunk."

I packed everything I owned into my 1969 Datsun and headed east. It was hard to leave my fiancé and parents, but I headed toward Washington with high expectations. My spirit of adventure was quickly deflated when my car broke down three times across the country. I hoped that these setbacks were not an omen of things to come. Although I was exhausted by the time I reached Washington and low on cash because of the car repairs, my excitement and enthusiasm returned when I began to work around the reporters and public figures I had seen on the evening news.

My job as a desk assistant was easy to learn and routine, so I began to observe the reporters and editors around me. Every fifteen minutes there was a deadline for the four ABC radio networks that went out of our newsroom. In this daily news bureau, the emphasis was on obtaining the official statements on what was happening in Washington and then getting them out. There was little if any time for any in-depth and behind-the-scenes reporting, and few chances to find out what was really causing an event or controversy. The idea was to get it fast, get it right, and get it out.

I realize now that I was observing a typical large news bureau in Washington, but at the time I was surprised and a little disconcerted. My editors executed the news with cool detachment and often indifference, regardless of how controversial or emotional the story. I have come to understand that this is an important part, if not the core, of journalism, but I would get personally involved in the news and eventually I began to see that I was not suited for it.

My idealistic view of the press and the news media began to crumble, too, when I was forced to acknowledge that journalism is a business and that most large news organizations are first and foremost corporations. Having never been exposed to how most corporations run, I found out, often the hard way, that there are written and unwritten rules of corporate life that you do not question, especially if you are at the low end of the totem pole. I had been raised by my parents with the freedom to question my surroundings and when I saw something that I felt could be done a better way or was given an order that I thought was unreasonable, I spoke up. Most of the time at ABC it was not to my benefit. I discovered that most of the reporters tolerated or accepted my questions or suggestions but many of the editors (ones who had never been reporters) and the corporate managers did not.

After ten months at ABC I realized that I was not suited for daily news work and did not have the right personality to move up the ladder in this large organization. It was upsetting to see the cutthroat competition that went on among my peers to gain favor with influential editors and producers, and promotions appeared to me to be based sometimes on favoritism rather than ability. I might have been interested in a research job in the more in-depth news sections at ABC, but those jobs were hard to come by.

Therefore I reluctantly began to look for a new job. One of the reporters in radio news, Tony Sargent, saw my predicament and suggested that I try for a temporary job as a researcher at the President's Commission on Coal. The radio manager agreed to give me a leave of absence from ABC, and I accepted a job at the commission.

I did not realize at the time that my experience at ABC would prove to be extremely valuable in working with the press and later with the Pentagon underground. First and foremost, I gave up my unrealistic idealization of the news media and was forced to see that as in any other profession, there are both committed and ineffective people in the media. I also learned that it takes a certain type of person to be a good reporter and another type to be a good editor or manager, and these two personalities often clash on the way to the goals of any journalistic endeavor. I saw that the best reporters are the ones who want to get the real story behind an event, no matter whom it affects, and they do not let power and influence deter them. But I also saw that the most successful editors and managers had other factors to consider, such as how a story will affect future relations with politicians whom they may later need to interview or use to get inside information for a story. Editors and managers especially have to anticipate how the corporate structure of the news organization will react to exposing facts that will seriously disrupt the status quo and the corporation's power in it.

I also discovered that reporters compete for time and space in the news media and must sell stories to their editors. Many public interest organizations do not understand this and are confused when a reporter is interested in their story but does not follow through with an investigation. The reporter cannot just write a story on any subject he wishes. If the story is not assigned to him, he must convince his editor to give him the time to pursue it, and if the story is controversial that editor must convince his senior editors and perhaps even the publisher or (in television news) the head producer or manager.

Since my involvement in nonprofit interest groups, I have been amazed at how blatantly such organizations try to "manage" or manipulate the media but alienate the reporters instead. In radio news I helped open the mail and was always amused at the standard Washington press release that was written like a news story but with self-serving rhetoric. At ABC, most of this stuff went into the trash. My experience there showed me that reporters want information without a lot of ideological baggage attached to it and they resent being used. Now, whenever I give information to reporters, I try to put myself back into the newsroom at ABC and imagine what approach to any story would get through to the reporters and editors there.

Although I knew I would miss the excitement of the daily newsroom, my four-month job at the President's Commission on Coal appeared to be equally exciting and much more challenging. To go along with their year-long study of the coal industry, the commission was sponsoring a project to study and photograph the living conditions of coal miners. My job was to help organize photographers in the various coal mining regions and go along with some of them to interview the miners and their families, keep track of the hundreds of photographs, and write captions for the photographs.

Surprisingly, this short stint helped sharpen my journalistic skills better than the previous ten months at ABC. My main job was to put the miners and their families at ease while the photographers took pictures of them. It was no easy task. Some of the miners in the back hills have a historical mistrust of anyone from the federal government and it didn't help when we showed up in official federal government cars. I learned how to approach and interview people who mistrusted me, to win their trust enough for us to take pictures, and to get them to open up about their present and past life-style. It did not always work, however. Once a miner who lived in a very remote area met our car by pointing a shotgun at us and his request to leave required us to back the car up half a mile before we could turn around.

I also learned firsthand some of the frustrations that average people have with the federal government. Almost every time I went down into a mine and talked to the miners, several of them would find out I was with the federal government and corner me to complain about the red tape and ineffectiveness of the federal programs geared to coal miners. I tried to explain to them that I was only on a study commission, not a regular bureaucrat, but they were so disgusted with the government programs that they insisted I take their complaints back to Washington. I wrote down their grievances to take back to my boss in Washington, but I wondered if they'd ever be forwarded. Sadly, getting no response would just make the miners more cynical about the federal government.

I finished my job with much personal satisfaction, but I wondered if the money that the commission spent for this project was really worth it or if the miners were really helped. Besides the four photographers and me, the project had seventeen field researchers and over a dozen administrative people in Washington. We produced a beautiful 232-page book on the coal miners and their families that is now registered in the U.S. archives and the Library of Congress.[2] The commission gave me a copy. It was an interesting book, professionally produced, but it was not read by the general public and I'm sure that even people interested in the subject don't know it exists.

I was told at the beginning of the job that the commission was running on a tight budget. Yet I was amazed at the salaries they were willing to pay researchers and the travel and administrative expenses. I know I was the lowest-paid researcher because of my lack of experience, but my boss apologized when he told me that he could pay me only at a GS-9 federal pay level that was about $16,000 a year. I had already shopped around for other jobs while at ABC and I knew I could not get that kind of pay in the open market with my small amount of experience.

Although the commission was only a temporary federal government office, there was a lot of administrative red tape and the other government agencies we dealt with worked at a decidedly slower pace than the commission. I discovered that there were very few ways you could speed up an unwilling bureaucrat. It was quite a change from the fast-paced world of news, and I could see why journalists and government officials often clash when it comes to the amount of time it takes to do a review or come up with a statement. On the one hand, the Washington press corps is dashing around to get the news out first; and on the other hand, appointed officials are at the mercy of slow-moving bureaucracies for their information. I could see that my impatience would also not make me a good candidate for government work in Washington.

After my four months at the commission, I went back to ABC temporarily and began to contemplate my next career move. I didn't want to give up on trying to become an investigative journalist. The fact that many of the special interest groups in Washington are not very good at convincing journalists to investigate their areas led me to track down the names of organizations that I thought were doing worthwhile work. One organization that was on my list was the National Taxpayers Union. I did not feel strongly about some of their issues, mainly because of my ignorance of economics, but I liked the fact that they appeared to be a grass-roots organization and that they did not shy away from questioning the status quo in Washington when they felt the taxpayer was not well served, so I made an appointment to discuss the possibility of a job.

The press aide, Donna Dudek, a bright woman in her mid-twenties, saw from my résumé that I had some press experience and she asked if I would be willing to write for the National Taxpayers Union newsletter, "Dollars and Sense." I told her straight out that I did not have any experience in economics, but she was interested in finding someone to investigate fraud and waste in government programs and write about it in the newsletter.

She took me to meet David Keating, a quiet man also in his mid-twenties, who was the research and legislative director for the organization. He repeated that they were looking for someone who could investigate government programs and prepare testimony on waste that they had discovered. Although I was ambivalent about some of the issues the NTU was pursuing, I was very interested in probing government programs for waste. I knew it would be good for sharpening my investigative skills and I thought it would be important and worthwhile work. I told them that I was interested in the job.

To my delight, I was offered the job and started work in August 1979, approximately one year after I had moved to Washington. To prepare myself for working at the National Taxpayers Union, I read their promotional literature. I learned that NTU was a nonprofit, nonpartisan organization—a legal definition that the Internal Revenue Service had given the organization when it was set up in 1970. Because the contributions to NTU were not tax deductible, the organization was allowed to lobby the Congress on legislation that they deemed important to taxpayers.

I am not sure whether anyone realized my basic neutrality on most of the issues the NTU was working on. I didn't have enough experience to commit myself to many of these issues, but I was willing to listen and learn. After all, I reasoned, working for a nonpartisan organization means I don't have to worry about unquestioning loyalty to party politics, which had disgusted me in the past.

I knew I would have to take a stand on what I would be concentrating on—government fraud, waste, and mismanagement. That proved to be easy because I realized that anywhere that power and a great deal of money come together, there are bound to be areas of excessive waste and fraud. I was sure that the federal government had not been able to overcome that aspect of human nature and that there was a huge area to be investigated. I spent most of my free time after I started the job looking at what had been investigated and written on fraud and waste and was surprised at how few reporters were assigned to the subject full-time. I should not have been surprised because so much news comes out of Washington every day. Fraud and waste investigation can take a lot of time and digging to get results.

My job was set up so that I spent half of my time helping David Keating with straight research. The other half of my time was spent setting up a waste and fraud file, trying to get some leads to begin investigating, and looking for pertinent material for articles for "Dollars and Sense."

I discovered that the federal government had an internal system to deal with fraud and waste and that this system was going through a major overhaul under the Carter administration. By the time I arrived on the scene in the fall of 1979, the Carter administration had set up a supposedly independent Inspector General office in most of the major government agencies. These Inspector General offices were to be funded independently from the main agency's budget and report directly to Congress. The Defense Department was the only major department that was exempt from the new law, and the most common reason given was that it was for national security considerations.

There were also various congressional committees that held oversight hearings on areas of their charters and occasionally a committee staff would uncover a large scandal. The hearings would usually receive a lot of press attention, but there was rarely much follow-up. Congressional oversight of the investment of the taxpayer's money was usually a luxury for the committee staff because of the enormous job of keeping the various government programs funded and running during each fiscal year. Most committee investigations did not have staying power unless a powerful member of the committee was championing the investigation.

The Inspector General offices of the various agencies were just beginning to issue six-month reports to Congress when I set up fraud and waste files. Those reports were rather slim, probably because the organizations were just getting started, but the Department of Health, Education, and Welfare submitted legislative remedies in their first report that could have saved over half a billion dollars in the health and welfare areas alone. I soon found that many of the legislative remedies were not likely to pass for political reasons. Exposing waste was much easier than eliminating it, especially if the wasteful program had a powerful ally in Congress.

Another area that was receiving attention at that time was the anonymous hotlines set up at the various government agencies to receive and track down tips on waste from inside the bureaucracy. The establishment of these hotlines was applauded on all sides, including inside the bureaucracies themselves, so I ascertained that they must not be very threatening to the status quo.

The government office that I found was the toughest investigator of government waste and fraud was one of the most unused sources. The General Accounting Office (GAO) issues monthly reports to the Congress on all types of waste and mismanagement in the federal bureaucracy and tends to suggest remedies. I thought many of the reports were quite tough and straightforward compared to the timidness of the new Inspector General offices. I found that most of the subjects they had investigated were not routinely covered by the press. Occasionally, a powerful committee chairman would order the GAO to investigate a subject of the committee's interest and he would then release the results during a hearing to get good coverage in the press. But the reports that the GAO generated themselves often uncovered large areas of mismanagement and abuse that the average person would never know about. I began to order and read these reports regularly. It was frustrating to see so many of them collecting dust in the library. However, I would later learn that even the GAO was underestimating the waste in government.

Among the last waste and fraud factions I met during this period were government whistle-blowers. Over the years, I had read about whistle-blowers trying to expose and clean up waste in their area of government, but I remembered few successful ones. I came to realize this was because most of the attention the whistle-blowers attracted was focused on their personality, their credibility, and their right to blow the whistle and receive protection. The object of their whistle-blowing was often mentioned only in passing because the excitement of the story was how the government agency was trying to harass them.

During this time I was able to make contact with some whistle-blowers after they had gone public. Because they were no longer on the inside it was hard to work with them. We couldn't get any supporting documents and they were understandably unwilling to have us contact anyone where they had worked for fear of getting someone else fired. By the time most of the whistle-blowers came to NTU, they were all wrapped up in trying to defend themselves and get another job. I did what I could to support them, but we didn't have any legal resources and that's what most of them needed. Most of the whistle-blowers seemed to me overly paranoid, and it was hard to get them to talk about anything but how the system was out to get them. I was somewhat leery of them, as I thought some of their charges were too outrageous to be true, but I realize now that I was having the typical reaction to them: I didn't have any way of knowing what they were going through, nor could I judge if their stories were true. Most of them didn't have current documentation to counter the agency's attempts to discredit them or claims that the problem had been solved.

My fascination with this whole new world of government waste and fraud so preoccupied me that I didn't pay much attention to other issues NTU was addressing and I didn't get to know too many others on the staff besides David Keating and Donna Dudek. After my experience at ABC, I had decided not to be as outspoken in my personal opinions, so I rarely had a political conversation with anyone. After all, I reasoned, as a nonpartisan organization we were not supposed to let our personal politics interfere with our work. I felt that my boss, Dave, set a good example. I knew where he stood on most tax legislation, but I didn't know his personal political views.

But as we approached the 1980 presidential election, it became hard to avoid presidential politics in Washington. One evening as I was finishing up the last few work items on my desk, I noticed that Jule Herbert, the vice-president of NTU, was flipping through some magazines in our file. I had not had many conversations with him and I felt that it was time to become better acquainted. I opened the conversation by commenting on President Carter's latest speech and he responded by making a face. Undaunted, I made another remark about Ronald Reagan's chances of making the presidency. Again he made a face. I asked him whom he preferred as a presidential candidate. He shuffled over to his desk and pulled out a "Clark for President" pamphlet that contained the positions of the Libertarian party candidate for president. I had never heard of the Libertarian party, not even at the University of California at Berkeley, and I thought that it was just a fluke that Jule was so interested in this third party candidate. It was only later that I noticed that Jule was listed on the pamphlet as the national treasurer of the Clark campaign, and I was surprised that he had accepted that position considering his job as a vice-president of a nonpartisan organization. I later discovered that the Libertarian party had many supporters on the NTU staff, including the people with whom I worked most closely.

I had a live-and-let-live attitude about the involvement of most of the professional staff in Libertarian party affairs, but I was surprised to find a staff of a nonpartisan organization publicly identified with any political group. But I decided that as long as my colleagues didn't let their political ideology interfere with their work at the NTU and as long as they didn't pressure other members of the staff, I could live with the situation. I now realize that I was extremely naïve about how nonprofit organizations were run in Washington.

In January 1980, I was contacted by a Henry Durham, who was given my name by a person at the Government Accountability Project (GAP), another nonprofit organization that concentrated on protecting the legal rights of whistle-blowers. Durham had been involved in blowing the whistle on the C-5A cargo plane scandal in the late 1960s. As a production manager for the Lockheed Georgia Company on the C-5A production line, he had become concerned about the large waste and poor quality control of the planes coming off the production line. After months of trying to correct the problem within the company, he was compelled to take his information to the congressional Joint Economic Committee that was investigating a large cost overrun scandal on the C-5A at that time. As a result, he ended up leaving his job at Lockheed and federal marshals were needed to protect his house in Marietta, Georgia, because of threats he had received while he was a congressional witness.

He was coming to the NTU because of his concern that the Air Force was considering a plan to pay Lockheed to fix a severe wing problem on the C-5A for which he felt Lockheed was responsible. He was angry that the Air Force would even consider "rewarding" Lockheed with a $1.5 billion wing fix after the scandal that had occurred in the late 1960s.

The story sounded complicated and technical to me, but Dur-

ham had solid documentation of Lockheed's poor past performance and the Joint Economic Committee had held thorough
hearings on the subject. I had not yet investigated any Department of Defense programs and I thought this might be a good
place to begin because of the history of the program. Besides,
$1.5 billion sounded like a lot of money for any one program.
Most of the federal programs I had looked at before were only
a small part of a bigger program and few of them were over the
$100 million range. If Durham's allegations were true, the
payoff to the taxpayer in stopping this program, or at least
reducing its cost, would be significant.

Dave Keating agreed with me and encouraged me to follow
up on this lead. It was easy enough to ask the public relations
people at the Air Force to send me information on the current
status of the C-5A wing fix and the original Air Force proposal
to fix the wing. I also found a very good book on the subject,
The C-5 Scandal by Berkeley Rice, and I settled down to read
about the whole affair. I was shocked by what I read. I mentioned to Dave Keating that the original scandal had revolved
around the testimony of an Air Force cost control analyst, A.
Ernest Fitzgerald, who was later fired by the Air Force for that
testimony. Dave was surprised that I didn't know who Ernest
Fitzgerald was. He told me Fitzgerald had been chairman of
the NTU and a major force in the taxpayer movement for many
years until he regained his job at the Air Force. He encouraged
me to give him a call.

For some reason that I cannot explain, I was reluctant to call
Fitzgerald. Perhaps it was because he had been connected to
the NTU and I wanted my investigation to be objective. I worried that if my findings conflicted with Fitzgerald's opinions I
would be at odds with the top people in the organization. Perhaps it was because I thought Fitzgerald would want me to
concentrate on his harassment as a whistle-blower and the past
scandal rather than the wing fix—a problem I'd had with some
whistle-blowers.

But I realized that I needed help if I was going to investigate such a complicated problem in an agency that I had never looked into before. When I picked up the phone to call Ernest Fitzgerald, I was unaware that I was entering a new stage of my career that would change my attitudes toward Washington forever.

3.

THE MENTOR

ERNEST FITZGERALD had been fired from his job at the Pentagon and then reinstated four years later. Since I had learned from Dave Keating that Fitzgerald had never completely regained his original stature nor gotten his duties back after the Pentagon was forced to rehire him, I expected a sour and bitter bureaucrat to answer the phone.

I couldn't have been more wrong. What I found was an enthusiastic, energetic man with a charming Southern accent and manner about him. He seemed pleased by my call and encouraged me to look into the C-5 wing fix, especially in light of the disastrous history of Lockheed's performance with this plane. But he didn't whine about his treatment and try to get me to start a crusade over his troubles. He was willing to help me on the substantive issues of whether the C-5 cargo plane should have its wings fixed and especially if Lockheed should be "rewarded" for fixing a mistake in their original design.

"You know, Dina, they don't let me look at that stuff on the C-5 anymore," he said with a chuckle. "I swear I don't know why!"

I was surprised and elated to find a whistle-blower who could laugh at a situation that had been plaguing him for eleven years. Although he didn't have any documents on the C-5 wing fix, he told me where some public reports were and gave me names to call to get some inside information and unclassified reports. He encouraged me to call him back if I found anything interesting or if I received any document I didn't understand.

After our short conversation I was inspired not only to dredge up any reports on the C-5 but also to learn more about Ernest Fitzgerald. I spent the next several weeks reading his 1973 book, *The High Priests of Waste,* and then some newspaper articles about his ordeal in the late 1960s and early 1970s. I also went to the U.S. district court to get some briefs from his case.

In November 1968, Ernest Fitzgerald, deputy for management systems for the Air Force, had been called to testify before the Joint Economic Committee's Subcommittee on Economy in Government and asked if it were true that the Air Force's C-5 cargo plane was $2 billion over the predicted price. In the tradition of a good bureaucrat, his answer was vague, but it generally confirmed that the plane was over-running what at that time was already an enormous sum.

Within a year he was fired for his testimony. The Air Force position was that his job had been eliminated in a reshuffle within the department, but since his job was the only one eliminated this excuse was clearly false. After four years Fitzgerald got a job back in the Air Force, but didn't have as much power and influence as before. When I met him he was in the process of suing to get his original job back and also suing former President Nixon and several of his staff for damages suffered after the illegal firing.

During the course of the Watergate scandals, Fitzgerald found out that someone in the White House had given the orders to fire him, so he filed the suit against Alexander Butterfield (of Watergate tapes fame) and nine John Does (unknown defendants). As more and more documents came out of the

White House during the Watergate investigation, he was able to follow the chain of command upward to learn who fired him. Finally, when President Nixon was forced to release transcripts of his office tape recordings, Ernie discovered that President Nixon had actually fired him on tape with the famous words, "I said, get rid of that son of a bitch."

When I met Fitzgerald in 1980, he was, ironically, fighting a Democratic administration to get his original duties back. In the 1976 campaign candidate Jimmy Carter had used the Fitzgerald case as an example of what had to be changed in an entrenched bureaucracy. But as president, Carter appointed Harold Brown Secretary of Defense. Brown, as Secretary of the Air Force during part of the C-5 scandal in the late 1960s, had been involved in putting down Fitzgerald. After that, Fitzgerald couldn't get any cooperation from the Carter administration.

My search for pertinent documents on the C-5 wing fix went well. Through the sources Ernie had given me, I found three reports that questioned the wisdom of investing $1.5 billion in the wings of an aircraft that had other maintenance and readiness problems. One report was a 1975 General Accounting Office (GAO) study[1] on the airlift effort the United States had provided for Israel during the 1973 Mideast war. The study claimed that 60 percent of the C-5 cargo planes were not able to be used or were inoperable for the airlift because of needed maintenance or parts. The wings were not the only problem of the plane. One of the big selling points of the C-5 cargo plane was its ability to airlift outsize equipment, such as tanks, to the battlefield. In reality, according to this report, the remaining 40 percent were able to deliver twenty-nine tanks during the airlift and only four tanks before the cease-fire was signed in this short war of only several weeks.

A 1976 GAO report addressed the future need of airlift and questioned the wisdom of spending more money on the C-5 before studies were done to compare the cost of the C-5 to commercial alternatives such as the Boeing 747 cargo plane, or to sealifting or prepositioning the needed war matériel. It appeared that the C-5 could be the costliest and least reliable alternative. The 1976 GAO report states:

> If the C-5A's are to be available for airlift through the 1980's, the wing modification and other modifications such as the aft cargo door, installation of a fire suppression system, and a lift distribution control system are apparently essential. The Air Force should firmly establish and present to the Congress the total costs associated with modifying and correcting all defects. That cost should then be compared with the cost of alternative methods of achieving the mission now assigned to the C-5A, such as prepositioning matériel, utilizing fast sealift capability, or procuring outside versions of the 747 (or equivalent) freighter.[2]

This 1976 GAO report referred to a so-called APEX[3] engineering report that had been done on the C-5's condition in 1975. Through several of the sources Ernie had given me, I found a dog-eared copy of the engineering section of the report. Apparently the APEX report had been put together by an Air Force study group. It listed at least nine modifications or tasks beyond the wing fix that the C-5 needed to make it safe. The APEX report did not put a price tag on these modifications, but the 1976 GAO report concluded: "The total cost to implement the APEX improvements is unknown at this time. We believe, however, a substantial cost will be incurred for the additional work resulting from the study."

I also found that the House Appropriations Committee's Survey and Investigations staff was studying this same problem with the C-5 and that the Air Force still had not compared the $1.5 billion cost of fixing the C-5 wing to the other alternatives in 1980. I was disgusted at the irresponsibility of this lack of action on the part of the Air Force and felt certain that if these facts were exposed, the Congress and perhaps the Department of Defense would not allow the Air Force and Lockheed to proceed with this questionable wing fix.

Although I had been talking to Ernie at least once a week to report my progress on getting the documents, we really had not discussed what I should do with them or what would happen if and when they were released. When I gave him my theory about the Congress and the DOD not tolerating the Air Force's irresponsibility, he was incredulous. "Dina," he exclaimed, "it doesn't *matter* what is responsible for the taxpayer in the Congress and the Pentagon. This is another make work and bailout for Lockheed and the Georgia congressional delegation. It is pure pork barrel. They aren't going to care about the facts."

"Well, what about the DOD?" I replied. "Aren't they going to get after the Air Force?"

Exasperated, he explained to me that the Secretary of Defense was Harold Brown, who had been Secretary of the Air Force during at least part of the past C-5 debacle. I countered that President Carter was against wasteful defense spending, so at least the White House would be against this sort of irresponsibility. I felt that I was beginning to uncover a major scandal. Then Ernie reminded me that the President was from Georgia, where most of the work on the wing fix would be done. He told me I wouldn't get much sympathy there.

I could tell that Ernie was getting irritated by my naïveté. He told me to go back and reread his book if I thought these things couldn't happen. I felt at the time that Ernie had been harassed for so long that he thought everyone was part of a giant corruption game. The corrupt people would not be able to get away with the same trick again, I thought, because too many other people wouldn't tolerate these shenanigans. I like Ernie a lot, but I thought he was too bitter and jaded to think realistically. Of course I should have realized that Ernie had been around for a long time and had gone through a lot, and that he was the realist and I the dreamer. It took a long time and many blatant examples of waste for me to finally admit to myself that he was right. At that time, though, I had many miles to go before I could even consider his conclusions.

I found another document in my search that was not necessarily germane to the case I was building, but it had a chilling impact on me. I knew that a C-5A cargo plane had crashed during the evacuation of Vietnamese orphans in April 1975 because the rear cargo door had fallen off. Ninety-eight young children had been killed in that crash, along with dozens of American personnel. I thought this was an accidental tragedy that really didn't have much to do with my investigation, so I was shocked to find out that the Air Force had a *1971* engineering report that warned in very strong terms about the danger of the C-5's cargo door system. One of the engineers wrote in the report that the complex rear cargo door mechanism was a "monster system that was unreliable and unsafe." He also recommended that the plane be grounded until the defect was fixed.

Repulsion and then outrage swept over me as I read the report. This was not just a matter of wasting money; people had been killed. Columnist Jack Anderson had written a column about this report in 1979, but otherwise it had not been reported widely in the media.[4] A court case by the civilian survivors of the crash against Lockheed and the federal government was in progress. The APEX report and this 1971 engineering report were among the important evidence for the trial.

I tried to compare this incident to a similar situation in the private sector, but I knew that the public would not tolerate such a defect in a commercial airliner. In this instance, mainly civilians had been killed, but the C-5 was normally operated and used by the average soldier. Who, I wondered, was looking out for him? My investigation took on a new moral tone. At the time, I was just beginning to understand that the soldier has very little representation or say about the weapons that he must stake his life on in a war. I decided to make this one of my new priorities in digging into this case and any other Pentagon investigation I might be involved in.

Dave Keating had been following my progress and instructed me to prepare congressional testimony on the subject as well as to write a story for "Dollars and Sense." I was excited and nervous about putting what we had found into congressional testimony. I had never had so much responsibility, and I knew that I would have to be very careful of the facts so I would not embarrass the NTU on Capitol Hill.

At the same time, Donna Dudek had also been following my progress and was interested in seeing if some of the media might be interested in what we had. She decided that our best bet was Bob Lisset, an acquaintance of hers who was a producer of the now-defunct *NBC Magazine.* Lisset was skeptical when Donna called him but he agreed to take a look at our documents. I was even more excited at the prospect of having a network do a piece on my work on the C-5. I still had a yearning to do television documentary work and this was the closest I had ever gotten to it.

Lisset was pleasant but cool at the beginning of our meeting. Although I was nervous, I carefully went over the documentation. Luckily, he was fairly knowledgeable about the C-5, so I could begin directly with the new documents. As I showed them to him, he asked probing questions and I could see that he was getting more and more interested. He took an armful of documents with him and said he would make his decision soon.

Shortly after the meeting he called to say he wanted to do the show—a twenty-minute "magazine" piece. I was thrilled, but then I began to have doubts about preparing congressional testimony and researching a show for a major network at the same time. It was a tense but exhilarating period for me.

In preparing the NTU testimony, I covered the three main reports on the C-5 wing fix and then asked why the Air Force had not compared the cost of fixing the C-5 to the cost of other types of transporting matérel. I also put in the history of the C-5 program, including a time line of past events in the back of the testimony. Dave wanted me to include specific actions that we thought the Congress and the Air Force should take before committing the money for the wing fix. I felt that adding these recommendations to the testimony was a good idea because I thought that it would not serve us well to be just naysayers, as all too many groups were.

We asked the Congress to:

—follow the House Appropriations Survey and Investigations staff report that called for an independent panel of specialists to reevaluate the wing fix program to see if it was the most cost-effective solution.

—stop funding on the C-5 wing fix program until such a study was done. We recommended that the Congress ask its Office of Technology Assessment to conduct the study.

I also added a sentence that raised a question of whether Harold Brown, then Secretary of Defense, could be objective in making a decision concerning the C-5 considering his past involvement in the program. It was a one-line throwaway comment that would become more important than I realized.

I also raised questions about the C-X, a new cargo plane the Air Force was planning to design and build for the next several decades of airlift. At my request the Air Force had sent me a fact sheet on the new proposed plane. I was amazed to see that the C-X's requirements were very similar to the original requirements of the C-5, which Lockheed and the Air Force were never able to meet. The requirements for the C-X called for it to carry "outsize" equipment such as tanks and to land on unimproved dirt strips near what the Air Force then called the FEBA (Forward Edge of the Battle Area) or in layman terms the front lines. The C-5 was never able to pass the tests of landing on a dirt strip, and common sense would show that it is very unlikely that you will be able to land a large, unmaneuverable, and unprotected plane anywhere near the front lines because of enemy fire.

I asked Ernie about the wisdom of the Air Force's trying once again to accomplish the same mission at which it had failed so miserably with the C-5. He laughed and told me that he once asked an Air Force pilot if he "could land this turkey [the C-5] in a cow pasture." The pilot answered, "Sure, once!" I liked the story so much that I added it to our testimony on the questionability of the C-X project.

Dave went over the testimony I had prepared, while firing questions at me to see if there were any weak spots. He was extremely thorough and I sensed that he knew it is not wise to take on the Pentagon unless your charges have no holes in them. He suggested that we meet with Ernie to make sure we had all the facts right and in the proper order.

I readily accepted his suggestion because although I had dozens of phone conversations with Fitzgerald, I had never met him. He agreed to see us and suggested that we meet him in his office in the Pentagon, which was another treat because I had never been inside the building. I expected it to be plush but warlike, with military men moving down the hall with supreme efficiency.

When Dave and I arrived at the concourse at the Pentagon, I was disappointed at the inside of the building, which, except around the offices of the Secretary of Defense, service secretaries, and the Joint Chiefs of Staff, looked old and a little worn. But I was even more disappointed with the people I saw there. I had been in other federal buildings and seen that the majority of the workers had what I called the bureaucratic shuffle—a lackadaisical, semi-bored, unhurried attitude. Clearly they weren't inspired by what they were doing and I, at the time, vowed that I would never become like them.

I expected the military crowd to be different. I was looking for the square-shouldered majors and colonels with a bright "can do!" attitude about their job of defending the United States of America. While I saw a few people like that, most of the military men and civilians in the building were afflicted by the bureaucratic shuffle, and I was shocked to realize that many of these military men were just bureaucrats in uniform. I later learned that a dedicated military man dreads assignment to the Pentagon. But, I also learned, the bureaucratic military men made their best career advancements there.

I certainly was not disappointed with Ernest Fitzgerald. He was extremely energetic in his manner and speech, and I couldn't get over how mischievous his grin appeared at times. He was of average build, in his mid-fifties, and had even more Southern charm in person. I was, once again, surprised at his unbounding optimism that something could be done to change the Pentagon procurement system. Several years later, when I became discouraged at the enormous task of trying to change such an entrenched system, I asked Ernie how he could keep fighting for so many years.

"I either do this or go back and sit behind the mule on my Alabama farm," he replied, and I gathered that he would be blackballed in the defense industry if he ever tried to search for work in his field of industrial engineering. As I got to know him, I realized that his unyielding sense of humor, even dark humor, kept him going.

He carefully went over the testimony with Dave and me in his office, looking for holes in it but appearing pleased with our work. He had been trying to get the NTU to look once again at the military from a taxpayer's point of view, as it had when he was chairman of the organization.

With Fitzgerald's approval of our case, we were ready to face the public. On March 29, 1980, *NBC Magazine* aired Bob Lisset's show on the C-5. In June 1980 we testified before the House Armed Services Committee during their public witness day, and the August issue of the NTU's newsletter had my report on the C-5 as the cover story. It had been an exhausting but exciting six months for someone who'd had fairly mundane jobs and I loved every minute of it. I was ready for more investigation and more action.

The airing of the NBC show was deeply satisfying. Bob Lisset had discovered on his own that the C-5 had recent severe engine problems and then sprung those facts on Hans Mark, the Secretary of the Air Force. Mark did not have any idea that this was the case and I was surprised by how unprepared he was on that program, even though he knew he was going to be interviewed about the C-5. This was my first glimpse of how little the decision-makers seem to know about specifics on weapons. I thought it was an isolated case. I would learn.

The show backed up our research on the bad shape the C-5 was in because of poor production control and design. Bob Lisset even got the Air Force and Lockheed to admit that the wings were faulty, with many stress fractures. But the Air Force and Lockheed did not admit to the other glaring problems in the plane. That should have tipped me off that something was fishy about their cooperation. Later I would find out what was behind the Air Force's willingness to admit the problems on the wings. But I was too inexperienced to pick up on that subtle message at the time and just basked in the satisfaction of getting my investigation on a major network. It was a heady experience for someone barely two years out of college.

Testifying before the House Armed Services Committee was an important step. I would not be testifying. Dave planned to be the spokesman, but I was nervous about even being up at the witness table with him. Although I had seen many rather dull congressional hearings, I could not help imagining that being at the witness table would be as scary as being a witness at the Watergate hearings.

The room was quiet as we entered and I calmed down a bit when I realized that public witness day is a very poorly attended event. Dave did well in presenting the testimony and at first didn't get any serious or challenging questions. Then a new member of Congress and the lowest-ranking member of the committee, Representative Larry Hopkins (R-Kentucky), honed in on Dave.

"Are you charging that the Secretary of Defense of the United States of America, Mr. Harold Brown, made a cover-up?"[5] he asked, referring to the comment I had included about Harold Brown's inability to fairly judge matters in the C-5 because of his past involvement with the plane. Dave and I were stunned. We had thought that the congressman would be interested in the shocking case we had just laid out instead of in only that one comment.

Dave was not going to take any chances, however, and merely replied that Harold Brown was involved in the past C-5 mistakes. Representative Hopkins then arrogantly lectured us young people on how we'd better have our facts straight when we came up before Congress. I was extremely angry and disillusioned because he didn't seem the least bit interested in our carefully laid-out arguments on how the Air Force might be wasting $1.5 billion.

The August issue of "Dollars and Sense" had a picture of a burned-out C-5 on the cover with the headline: IS THIS ANY WAY TO RUN AN AIR FORCE? I was thrilled but also a little worried about the reaction of the fairly conservative NTU membership. The staff were all surprised that my article produced only positive responses.

Shortly after the airing of the NBC show, Bob Lisset received a call from a Dr. Paul Paris, a St. Louis University professor who was an expert in fracture mechanics—that is, the study of fatigue stress in metals, especially airplane structures. Lisset passed the call on to me. Dr. Paris told me that he had served on a 1977 Structural Information Enhancement Program (SIEP), which was set up by the Air Force to begin studying the C-5 wing problem and what could be done about it. He suggested that this group, along with other study groups in the Air

Force at the time, did not always have impartial people to review the problems. In fact, he claimed that he was the only member of the SIEP group who was not directly employed by Lockheed or the Air Force. He also claimed that these review groups were limited in the amount of technical information they were given by Lockheed and the Air Force and that the groups' study area was limited to only the most expensive and thorough fix for the C-5 wings.

His bottom line was that Lockheed and the Air Force had *overemphasized* the seriousness of the wing cracks in order to get the most expensive fix for the plane. He told me that the wing fix the Air Force was proposing was a total replacement of the wings rather than just repairing them. According to him, the fixed wings from the Air Force's proposed program would last much longer than the rest of the plane possibly could. He likened it to putting a set of tires with a 50,000-mile guarantee on an old car that had, at best, 10,000 more miles of life in it. He said that he had raised these concerns when he was a member of these committees and was now disgusted that Lockheed and the Air Force were willing to waste precious airlift resources for a complete rewinging of an airplane that didn't need it.

If these charges were correct, they would explain why the Air Force and Lockheed had been so willing to cooperate in showing how badly the C-5 wings were cracked to get the bailout for Lockheed, but were silent about the other glaring flaws in the plane. But why would the Air Force purposely waste the money? Could Ernie possibly be right that it was another bailout for Lockheed?

I knew that Senator Sam Nunn (D-Georgia) was heavily promoting Lockheed as the company to build the proposed C-X by claiming in a speech that "Lockheed is airlift."[6] But it was hard for me to believe the Air Force would go along with him, considering the terrible publicity and embarrassment they had gotten from the original C-5 purchase. I felt that I had been trumped by the Air Force and Lockheed. Here they were over-stating the wing problem, while ignoring or hiding the other problems of the C-5.

I asked Dr. Paris if he had any documentation to support his claims. He said he did but that some of it was classified. I told him on the spot that I didn't want anything classified, thus setting a precedent that I would follow for years. He said that he would send me a letter outlining his claims and any documentation he had that was not classified.

After several weeks of reviewing his work and checking his documentation, Dr. Paris advised us that he would be in Washington on a business trip on April 8, 1980. Although I was too ill to meet with him that day, Dave did and was impressed with his general knowledge and encouraged me to pursue his claims when I came back to work.

I called Ernie and told him the story. He was not surprised by the trick Lockheed and the Air Force had pulled, but by hearing that someone in Dr. Paris's position had been willing to come forward. I discussed with Ernie whether Dr. Paris should go public with his complaints, if we felt they were justified, and he advised against it. He said that it was just too hard on the person who goes public.

Since Ernie did not have any experience in the area of fracture mechanics, and could not get access to any documents in the Air Force, especially on the C-5, he encouraged me to contact Richard Kaufman, the major researcher on such matters for Senator William Proxmire (D-Wisconsin). Senator Proxmire, then the chairman of the congressional Joint Economic Committee, had held hearings on the charges of Henry Durham, the former Lockheed employee, and had Kaufman research—and discover—the original C-5 overrun. Ernie said that if Dr. Paris wanted to go public, it would be safer to do it in front of a congressional committee because he would at least have some legal protection against retaliation.

Dr. Paris agreed to work with the congressional committee

staff people if they were serious about trying to solve the problem. I called Richard Kaufman, who agreed to look at our material, so I went over to his office. Kaufman, a shrewd and competent staff member, did a good job of trying to poke holes in Dr. Paris's story.

After a long discussion Dr. Paris decided to testify at a hearing. He later told me that it was because the NTU and Senator Proxmire wanted to make an honest evaluation of precisely what kind of C-5 wing fix, if any, was needed. Dr. Paris, Kaufman, and I spent several weeks preparing for a hearing and trying to find more information on the whole wing-modification plan.

During that time several financial documents on the wing fix were, surprisingly, given to me by an officer at Wright-Patterson Air Force Base. These documents showed, among other things, that the Air Force had not held a true competition on the wing fix program as they had said they would. The Air Force had decided that Lockheed would receive the research and development contract on the wing fix and then the other airplane manufacturers would bid competitively on the rewinging contract. The problem was that the other companies were only interested in bidding if they could also do the research and development since it would be too hard to overcome Lockheed's advantage as designer of the new wing. As a result, the other major airplane companies declined to bid on just the rewinging contract.

To my surprise, the Air Force was still calling the rewinging contract a competitive contract because they took labor rates and various manufacturing data from other companies and estimated what bids they might have made, and came to the conclusion that Lockheed had the lowest offer. It was hard for me to believe they could pretend that this exercise had any resemblance to true competitor. I turned the document over to Kaufman, who planned to use it in the hearing.

The hearing took place on August 25, 1980. That morning

Kaufman remarked to me that it was being held in the same room where Fitzgerald had testified in 1969, with the same committee, the same staff aide (himself), and the same senator (Proxmire). He marveled that this plane continued to create scandal after scandal. Little did I know that the C-5 would come back to haunt me again and again in the years to come.

Dr. Paris testified first about his experience on the various review committees for the wing modification and about his attempts to get information on the plane from the Air Force and Lockheed. He told how, at the beginning of the review for the wing fix, the committees had outline modification plans A through H, with the H-modification being the most extensive and expensive. Shortly after that, the review committees were told that they were to consider only the H-modification plan in their review. Dr. Paris ran into a lot of problems when he began to ask why and wanted to see the numbers that backed up that decision. He was never able to get access to Lockheed's numbers to see if the conclusion was sound scientifically instead of politically.[8]

In his statement he said that the number given for the C-5 wing life before the fix was needed was "based on Lockheed data" and that he "was the only member on the Steering Group who was not a regular Air Force or Lockheed employee," by which he implied that there was opportunity for much conflict of interest. He was concerned that in "August 1977 at the first meeting of the Steering Group, the Lockheed-Georgia people outlined the tasks and in each case the tacit assumption was made that since the H-mod[ification] of the wing was going to be done, other less expensive options were not going to be considered."[9]

According to Dr. Paris's testimony, the more he complained the more he was shut out of the process. Later in the hearing, Senator Proxmire got the Lockheed-Georgia president, Robert Ormsby, to admit that the wing problem was caused when Lockheed took 10,000 pounds out of the original design in order to meet the Air Force requirements and win the original contract back in the late 1960s, and to concede that Lockheed was going to make $140 million out of the $1.4 billion contract for the H-modification.

It was amazing to me and others in the room that the Air Force decision on how to fix the wings was based on Lockheed's assumptions and numbers. I began to remember what Ernie had told me earlier: this was merely more work for Lockheed and Air Force officials wouldn't be outraged by my revelations because the Air Force was part of the problem. This was not the last time Ernie's seemingly cynical remarks would turn out to be right on the mark.

When Dave Keating testified he emphasized the message that the wing modification was sending to contractors. He asked in his testimony:

> Lockheed now has the contract for the H-Mod wing fix . . . If any profit is being paid to Lockheed for the H-Mod, we are setting a terrible incentive system. We will be rewarding Lockheed to repair a part that is clearly deficient. What type of example will we be setting for other defense contractors? The more inefficient you are—the more profit you make. Build failures into the system and you'll be rewarded. By rewarding failure, such a system encourages waste and inefficiency. . . . Finally, because the H-Mod wing fix may very well be unnecessary, could it be that [the] H-Mod was intended to be a multimillion-dollar bailout for Lockheed?

Later in the hearing Senator Proxmire called me forward from the audience to answer questions on the bidding document I had discovered. (I wasn't expected to be needed in the hearing, so I hadn't sat with Dave at the witness table.) Although I was nervous and thought my answers to Senator Proxmire's questions sounded incoherent, in looking back at the transcripts, I am surprised that I made sense.

I was delighted by the press coverage of this hearing, especially since it dealt with such a technical subject. Although the press coverage would be considered average by Washington standards, at the time I thought it was a coup for the NTU. Very little that NTU had done during my tenure there had received so much press coverage. There were stories in *The Washington Post*, the *Washington Star*, *Aviation Week & Space Technology*, and *Defense Week*.

The president of Lockheed-Georgia, Robert Ormsby, testified after we did and the Air Force was scheduled to testify on September 16, 1980. Both groups appeared calm as they told the senators that Dr. Paris was wrong and the H-modification was the correct solution. The Air Force representative did not want another evaluation of the numbers as suggested by Dr. Paris, the NTU, and Senator Proxmire. Their excuse was that the C-5 was too vital a weapon to permit a delay in an operational decision, but Senator Proxmire was determined to get the GAO to review the facts. Unfortunately this took more than a year, long after the Air Force was able to get the appropriations for the wing fix through the Congress.

I learned from this hearing and investigation that you can do a very thorough job and prove with large numbers of documents that you are right, but once one of the Pentagon's weapon system programs has momentum it is extremely hard to stop. I also learned not to be so outraged that the Congress was not more concerned with this kind of decision-making by the Pentagon.

However, I was still elated over what we had accomplished on the C-5 story, even though the funding on the wing fix had passed. I was disappointed that we had not delayed or killed off this questionable program, but I realized that we had come in too close to the end of the decision-making process to realistically hope that we might get them to change. At least, I felt, we had put the Air Force and other government agencies on notice that we were watching them closely for waste.

I believed that the best payoff for the NTU was in the military area, because of the amount of money involved and because President Jimmy Carter and candidate Ronald Reagan were on the 1980 campaign trail trying to outdo each other in promising how much money each as president was going to give the Pentagon. I was convinced that the result would be that the military bureaucracy would get a windfall profit from this debate and that we should watch the Pentagon carefully for waste.

I had found a recently released report on the Army's experimental M-1 tank and wanted to begin to look into it after the C-5 hearings. Reagan had won the election and I knew that everyone else on Capitol Hill and other investigative agencies would be looking for the "welfare queens" in the government's social programs. But I found that Dave was uncharacteristically negative toward my suggestions and vague about when I should start my next Pentagon project. I was puzzled and disappointed when he assigned me to look at the comparative pay scales of government and private employees, especially since I had little background in economics. But I accepted the assignment and began to research and prepare an article on the subject for "Dollars and Sense."

Just about the time I had gathered enough facts to begin to write on the subject, Dave told me that the NTU chairman, James Davidson, had given a speech claiming that federal workers earned on the average 67 percent more than comparative workers in the private sector. Dave said that Davidson claimed he had gotten this figure from our department in NTU. I knew that I had not given him such a number: the most reliable number I had found on the subject was 44 percent from a well-respected economist at the U.S. Chamber of Commerce. Dave told me that government employees' unions were asking to see Davidson's justification for his figure and I had to tell him that the best number I could come up with was 44 percent. Dave wanted me to recheck my numbers and perhaps add benefits to the number to see if I could get it near 67 percent.

I rechecked my sources and had a long talk with the economist at the Chamber of Commerce about adding in benefits. He told me that he didn't think he, as an economist, could put a credible monetary value on federal benefits because some of them were too intangible to calculate realistically.

After I told Dave that I believed the 44 percent figure was the only one we could credibly use, he grew uncomfortable. I surmised that Davidson was putting pressure on him to justify the 67 percent statement. When I wrote the story for "Dollars and Sense" based on the numbers I could back up, I was told by the editor that Davidson wanted to see my story. It came back a few days later with a line drawn diagonally across the first page and Davidson's comment "Unacceptable" on it. I was afraid that to get the story past him, I would have to use his unverified numbers: I was being tested for loyalty. I didn't know what to do, and Dave avoided me when I broached the subject with him. I had the feeling that I might be fired if I didn't comply.

About the same time, Ernie heard from Davidson about Ernie's possible participation in an economic conference that the educational arm of the NTU, the Taxpayers Foundation, was sponsoring. Only later did I learn that Ernie had become convinced that the NTU leadership was beginning to throw in its chips with the new Reagan administration. That certainly explained why I hadn't been encouraged to uncover more Pentagon waste. Ernie explained the problem a few years later in the book *More Bucks, Less Bang:*

> As the [NTU] staff analysis [on the Pentagon] began to bite, it appeared to me that the NTU hierarchy became uneasy. In a dramatic departure from past policy, the NTU became intensely partisan during the 1980 presidential campaign and for a year or so thereafter. They became ardent Reaganites. The NTU had long led the taxpayers' campaign for a balanced Federal budget to be achieved by good management, frugality, and generally bringing the Feds to heel. Ronald Reagan promised to do this.

Despite pledges to cut the then-current Pentagon spending plans of about $99 billion by $5 to $7 billion in the 1976 presidential campaign, Jimmy Carter and his Secretary of Defense, Harold Brown, opened the Pentagonal money sack at both ends after Carter won the 1976 election. Then, during the 1980 campaign, the two major candidates tried to outdo each other in promising increased military spending.

President Reagan kept this promise but the balanced budget promise went by the board, and NTU was left supporting by implication a projected increase of over one trillion dollars (that's $1,000,000,000,000 or the entire estates of one million millionaires, or about $20,000 for every family in the United States) in bonded debt of the United States.[10]

Ernie had been invited to attend this Taxpayers Foundation conference and he asked me to come along with him. I was uneasy because of my conflict with Davidson, but I decided to go anyway. There were a lot of think tank intellectuals and economists as well as Jim Davidson in the room when we arrived. Ernie and I sat together and listened carefully to the group's discussion on what could be done economically and structurally to change the current defense procurement system. After my experience with the C-5 pork barrel wing fix and the factors that fueled it, the discussion seemed academic to me and I turned to see Ernie's reaction to these experts.

To my surprise, Ernie had raised his hand to speak. After being recognized by Davidson, he started his comments by saying that he thought the discussion was "a little unreal."[11] He told them that their suggestions for improving the procurement process were good but until they realized that it was the money and the pork barrel that were steering the weapon procurement process, all their reforms would be ignored by the bureaucracy in the Pentagon.

By working in the Pentagon he could see that money was no problem there. "We have, in fact, horsewhipped the managers to spend money faster," he explained. Most of the conference participants appeared uncomfortable with Ernie's straightforward description of the problem. He was bringing a taste of the reality that he had to live with every day to these men, some of whom spent most of their time in sheltered academic settings.

Finally, one of the participants asked Ernie how he would start to solve the problem and he told them that he would start by saying the magic word "no" to the Pentagon. He said that the Pentagon could work well if someone would only say no to their boondoogles.

Jim Davidson appeared stricken that a little dose of common sense had invaded his academic conference. The participants reacted with nervous laughter and the session ended quickly. Ernie offered me a ride home. I could tell that he was disappointed to see the National Taxpayers Union spending so much money on a conference with participants who, in his view, were part of the defense acquisition problem. He told me that when he was chairman of NTU, it was much more of a grass-roots organization.

As we chugged in his old orange Vega station wagon toward my apartment on Capitol Hill, I told Ernie about my conflict with Davidson on my federal salary story for the NTU newsletter. I said that I thought I might be fired if I didn't give in, but that I knew Davidson was wrong. Ernie sat quietly as I explained my dilemma, then he suddenly pulled the car over to the curb when we reached Stanton Park.

"Dina," he said, "how much money do you make at the Taxpayers Union?"

"I make $10,500 a year," I told him.

"Listen," he replied, "if you're going to sell out, go to Lockheed and sell out for at least $100,000 a year. If you sell out to the Taxpayers Union for only $10,500, I won't have any respect for you. If you sell out to Lockheed for $100,000, I won't like you but at least I would respect your judgment about money."

With that he started up the car and proceeded to drive me home. I laughed but the impact of the statement hit me hard. For the first time since I had come to Washington, someone had enforced the belief I had grown up with that you had to do the right thing no matter what the consequences. I had considered sliding over that line I had drawn between right and wrong. Ernie's statement cleared my mind, muddied after two years of trying to survive in a job in Washington.

That night I decided that I was going to take the high road in this conflict and that if I was fired, I would be better off with my integrity as a journalist intact. The next day I told Dave that if Davidson insisted on keeping those unsubstantiated numbers in my federal pay story, I would insist that my name be taken off the story and I would not answer any questions from the public on the story. The NTU eventually printed the story without my byline, but to Dave's credit he used my figures rather than Davidson's.

At that point I realized that Ernie had truly become my mentor and that I wanted to adopt his standards for personal integrity. Once I had made that decision, I felt a great burden had been lifted from my shoulders and my life became much less complicated. It's easier to make decisions when you know that you will not compromise yourself.

I felt good about working with Ernie, because I felt what we were doing would directly help the American taxpayer and the soldier who has to use the equipment the Pentagon buys. Ernie eloquently put it into terms I could identify with in his testimony before Congress in 1984: "Bad management has shot down more airplanes, sunk more ships, and immobilized more soldiers than all our enemies in history put together."[12] After the crazy experience with the C-5 wing fix, I was beginning to believe it. I knew that I wanted to do more.

4.

THE EXPERIMENT

I WAS STILL BROODING over the fact that I wanted to do more military investigations when I received a call from Ernie a few mornings later. He wanted to know how my conflict with Jim Davidson had turned out. I told him I was surprised that I hadn't been fired. Then we began discussing the discouraging fact that the NTU leadership didn't seem interested in having me uncover Pentagon waste, even though we had been so successful at publicizing the problems of the C-5.

Suddenly Ernie asked if I would consider starting my own organization to look at Pentagon waste and fraud. I was astonished: I couldn't imagine that I had the capability or sophistication to start my own organization at the age of twenty-four, but at the same time I was extremely flattered that Ernie would consider the idea. He told me that a group of people inside the Pentagon needed a way to let the public know about the scandalous situation in the Department of Defense so that pressure could be brought from the outside to make the DOD work better. They had tried to change the system internally but couldn't get anyone to pay attention, he said, and it usually hurt their careers even to protest that far. He told me that very few were willing to be whistle-blowers anymore because "whistle-blowing is a dead art . . . it does not work."

Ernie outlined how such an outside organization could release documents as a "front" for, as he called them, the "closet patriots" inside the Pentagon, so that attention would focus on the scandal rather than on the personality of the whistle-blower. If the organization could protect the identities of these sources, then they could remain in a position to continue to investigate the problem and provide more inside knowledge.

I liked the idea that the source could continue to provide documentation during an investigation, particularly because of my frustration trying to prove that the Pentagon had not fixed a problem when a whistle-blower came forward and was no longer on the inside.

I told Ernie that it was a great idea but that I didn't have the slightest notion how to start such an organization. He replied that he had brought up the idea with the board of directors of the National Taxpayers Legal Fund of which he once was chairman and was still a member and that the board appeared enthusiastic. The problem was that the Legal Fund was in debt and if I became affiliated with it I would have to raise my own money. I responded that I didn't know anything about raising money, and he gave me a few names of board members of the Legal Fund and asked me to think it over.

After I hung up I sat back and rolled the idea of my own organization around in my mind. It was a thrilling but frightening offer. I didn't know much about running anything, since I had always been at the low end of all the organizations I had worked for. But I pushed my fears to the back of my mind and began to explore the possibilities of such an organization. I knew it could be done at minimal expense because I would really need only office space with a phone and a desk to get started. I had a few press contacts from the C-5 wing fix project and I had learned a lot about the Washington press corps from

Donna Dudek. To start with, I mused, I would be able to take on only one weapon at a time and build a reputation slowly from my first investigation.

I fished around my desk for the GAO report I had received on the Army's M-1 tank and decided that it would be a good place to start. The price of the M-1 tank had jumped dramatically in just one year and the GAO report was not optimistic that the price would remain under control. I figured that someone on the inside must be upset at this development, and that it would be best for me to investigate a weapon that Ernie wasn't involved in so that my facts couldn't be traced to him and the other dissenters in the Air Force.

But what about money? I asked myself. And what about the uncertainty of such an undertaking? Maybe this idea is just too unrealistic, I thought. I decided to bounce the idea off my husband later that evening. To my surprise, he didn't think it was unrealistic. He had a full-time job and he encouraged me to try to get funding for such an organization. Pretty sure that I wasn't going to be allowed to do more military investigations at NTU, I thought I'd go ahead and take the risk.

I decided that to be able to set up an organization that might work, I couldn't be at the NTU full-time so I asked Dave Keating if I could work part-time for three months. He agreed but told me that I would have to leave the NTU at the end of that time whether or not I had funding for the organization, since he needed someone working full-time. I accepted that and with this step realized that I was now committed.

Ernie had given me the names of two board members at the National Taxpayers Legal Fund (NTLF), Anne Zill and Jule Herbert, whom I already knew from working at NTU. I decided to pursue Anne Zill first since I didn't feel that Jule was too approachable and I wasn't sure that he was enthusiastic about my work at the NTU.

Anne Zill is the Washington representative for Stewart Mott, a well-known philanthropist from New York City. I did not know what sorts of projects Mott helped fund, but Ernie had spoken highly of Anne and her knowledge of the public funding field. Ernie had told me that she was also concerned about the debt the NTLF had accrued and was anxious for NTLF to have some future programs that would be attractive to funders.

Anne Zill's office is at the top of a big mansion on Capitol Hill that Mott had bought to house the various organizations he supports. As I climbed up three flights of stairs to her office, I became increasingly nervous because I was wholly ignorant about fundraising. And I was also concerned that it would be hard to convince anyone, especially someone as savvy as Zill, to invest in anyone as young and inexperienced as I. I felt that I was in over my head.

Anne is a young-looking, energetic woman in her thirties and I was impressed with her accomplishments and position. She let me know that while she would be happy to guide me in setting up an organization, I would have to learn how to raise the money to support it. She gave me some pointers on how to approach various foundations and to do direct-mail fundraising, and we agreed to have another meeting. Although she had done her best to be helpful, I wasn't optimistic of success. Fundraising struck me as the sort of work I would never be good at.

A few days later, when I was putting in my half day at the NTU, Jule Herbert approached me and, to my great surprise, said that he'd been talking to Ernie and liked the idea of our proposed organization. A wealthy funder named Charles Koch might be willing to provide the seed money for such an organization, Jule went on, and if I wrote up a proposal for the organization, he would send it to Koch. I later learned that Koch was one of the major backers of the Libertarian party and had given a large amount of money to their 1980 presidential candidate, Ed Clark. I was leery of the Libertarian party, but I reasoned that if I laid out the clear intent of the organization and stuck to the guidelines, there wouldn't be any Libertarian slant to the organization. I also knew that Ernie was viewed as the mentor to the proposed organization and to me. He wasn't a Libertarian zealot and wouldn't want politics intruding on a nonprofit research and public educational project.

Having the freedom to mold an organization to my own ideas was thoroughly satisfying, but I had to think about what I wanted to accomplish. One of my few constraints was that since the outfit would be a project of the NTLF, a nonprofit, tax-deductible organization, the law allowed such a project to lobby only 20 percent of the time. I decided at the beginning that I was more interested in publicly exposing the scandals in the Pentagon than in lobbying, so that solved most of the problem. The NTLF director, Dan Lewolt, told me that if a member of Congress asked for our information and we supplied it on request, that was not considered lobbying according to the Internal Revenue Service's rules.

After much thought and discussion with Ernie, I came up with five goals for the project. First, I decided that we didn't want to get involved in foreign policy because I wasn't experienced in that area and it had nothing to do with military procurement. Also, Ernie and I agreed that my sources inside the Pentagon wouldn't be interested in promoting a particular group's views on foreign policy. The approach was similar to the impartial taxpayer concept followed at the NTU: I felt that reporters had been interested in our material on the C-5 wing fix mostly because we didn't try to inject any war or peace ideology into our findings.

I submitted the proposed five goals to Jule for his comments because I wanted him to be clear on where the organization would stand. He changed a few words that, to my surprise, strengthened the narrow track Ernie and I wanted to take, and gave the proposal back to me with his approval. The goals were to:

1. Awaken public awareness to the waste, fraud and fat in the military budget.

2. Encourage close public and congressional scrutiny of large military outlays, including major weapon systems.

3. Reform the military procurement system toward an effective and reliable defense of the United States.

4. Save the American taxpayer as much money as possible without jeopardizing U.S. defense.

5. Encourage and assist whistle-blowers in the military establishment to expose ongoing fraud and waste.

I sent the proposal to Charles Koch, our possible funder, stressing that the organization would be a low overhead operation because in the beginning I would require only office space with a desk, a phone, and a part-time secretary.

I also had to give the organization a name. Several people at the NTLF came up with Taxpayers Against Military Excess (TAME), but I thought that was too cute and had a liberal sound to it. I wanted a name that would sound as politically neutral as the organization would be. After a few false starts I came up with the bureaucratic-sounding Project on Military Procurement. I wanted the name to be vague enough so that people in Washington, especially journalists, would not automatically give the organization a political label and would listen to what we were saying to find out what we were all about. Later, I would find that another benefit of the organization's name was that at first many people, including government employees, assumed that we were a government entity and were not suspicious of our requests. I gave the finished proposal to Jule and waited with hope.

In the meantime I was learning about the traditional world of fundraising and found it very discouraging. Most of the foundations that could be expected to give us money met only twice a year, not in time to fund me before my three months were up at the NTU. I could also see that successful grant writing was an acquired skill but not one that I wanted to spend my time learning. I wanted to investigate and report. But I saw it as necessary to reach my goals, so I began reading books on writing applications for grants. Occasionally I played hooky from that and began researching the background of the M-1 tank.

To my surprise, Charles Koch agreed to give me seed money. Jule shuffled into my office to announce the approval of the Project and asked me how much I wanted in salary. I could hardly believe it. The money would be donated to the NTLF and in the last week of January 1981 the board of directors agreed to adopt the Project.

January 30, 1981 was my last day at the NTU. I was excited about my new start, but I realized that I had learned a lot about investigation and the press from Dave Keating and Donna Dudek, and didn't regret my tenure at NTU. Dave, now vice-president of the organization, taught me caution and discipline in investigative matters. I have the utmost respect for his careful investigations.

On February 2, 1981, I started as the project director of the Project on Military Procurement. The title carried no weight and the organization had no substance. It meant only a $16,000 a year salary, but there was the promise that I could mold the job into something that could make a difference, that might improve the defense of our country. Ernie and I were pushing toward our goals and I felt that the Project's only limitations were our own hesitations. I was ready to put fundraising behind me and produce something of value people would *want* to fund.

At first, I spent most of my time researching the M-1 tank. This led me to Andrew Cockburn, a New York–based journalist who at the time was writing for the trade publication *Defense Week*. I had worked with him briefly on a story there on the C-5 wing fix. He had produced an exposé on the technical problems of the M-1 for ABC's news magazine *20/20*. He gave me some good background on the M-1 and encouraged me to keep working on the story.

Unbeknownst to me at the time, Andrew informed a group of men inside the DOD who were becoming increasingly alarmed at the test failures of the M-1 tank that I, too, was looking at its problems and that I might be able to help publicize them. Thus, I met and began to work with one of the major factions of what I now call the "Pentagon underground." This group, which so successfully led me through the maze of the M-1 tank tests and other documents, was mainly concerned that our weapons were overly complex and expensive, unreliable, and often ill-conceived for the battlefield.

Coincidental with the start of the Project, a group of these men, after years of trying to reform the system from within, had decided that they had to go public to force some reforms of the weapons procurement system before soldiers died unnecessarily. Some of this group worked closely with James Fallows when he wrote *National Defense.* Others stumbled onto me and my fledgling organization. Over the past four years I have worked with many groups in the underground and have been amazed that many of them don't know about each other or have not thought about working together.

Ernie Fitzgerald was the natural head of a group inside the Pentagon who were concerned about the inefficiency of the weapons procurement system and the unnecessary waste of billions of dollars each year. The group I met while researching the M-1 were investigating the technical failures of the procurement system that directly hurt military effectiveness. Over the course of four years I met half a dozen small undergrounds concerned with fraud or mismanagement in their area. These groups merged into a single purpose under the Project: to buy more effective weapons at a lower cost. This combined approach has had a powerful effect on the press and the Pentagon.

It took quite a while for this combined underground to get

rolling under the Project because I had much to learn about how the military procurement system does and does not work. Each new group of the underground was leery of me at first and I, in turn, had to be convinced by their documentation that their accusations about the Pentagon were sound. They tested me with certain issues or weapon systems to see what I would do with the material and I carefully checked each one of their claims. I didn't assume that they were automatically right. I found each group had a bias that I had to sort out before I approached the press with the material, so I often checked the claim of one group with another group that was not involved with the claim.

Through it all, Ernie was a great advisor and mentor. Although he wasn't personally involved in any of the programs that I was investigating, his nearly thirty years of monitoring procurement gave me good insights into how the Pentagon system works and how it covers up its mistakes. His knowledge of the system saved me from having to learn some valuable lessons the hard way. It was, nevertheless, often a maddening experience, because I would call him up with what I thought was a new kind of scandal only to learn that the Pentagon had used the same methods of deception on a related matter ten years earlier. He always seemed able to predict the outcome of such scandals, even though I thought at the time that he was way off the mark or too outrageous. I learned from him that the Pentagon bureaucracy's failures in procurement were amazingly predictable, whether it was the Army buying a tank, the Air Force buying a plane, or the Navy buying a ship.

By the summer of 1981, a budding underground had formed. We had a few successful exposés on various types of problems, and with the M-1 under our belt, more and more reporters were becoming interested in our information. I knew that it was time for the Project to grow and take on other weapons investigations. Jule Herbert agreed that I should get a summer intern. Since Jule had become the working president of the NTLF, I passed administrative decisions through him and his executive director, Michael Burch. Both of them seemed delighted with the publicity the Project had received and encouraged me to press on.

I interviewed a few possible interns and was most impressed by a woman from American University named Donna Martin, who had been referred to me by a journalist. She was a small, pretty woman with a surprisingly no-nonsense attitude, and remarkable poise for a college student. She was working for a master's degree in international communications and had been a television reporter and weekend anchor at a local news station. She already had a master's degree in radio and television. Then I was surprised to learn from her résumé that she was thirty years old. I was flattered that such an experienced woman would be interested in a summer job with the Project and I promptly hired her.

I assigned Donna to look at Navy programs so that she would become familiar with the department's new weapons and their possible problems in case we found an underground in the Navy. She threw herself into the task, which, of course, was difficult because she had no previous experience in military weapons. She found out that there were a series of classified General Accounting Office (GAO) reports on the problems of the guidance system of the soon-to-be-deployed cruise missile program.[1] I had established a policy that the Project would not accept any classified documents because I believed that we had no right to break the law. Donna found out that the GAO was willing to "sanitize" the documents, which means that the classified sections would be cut out.

I told her to get the santizied documents, but I didn't think that there would be much revealing information left. I also didn't think that the missile would be publicly considered a technical failure because so many of the peace groups were condemning it as an effective and destablizing nuclear weapon.

When Donna finally received the sanitized reports, I saw that

I could not possibly have been more wrong. The five reports, which spanned three years, consistently warned, among other things, that the guidance system for the cruise missile had considerable problems that might not be fixed by the time the missiles were deployed in Europe. I checked with my sources and found several people with the technical experience to explain the reports to me and to verify that this problem had been known internally for some time. I was surprised that my sources had not mentioned this problem, but they told me that they had not brought it up because the documents were classified.

I passed the documents to three journalists from the *Chicago Sun-Times,* the *Boston Globe,* and the *Chicago Tribune,* who wrote stories about the GAO's concerns on the cruise missile. I expected the Navy and the Air Force to be upset, but instead they sent the reporters to the Joint Cruise Missile program office, which stated that recent tests showed the GAO to be wrong; the tests could not be released because they were classified. My sources assured me that the GAO reports' conclusions were still valid, but they could not help me get the documents to prove it because of the classification problem. The Joint Cruise Missile office did not answer all the questions we had raised from the GAO reports, but when they chose to ignore us it was hard to encourage reporters to do follow-up reports without any documents. It was very frustrating.

Jule Herbert, however, was elated with the Project's ability to get front-page stories. He sent the front-page headline story in the *Chicago Tribune* to Charles Koch, the man who had given the seed money for the Project, and to other potential funders. The NTLF board of directors seemed pleased at the progress we had made in the first seven months of existence with our investigations of the M-1 and the cruise missile.

Although the executive director of the NTLF, Michael Burch, was a little gun-shy about the Project's work and the political effect we might have on Capitol Hill, Anne Zill, Ernest Fitzgerald, and Jule Herbert encouraged me to continue to get the word out to the press and the Congress. In my initial budget for the Project, I had recommended that the Project, through the NTLF, hold a conference on military waste and ineffectiveness. Since we were getting a lot of requests from Congress after the recent publicity, I felt that a conference might be worthwhile if I could find speakers who were willing to talk about these problems in public. I drew up a preliminary plan for topics and speakers for a conference, and Ernie and Jule encouraged me to put one together.

Because the staff at the NTLF was so small, it took a few months to work out the details and logistics of the conference. Each step of the way I informed Jule about the subject and the tentative speaker list. The conference involved a lot of work, but I felt that it was worthwhile because of the impact we could make on reporters and congressional staff who were expected to attend. I had no idea that the real impact of the conference would be on the Project itself instead of on the audience.

To my surprise, we were able to get two Republicans, Senator Mark Hatfield of Oregon and Senator David Durenberger of Minnesota, along with two Democrats, Representative John Dingell of Michigan and David McCurdy of Oklahoma, to sponsor the conference. I felt this showed we were truly a nonpartisan organization.

I was also elated that several men who were familiar with the issues agreed to appear at a public conference and discuss what was considered heresy in the Pentagon: that our weapons were not working and that they were costing far more than they should.

I asked Ernie to be the moderator at the conference because of his overall knowledge about defense. The rest of the panel consisted of Pierre Sprey, a consultant of the Pentagon and the codesigner of the F-16 fighter; Thomas Amlie, the former head of the Naval Weapons Laboratory at China Lake, California, an expert in most Navy and Air Force missiles; Paul Hoven, a former Vietnam helicopter pilot and consultant on land warfare strategy and coauthor of a paper on the Bradley Fighting Vehicle; and Loebe Julie, a small businessman and engineer who had been battling the Army for seven years to get it to buy his proven calibration system. I felt that we had good representation of all the groups in the Pentagon underground and were covering topics that directly related to the Project's goals of a better defense for less money.

The conference's name was designed to convey a constructive examination of our defense buying: "The Taxpayer and National Defense: Are We Getting a Good Return on Our Pentagon Investment?" The conference was broken into a morning session in which each speaker gave a paper and an afternoon session devoted to questions and answers and general discussion.

The conference took place on March 10, 1982. The turnout was good for such a young organization. We had an interesting mixture of congressional staff, reporters, and, I suspect, a few of the Pentagon underground I had not met before who sat in the back listening.

Just before Sprey gave his morning briefing on the quality and quantity of our weapon systems, a tall, nervous blond man who was dressed in civilian clothes but had a military haircut appeared at the press table and began handing out a stack of papers to the reporters. I immediately went over to question him, but he quickly vanished when he saw me coming. One of the reporters gave me the distributed paper, which was a point-by-point Army rebuttal of an earlier briefing Sprey had given to members of Congress. I slipped a copy to Ernie at the front table with a note describing what had just taken place, and he relayed the information to the audience. Heads turned to see if the man could still be spotted. The panel members, including Sprey, made a joke that the Army had rebutted the wrong briefing. But I was still impressed that the Pentagon had noticed our conference and was worried enough to prepare a rebuttal of at least one of the speakers. I was surprised that they were willing to reveal their concern about our activities to the press and pleased that they stopped pretending to ignore our work.

In the afternoon session, the questions to the panelists ranged from reducing the costs of weapons to trying to make more effective planes and missiles. I was especially pleased to see my former boss from the NTU, David Keating, who asked several good questions from the taxpayer's point of view. Paul Hoven, the combat veteran, kept the discussion from rising into the clouds by telling some stories of what happens in battle when procurement policies fail. I was happy to see that this conference, unlike many conferences I have attended in Washington, stuck close to the facts and did not get wrapped up in esoteric arguments while the Pentagon continued to waste millions of dollars.

I noticed that one of our board members, Edward Crane, had come in for the afternoon session. The head of the Cato Institute, one of the major Libertarian think tanks in Washington, he had never discussed the Project with me and we had met only twice, so I was pleased to see that he was taking an active interest in our conference. About the same time, one of his companions asked the panel about the underground's reaction to the effect of the military budget and U.S. foreign intervention on U.S. weapons procurement policies. I was concerned that we keep foreign policy out of the conference because it didn't have anything to do with the procurement policies we were trying to reform. I thought that Sprey gave the best answer when he said:

> When you get into those areas, like should we be in Europe, or should we have a larger or smaller presence in Europe, and those other things that in theory are supposed to control our defense posture, and those are important questions—I don't intend to minimize them—however, I think it's very important for people here to understand that they have no connection whatsoever with what we buy. . . . [W]e buy for totally different reasons

because it's good stuff and we like it, and certain bureaucracies have certain interests. Afterwards, we make up
foreign policy justifications for why that was the right stuff
to buy to meet our commitment in the Indian Ocean or
commitment . . . [a]nd it's a terrible illusion to think that
stated foreign policy of the State Department or anywhere else has any real impact on what, in fact, is the
defense budget.[2]

A few minutes later Crane strode out of the room looking
grim, but I was so absorbed in the discussion I didn't pay much
attention. The conference ended on a positive note as each
panel member gave some concrete suggestions on how to begin
to solve the problem. All the participants felt that the conference was a great success. I had no idea that a bomb was about
to drop on the Project.

Two days after the conference, as I was cleaning up the final
details, I received a call from Ernie. He was surprisingly somber
as he told me that Ed Crane had written a memo severely
criticizing the Project and was laying plans to get the Project
ejected from the NTLF. He told me that Crane had written in
his memo to the board of directors of the NTLF that "the
Project on Military Procurement is attempting to increase the
efficiency of our fighting machine. From my perspective it is
already grossly too efficient. I'm also skeptical of arguments that
we can actually save the taxpayer money by telling the Pentagon on [sic] how it can save money." Crane also said that the
chairman of the NTFL, Eugene McCarthy, felt that it was
"more important to cut the Pentagon's lean than its fat." He
believed that if the Pentagon was weak, the United States
would not be able to have an interventionist foreign policy. This
was not the first time I had heard this complaint, but I thought
it had been resolved in the organization months earlier.

The Project received a grant to start a newsletter about our
current investigations. Since I was busy with investigations, I
hired an assistant named Ben Lay, after Donna Martin left for

the summer, to write and design the newsletter. Although the Project had raised the money for this newsletter by itself with the help of board member Anne Zill, I agreed to have the first edition approved by Jule Herbert and Michael Burch.

They rejected draft after draft, telling me that it was poorly written or that the stories were not well documented, which I was confident was not the case. I had two lengthy discussions about the problem with Jule, who finally admitted that he wanted me to put some foreign policy and war and peace articles in the newsletter. I reminded him that the Project goals did not address these issues and that I had promised my sources not to use the publicity the Project's investigations generated to push any foreign policy ideology. He seemed to back off the issue but he and Burch continued to stall the newsletter. Jule told me that I could not discuss the issue at the next board meeting because no employees were allowed. Later, I found out that Burch had been at the board meeting and criticized the newsletter's quality. This angered me, but at the time I decided to ignore the problem and delay the newsletter until they either forgot about it or we were pressured to use the newsletter grant money. I knew that I had come too far to ever consider breaching the agreement I had made with the underground. Besides, Jule was obviously too happy with our publicity for me to become concerned about the future.

It had become apparent that Ed Crane was a major reason behind Jule's resistance to the newsletter. I found it hard to believe that Crane could really believe that a weak and wasteful military would convince our top decision-makers not to intervene overseas. It certainly did not stop us in Vietnam.

Ernie told me that this attitude was not new. In *More Bucks, Less Bang* he later recounted Crane's attitude of cutting the lean, not the fat, in the Pentagon: "This was the limousine liberal cocktail chatter from the early 1970's. Those of us who lived through the efforts to control military spending in the late 1960's and early 1970's recalled that same argument being made by representatives of the big foundations, the labor unions and establishment liberals.[3]

Ernie told me that Ed Crane, Jule, Anne Zill, and he had agreed to meet in three days, on March 18, to settle the matter. I told Ernie that my position was clear: I had carried out the agreed-upon goals of the organization as approved by the board; and I could not morally renege on the arrangement I had made with the underground. Ernie agreed, and since I was not asked to present my views, I knew that he would tell the group how strongly committed I felt to the underground.

The rest of the week I was surprisingly calm as I went about the normal work of the Project. I guess that I thought the Project had been too successful to justify firing me. Until then everyone had been ecstatic about our success, and I thought this was just a minor bump on the road to our successfully exposing Pentagon waste.

Three days later I wished Ernie good luck with his meeting and went home for the evening. I had just settled down to a long bubble bath when the phone rang. It was Ernie: in a quiet and depressed voice he told me he thought he'd just gotten me fired. Incredulous, I asked him what had happened. He said the discussion had started out cordially but that Ed Crane started complaining extensively about the Project's approach to the problem. Ernie told me he started to get angry because, up to that point, Crane had never been involved with the Project either to help or to criticize it.

"You know," Ernie said, "he's one of those people who sit in lounges and criticize the world instead of going out and being in the trenches like you and me."

Still very serious, he told me that he thought that I would be fired soon. We talked about options for the Project and then ended the conversation.

I was strangely calm about this piece of jarring news, perhaps because of the success I'd had in standing up to the NTU director, Jim Davidson. But I also felt if the NTLF would not let me run the organization as I had promised the underground, I would rather not do the job at all. I didn't want to get so addicted to the heady feeling of the Project's success that I would continue to run it at any cost.

Jule had written a memo to the board on March 19, 1982, and was nice enough to furnish me with a copy. Although many of his complaints were similar to Crane's, he was much more conciliatory about working out a solution. He had talked to Ernie earlier and admitted that the Project was the most successful NTLF endeavor and he did not want to lose it. So I went home for the weekend to celebrate my twenty-sixth birthday, more hopeful than I had been all week.

Jule returned Monday a changed man. Around mid-morning, he shuffled into my office to tell me that I was dismissed because he was tired of "this Fitzgerald thing." Assuming that he was talking about Ernie's argument with Ed Crane, I replied that I thought the board of directors should vote to eject the Project, but he shook his head and turned to leave. The discussion began to sound more like a divorce than a firing when I told him that I planned to keep the Project's name and continue it. He told me I couldn't keep the Project's name, but I countered that I would simply tell the reporters the Project no longer had the special relationship with the Pentagon underground, and the substance of the Project was the connections listed in my Rolodex, which went with me. I figured I had nothing to lose by acting so boldly.

It worked. Jule later agreed to let me keep the Project name and to take over the lease on the office after I threatened to rent the space right next to the NTLF main office. The next day I wrote a parting memo to the board on why I could not compromise the Project goals. Here are some excerpts from that memo:

> . . . From the very beginning of the Project I have been extremely careful not to involve the Project in defining

the "defense of the United States" from a foreign policy point of view for the following reasons . . .

. . . the Pentagon has used the emotional aspects of foreign policy to muddy the waters on any discussion of weapons procurement for years in order to distract and separate taxpayers, while the Pentagon quietly robs our coffers . . .

. . . by removing foreign policy as an issue, I have been able to tap the resources of a wide and varied group of people in the Pentagon who would not normally go public with their information and documents. They have come to the Project because they know we will not push a foreign policy doctrine with their material, but rather use their material to expose the Pentagon for what it is: a bureaucracy that has gone wild with the taxpayer's money, full of fat, fraud, waste, and useless weapons. The Pentagon really does not know how to react to us because they cannot label us in the traditional dove-hawk manner, nor can they discredit us to their employees by distorting our foreign policy views. I believe that this is exactly why the many anti-Pentagon groups have failed in the past to stop the overspending by the Pentagon, and the conservatives have been unable to build weapons that will defend anything, even the continental United States . . .

. . . Our success with the press is also linked to our unique position of not addressing foreign policy. Reporters seek information about weapons procurement from groups such as ours and I have seen them turned off because they are cornered into hearing a long lecture on foreign policy doctrine. These reporters are *defense* reporters, they cover the Pentagon, not the State Department. The Project provides a place for the reporters to come and find out about the real story on fat, waste, and porkbarrel, to teach them how to catch the Pentagon in its own lies, and how to critically evaluate weapons effectiveness in a battlefield situation. These reporters in turn inform the taxpayer on how and why the Pentagon is failing . . .

. . . As a taxpayer organization, we represent a very diverse group of people who have invested in some form of "national" defense. By keeping our focus narrow, we are able to appeal to a large group of taxpayers, and I believe that only this large group of enraged and disillusioned taxpayers will be able to stop the Pentagon's outrageous and dangerous spending habits. . . ."

Then I had to do some serious thinking about my future and that of the Project. My husband, Thom, and I sat down to assess what we had. I had the name of the organization, a lease on an office, and some office furniture. But I knew that the workload for the Project had grown with our success and publicity, and I couldn't handle the work on my own. The Project had no funding, no nonprofit status, and no staff. The firing came at an unfortunate time for my husband and me because he had recently quit his job to try to build up a consulting service in forestry. Now neither of us had a salary.

But neither of us was ready for the ground swell of support for the Project that occurred. Many reporters called with their condolences and asked if I was going to try to continue. I automatically answered yes while I reassessed our position. Reporters from the *Chicago Sun-Times, The Washington Monthly,* and the conservative *Human Events* did stories on the Project showing that I had been fired for trying to make the military more efficient.[4] I am sure the Pentagon was furious with these stories because they had been trying to convince the press that the Project was trying to harm military effectiveness.

The underground also called in support of continuing the effort. They had been pleased with the Project's success in getting the press and public interested in the problems of procurement and did not want to lose the momentum. So Thom and I decided to take a calculated risk: he would set aside his plans to start his consulting business and work for the Project free for three months, and we would fund the organization from our savings. I would also work without a salary and try in three months to find sponsorship for the Project. I called Ernie and other members of the underground with our decision and they pledged to help. Ernie sounded especially dedicated to the continuation of the Project, and I think that both of us were motivated to not let Ed Crane and the others on the board involved in the ouster win. Several acquaintances told me that Crane was predicting our demise, and it made Ernie and me all the more determined that the Project live.

The encouragement of the underground was especially touching during this stressful time. One underground member told me that I should let them know when my savings ran low and they would pass the hat among themselves. "Don't take on the financial burden by yourself," another told me.

I also received a call from a friendly senator who offered me a job on his staff at a much higher salary than I had received at NTLF. I thanked him profusely but told him I wanted to give the Project a chance. He said that it was a standing offer and it eased my mind that I would have a job to go to if necessary. I will always be grateful to him.

Thom and I worked long, hard hours that summer to give the Project the semblance of normalcy. While I continued to make contacts, look for documents, and seek new funding sources, Thom did all the rest, including setting up an office, keeping track of the Project's finances (from our money), answering the phone, writing letters, and doing all my needed background research. It was certainly not gratifying work for a man with a master's degree in forestry, but he organized the Project as it had never been done before. We were definitely still in business.

The underground continued to grow and produce. During that summer and fall of 1982 I had some of my best releases and stories in the press on such subjects as the C-5 cargo plane, the M-1 tank, and the Maverick anti-tank missile. I found a whole new underground who were concerned with the debate on whether to buy another run of the infamous C-5 cargo plane or to look to an alternative, and they leaked massive amounts of significant documents to me.

But by early June, Thom and I began to become concerned

about our finances. Things were getting extremely tight. Then in June, with just $30 left in our checking account, Anne Zill and Ernie called me to say that the Fund for Constitutional Government had offered to sponsor the Project. The Fund for Constitutional Government was set up to expose fraud in government after the Watergate scandal and seemed to be an ideal place to go. Ernie is on the board of directors and Anne Zill is the president, so I knew that I would have support, but I was leery about jumping into another situation with an organization that might have a hidden agenda for the Project and the publicity we generate. I very clearly laid out the objectives and goals of the organization to the fund and told them that I could not compromise the special relationship I had with the Pentagon underground. They agreed to my terms and adopted the Project. To the board's credit, they have never reneged on this agreement and their stewardship is responsible for the continuing success of the Project.

Thom stayed on without pay to help me for several more months until the fund could help me raise enough money to hire a part-time secretary. We were partially reimbursed for the money we spent on the Project, but our savings did not totally recover from the loss of interest and out-of-pocket expenses for which we did not get reimbursed. For the next two and a half years the Project has continued to give the Pentagon a run for its money. Along the way I have learned, sometimes the hard way, how the Pentagon, the press, the Congress, and the public have dealt with the perplexing problems of buying an effective and reasonably priced defense system for this country. I have learned how our system does and does not work. And the Pentagon underground has given me a unique inside view I want to pass on to the public. Much of the information contained in the next pages is information that the Pentagon and sometimes the Congress do not want you to know, but as citizens and taxpayers, it is your right.

5.

FOOLING ALL OF
THE PEOPLE
ALL OF THE TIME

THE CLOCK RADIO jarred me out of my sleep. As I shook myself awake and began to remember why I was rising so early, the excitement and fear began to pulse through me. I was to appear on the ABC morning news show *Good Morning America*. The subject I was to discuss I knew well: whether or not to establish an independent office inside the Secretary of Defense's office to test the weapons separately from the bureaucracy that develops and builds them. A year before, I had written an article for *Reason* magazine on the subject of testing weapons in which I suggested that such an office be set up as a check and balance system between the builders and the testers of our weapons. Senators David Pryor (D-Arkansas) and William Roth (R-Delaware) had written a bill to do just that and were planning hearings on the subject. The morning of the hearings, June 23, 1983, I was to appear on the show with Senator Roth.

I was nervous because I was also to meet and debate on national television the man whom I considered probably my biggest antagonist in the Department of Defense, Dr. Richard

DeLauer, the Undersecretary of Defense for Research and Engineering. Perhaps the highest procurement officer in the Pentagon, he was responsible for overseeing all procurement as
well as the testing of weapons. This bill would take authority for
operational testing (battlefield-type conditions) away from him
and place it under the DOD Undersecretary for Operational
Testing, who would be at the same bureaucratic level as he. We
were definitely invading his turf and he had already made it
known to the Congress that he was bitterly opposed to the bill,
as were most of the Pentagon's high-ranking officials.

By the time the ABC limousine came to my door to pick me
up at around 6:30 A.M., I was well-dressed with a heavily made-
up face and coiffed hair. I looked much more official and secure
than I felt. When I arrived at the studio and walked into the
waiting room, Senator Roth greeted me warmly and Dr.
DeLauer nodded his head in acknowledgment of me.

The interview, I felt, was interesting and fair. We were sitting
very close to each other at right angles and Dr. DeLauer's
elbow practically touched mine as we spoke. Each one of us had
a short opening statement and then we started around again
debating the merits or detractions of the proposed testing bill.
As my second turn approached and Senator Roth was speaking,
I began to flip through a book of journalism articles that the
Project had put together, looking for another example of poor
testing practices. I noticed Dr. DeLauer giving the book an
unfriendly look. It was his turn to speak again and he spoke well,
presenting the Pentagon's objections to the bill.

By the time Dr. DeLauer finished his point, reporter Steve
Bell informed us that they were out of time. Though disappointed that I had not gotten a second chance, I realized that
a senator and an undersecretary of defense have more weight
than I do. I was happy that we had a clear and important airing
of the issue. I did not realize that the fireworks were about to
begin.

As we rose from our chairs at the end of the interview, Dr.

DeLauer grasped both of Senator Roth's arms and began to exclaim how the bill was not a good idea. I walked over to try to help Senator Roth, who appeared to be a little flustered by Dr. DeLauer's intensity.

"Dr. DeLauer," I said, "the evidence for the need of a new testing office comes from your own [DOD] documents."

At that moment I felt his anger turn on me like a laser. Senator Roth quickly left the room with his aides. Dr. DeLauer grabbed my book from my hands and shook it in my face. "This book," he said, "is full of misleading innuendo." Furiously, he began to flip through the pages while muttering that he would show me an example. As he grew louder, I decided to make a quiet comment and leave this unwinnable situation.

"Dr. DeLauer," I said again, "I have your own test results to back up our claims." He quickly retorted that I could come to his office anytime and he would show me where I was wrong. (Later, when I tried to take him up on this offer, he never returned my phone calls.) I was edging toward the hall and the television crew was eyeing this confrontation with a combination of amusement and concern. Dr. DeLauer started each statement to me by yelling, "Listen, lady!"

I turned down the hall to meet my associate Donna Martin (who had recently returned to work with me fulltime) coming up the hall. Then I heard Dr. DeLauer retort that I was fooling all the reporters with my misinformation. I swung around and answered, "You mean that I am fooling *The New York Times, The Washington Post, The Wall Street Journal,* all the other papers and the networks . . . all simultaneously?"

"Yes, yes!" he retorted. "You are fooling all of the people all of the time!"

It was quite a scene with Dr. DeLauer's aides trying to pull him away and a stricken Donna Martin, who had come into the middle of this argument. But I could not resist a parting shot. I turned to him and in a very quiet voice, with my hand on my chest, said, "Dr. DeLauer, I'm just not that talented."

He sputtered something that I could not hear as I turned away from him to get out of the news bureau. Later, in the car with Donna, I had time to be upset. I was amazed that a man of Dr. DeLauer's position would find our work so threatening as to make a public scene. Yet in a way, his reaction validated our work: the Pentagon had acted for so long as if they were ignoring our work that it was gratifying to see they were paying attention.

But what stuck in my mind was Dr. DeLauer's statement that we were fooling all of the people all of the time. He certainly gave us a lot of credit if he thought we could even attempt to fool the press for several years with our minuscule resources. Ironically, I thought that the statement was much more appropriate for the Pentagon and their attempts to deal with the press, the Congress, and the public. I would not want to be on the Pentagon's side of the weapons debate because their emphasis on smooth public relations sometimes doesn't remotely resemble what is really going on. This carefully woven public relations cover is often torn apart as the Project and other sources confront them with their own documents that do not follow their public line.

But they continue to try to fool all of the people all of the time. Even when it is easier to fix a problem rather than cover it up, the public relations section will sometimes still choose to try to cover up the real problem. In working through several weapon scandals over four years, I have discovered that the Pentagon, along with other government bureaucracies, often cannot admit they have made a mistake. They seem to try to defend every decision and every weapon as though it was the last word. They try to deny that the Pentagon is run by human beings who are capable of mistakes, errors in judgment, and greed. I was determined to show, by weapon failures, that something is terribly wrong with the system they are trying so hard to protect.

As I began to take on more and more technical investigations of weapons, I ran into problems because I did not have enough training to analyze the highly technical material that was reaching the Project. It was fairly easy for me to take the time to learn about the technical details of the M-1 because I was tackling only one weapon system. But as more and more documents showed up at the Project's door, I realized that I needed help from someone who already had a basic knowledge of the technical side of the weapons procurement system. Although the sources in the underground worked long hours for free to help me with the great number of documents I received, sometimes I needed their expertise to help me with a question from a reporter or a congressional office and I could not reach them.

I decided to hire Paul Hoven and Joseph Burniece to aid me with the backlog of technical information and to work with the underground to evaluate whether the weapons the Pentagon was buying would work on the battlefield. Both men had been sources for me on the aluminum-armored M-2 Bradley Fighting Vehicle and the great danger that vehicle design posed for the troops riding inside it.

At the time I contacted them, they were running Summit Simulations in Minnesota, a small consulting firm that had contracts to make war game equipment and scenarios for the military. In the course of their work on war simulations, they began to discover that many of the Army's new generation of weapons, especially the M-2 Bradley vehicle, were not performing as well as the equipment they were replacing. The Bradley was costing about eleven times more. Hoven and Burniece wrote a lengthy paper on the Bradley and sent it to the Army and many members of Congress. Nothing happened until a congressional staff aide passed their work on to me. I checked their analysis with several of my sources and was told that it was sound, so I put John Fialka of *The Wall Street Journal* together with them. The result was a lengthy story in the *Journal*.[1] After that Paul and Joe helped me check on the validity of some of the test results I was receiving, especially with Army weapons. They came to work for the Project in 1983.

Paul brings a unique background to the Project. He was involved in heavy combat in Vietnam in 1968 as an assault helicopter pilot and was awarded thirty-four air medals and the Army's distinguished flying cross. He saw graphically firsthand what happens when weapons procurement policies and officer leadership fail. His combat experience brought a legitimacy to the Project in the eyes of some of in the underground and the Congress who were leery of a project run by two women who were trained as journalists.

Joe is also an asset to the Project because of his extensive background in military history and his ability to keep abreast of and understand the current literature on weapons from around the world. He is considered our main researcher in weapons and is invaluable to reporters who need background information on weapon programs and the older systems they are designed to replace. His background in tactics and strategy adds to the information we give reporters on why a weapon is not suitable on the battlefield.

Sometimes having Joe or Paul talk to a new source, usually a military one, has been more fruitful than if I had approached the person myself. The Pentagon had for some time tried to portray me as an uninformed, liberal do-gooder, and bringing Joe and Paul into the organization helped dispel that fear with the remaining skeptics.

However, Paul's combat experience has not been his greatest contribution to the Project. His ability to work with Joe and combine their military experience to figure out whether or not a source's claim is legitimate has saved me many hours of extra research and has made it possible for us to give reporters a more balanced picture of how these failed weapons will affect true military ability. They also helped the Project and the sources to go beyond criticism of weapons to suggest constructive alternatives to any weapon system we exposed as unworkable. It has always been the policy of the Project to suggest realistic alternatives to bad weapons and they reinforce that policy.

The key to the problems at the Pentagon is procurement, the buying of weapons and the pressures and forces on the people who do so. The Pentagon's stated purpose is to buy weapons that work to defend our country, but somewhere along the line a bureaucratic survival instinct takes hold and makes normally patriotic men hide facts, ignore bad test results, and even commit illegal acts while waving the flag even higher to cover their motives to the public and even themselves. It is an enormous and complex system of pressures and I, too, was at first intimidated at trying to figure it out, let alone pretend to be able to explain it to others.

The best way I know to explain how the system motivates men to act the way they do is to look at many examples of failed procurements and try to identify the common ingredients that led to those failures. Probably no one problem in procurement causes failures, but rather a group of forces continues to cause the players to perpetuate the myth that the weapons they are buying will work on a battlefield. But first it is important to know how the procurement system is supposed to work.

I once described the weapons procurement process in the following way:

The process the Pentagon uses to procure our weapons is an enormous bureaucratic mass, full of charts, chains of command, and acronyms. But in a simplified form, the basic components are these:

First, after a service (Army, Navy, or Air Force) decides, with congressional approval, to build a weapon, a program manager is selected. He sets up an office with a staff of perhaps 200 to 500 people in the research and development command of the service to implement the development and production of the new weapon.

At "milestone" points scheduled by each service, it is

decided whether or not to continue with the weapon. At Milestone I, the initial decision to begin the program is made. Between Milestone I and II, advanced development begins, with separate components of the weapon being developed at the same time. At Milestone II, the issue is whether to proceed into "full-scale engineering development" (usually a billion-dollar-plus commitment). Few weapons are ever cancelled once full-scale engineering is approved. Between Milestone II and III, the prototypes are redesigned and tested to provide the basis for a production decision. At Milestone III, the service decides whether to engage in limited production and further R&D [Research and Development] or to proceed to full production of the weapon.

The milestone decisions are made in each service by a council representing several appropriate commands. Those decisions are reviewed by DSARC, the Pentagon's Defense System Acquisition Review Council.[2]

Each service has its own designations for the various milestones and may conduct business in a slightly different way, but for the most part, that is how the weapons procurement system is supposed to work. But in the real world of the Pentagon bureaucracy, a weapon system that proceeds to a prototype stage and has a potential contractor has developed a constituency and becomes almost impossible to cancel. Anthony R. Battista, a House Armed Services Committee staff member, told *Washington Post* reporter Morton Mintz that "[p]rograms are freight trains. . . . [o]nce they get started, it's very hard to turn them off, even if they don't make sense."[3]

The following examples of how our weapons procurement bureaucracy operates and the problems this system generates are not an inspiring picture, but a study of them is necessary to understand why the end product is so disastrous to the defense of the country. Many of these symptoms of the procurement disease are closely related and a cure of one symptom may just open the door for abuse in other areas.

Testing

The testing of our weapons is a very important and often overlooked part of sound weapons procurement. A weapon system usually goes through two stages of testing, developmental and operational. Russell Murray, former head of the Department of Defense Program Analysis and Evaluation, describes the difference between the two types of testing in this way:

> The object of development testing is to find out whether a new weapon meets its technical specifications. The object of operational testing is to find out if the weapon— even if it does meet its specifications—will really be useful in combat.
>
> Development testing is conducted by highly trained scientists, technicians, and specialists under tightly controlled, laboratory-like conditions. Operational testing is conducted out in the field by run-of-the-mill servicemen under conditions simulating wartime as closely as possible.[4]

Operational testing is supposed to determine if a weapon that works on paper and in the laboratory will work on a battlefield under dust, noise, and confusion. For example, the Copperhead, an anti-tank, laser-guided artillery shell, which worked in theory, failed miserably in operational testing. The Copperhead is guided to its target by an infantryman pointing an infra-red laser device at the target, "painting" the target with the light beam so the shell can seek the reflected light on the target. It was designed to replace the old-fashioned free-flight shell that is fired by "guesstimate" coordinates given by a forward observer. When using the Copperhead, an infantryman, who is scouting ahead, carries the 90-pound, $400,000 laser device. Once he spots the target, he shines his laser on it while communicating his approximate position back to the artillery division. When the

Copperhead shell is fired, the forward infantryman must continue to "paint" the target to guide the shell to a hit.

As we could tell from the Army's 1979 operational test report, even when the weapon was tested under favorable combat conditions, it had some serious shortfalls. The rest results, called Cannon Launched Guided Projectile, Copperhead, XM712, Operational Test II (U), showed that the weapon system could not work in combat for the following reasons:

—"The system does not function in anything but perfect weather. Fog, snow, heavy rain severely hamper versatility of it and render it quite useless."[5] Very few enemies can be counted on to wait for clear weather for our Army's artillery shells.

—Once the Copperhead is fired by standard field howitzers, it flies for several miles and then connects with the reflected laser light bounced off the side of the enemy tank by a U.S. forward observer. The laser light reflection must remain at least thirteen seconds (a long time in combat) to guide the shell to the target. Then the forward observer must also maintain contact with the howitzer crews several miles away for up to thirteen minutes, placing him in an extremely vulnerable position. In using any infra-red device, the enemy will spot the laser light and can track the beam back to the forward observer. It is also fairly easy for the enemy to jam the radio signals between the observer and the howitzer crew, thus rendering the Copperhead useless.

—When clouds were below 2000 feet, the Copperhead round could not see through them. Northern Europe, an area in which the Copperhead will be used in a land war, commonly has clouds at that level or below.

—The dust generated by several Copperhead hits on dusty ground blocked laser beams guiding subsequent rounds. If the Copperhead itself made too much dust for following rounds, the shell would be in major trouble on a real battlefield that is full of dust and smoke.

In short, because of the length of time required to focus the laser on the target and the time it took for the necessary coordination between the gunner and the forward observer, an enemy tank in real combat would have reached the soldier well before he was able to obtain a hit with the Copperhead projectile. It was obvious from the test result, which was the last operational test given on the Copperhead, that the program should be reevaluated or probably canceled because of its impractical use on the battlefield.

The Copperhead program has also been riddled with cost overruns and delivery delays.[6] In 1983 the Army recommended that the program be dropped (but later reversed itself). The Secretary of Defense's office rescued the Copperhead, partly for political reasons and pressure from the contractor, and made it a part of the Army's land units. Despite the Army belief that the Copperhead is not suitable for the battlefield, as many as half the guns in each battery will be Copperhead-configured, meaning that effective artillery guns on artillery units will be replaced by the Copperhead. The Copperhead's bad test results were ignored by the DOD bureaucracy, even after we made them public.

A simple way to eliminate the bad news of operational test results is to alter the tests to fit the weapon. As we have seen with the M-1 tank, the procurement bureaucracy is perfectly capable of fudging or downright cheating on test results. The Maverick missile is another good example of how the bureaucracy cheats on the tests to make the weapon look good.

The Maverick is an air-to-ground anti-tank missile mounted

on the A-10 ground assault aircraft and the F-16 fighter. While flying the aircraft, the pilot looks through a sensor in the nose of the missile to find tanks and other targets on the ground. At first, the Maverick had an electro-optical (television) sight in its nose that worked poorly in Vietnam, so it was replaced with an infra-red sensor that seeks out heat images. The inherent problem with the Maverick is that a single pilot must fly the airplane, watch for anti-aircraft fire from the ground, look for enemy tanks through the small sensor, lock onto a target, and hold the image for up to fifteen seconds (enough time for an anti-aircraft gunner to track the plane and shoot it down) before he fires and breaks away to safety. Several of my sources liken the use of the Maverick sensor to trying to sight a tank by looking through a straw.

The Pentagon had cheated on two major operational tests for the Maverick in order to make the weapon look good. *Washington Post* reporter Morton Mintz wrote about the dubious conditions at both of these tests:

> At Fort Polk five years ago [1976], a small (1.5 by 2 kilometers) area was set aside at the test range. Numerous visual cues to the pilots and thermal cues to the heat-seeking IIR [Infra-red] sensor were on the ground—burning armor hulks, smoke, night-time flares, tanks firing their guns, muzzle flashes and forward air controllers on the ground to tell the pilots where the tanks were in relation to the aircraft and where they were heading.
>
> Another clue was PAVE PENNY, a device in the nose of the aircraft that swings back and forth looking for a "spot" put on a tank by a laser designator, a large, powerful, infra-red "flashlight" operated—at great peril in actual combat—by a soldier.
>
> "After the first couple of nights, the pilots learned the layout . . . how to beat the system by learning where the tanks are, where they go back and forth," says a source familiar with the test. "This is not dishonesty," he

stressed. "They simply wanted to look as good as they could."

The pilots made 123 "captive-carry passes" in which they tried to "lock on" to targets electronically without actually launching missiles, according to the sanitized version of a secret 1978 GAO report. Practice runs—possibly fatal in battle—weren't counted. "That's how you get excellent results, only counting the successes and throwing out the unsuccessful passes," says a retired Air Force combat pilot.

Be that as it may, less than 60 percent of the counted passes produced lock-ons on true targets; the rest produced no lock-ons at all, or lock-ons on false targets, such as fires, smoke burning bushes, and sun warmed objects. Any of these can appear as tank lookalike images on the five-square-inch videoscreen in the cockpit. At times after "launch," even "hot snow"—the steamy result of the passage over snow-covered ground of a tracked vehicle— defeated the IIR. . . .

. . . Trying to recover from the set-backs in Louisiana, the Air Force ran the new test at Baumholder Air Force Base, Germany, in January and February 1978, permitting no outside observers. The temperatures were above freezing, and no snow that might deceive the second-generation seeker was on the ground.

Visual cues and battlefield thermal clutter, such as burning armor hulks, were provided, but some realities of combat were not. For example, the Air Force denied requests for simulation of an artillery barrage such as would normally precede a tank assault, so the hot shell holes that can deceive the missile were absent.

In symmetry not often found in combat, the pilots flew over, and tanks traveled on, the same prepared lanes every night. Again, practice runs, 317 of them, were made but not counted. . . .

. . . Of the 215 "active" passes that the Air Force did score, published congressional testimony shows, only 113 —53 percent—resulted in lock-ons, but more than one-third of the lock-ons broke. Of the 113, nearly one-third had been cued by PAVE PENNY. Overall, the ability of the new centroid seeker to detect and lock on to a target was inferior to the original seeker used at Fort Polk.[7]

When I was investigating the Maverick, one of the areas of cheating on the operational tests that I thought was especially dishonest was allowing the pilots hundreds of dry runs over the targets to memorize them before the first shot was fired. That might have been acceptable in a development test where the engineers were fine-tuning the weapon, but it was inexcusable in an operational test because no enemy is going to allow hostile aircraft to fly over its territory and memorize the landscape. In fact, to truly simulate combat conditions, someone should be assigned to think like the enemy and try all types of evasive countermeasures to defeat the weapon. But this is rarely done even in operational testing.

After watching one troubled weapon after another pass the Defense System Acquisition Review Council (DSARC) system without a hitch, I began to think that the decision-makers at the DSARC meetings did not have all the facts about the weapon they were deciding on. But in the case of the Maverick missile, I was leaked the DSARC briefing charts that showed the high officials at that meeting, chaired by Dr. DeLauer, had very discouraging news on the ability of the Maverick and passed it anyway.

I received these sensitive yet sanitized briefing charts on October 6, 1982, and released them to several reporters. The charts showed that each of the departments concerned with the procurement and deployment of the Maverick was seriously concerned about its ability to work and be maintained on a battlefield. Some examples from the DSARC charts:

USD [Undersecretary of Defense] (POLICY)—The operational effectiveness and suitability under European weather conditions have not been resolved

D (DT & E) [Director, Development Test and Evaluation]—Operational realism of most test scenarios was constrained

ASD (COMP) [Assistant Secretary of Defense, Comptroller]—Production cost increases have occurred and are reflected in quantity buy decreases in FY [fiscal year]-§83 (1335 vice 2560) and FY-84 (2600 vice 3375)

ASD (MRA & L) [logistics]—Test equipment evaluation criteria and quantitative performance requirements are not adequate

ASD (MRA & L)—Reliability, maintainability and readiness objectives of the missile and TGM [terminally guided munitions] have not been met

Dr. DeLauer told Morton Mintz that he was confident of the Maverick's ability because he had been reassured of its merits by his predecessor in the undersecretary job, Malcolm Currie. However, Currie was a key player in the Maverick missile project at Hughes Aircraft before he took the undersecretary job in the Carter administration and then returned to Hughes as a corporate vice-president. Dr. DeLauer commented to Mintz:

> I've looked at the design. One of the guys who designed it sat in that chair. I have high confidence in his technical ability and his honesty to me . . . He and I went over the whole goddamn design. And, you know, we talked what the hell is the problem and how we can get [a component] to work a little better, and what the production problems are. You know, we sat there as a couple of engineers. That's my goddamn life.[8]

Dr. DeLauer did not seem to understand Currie's bias and motivation in making him believe the Maverick worked. The Air Force's poor test results and the negative recommendations of DOD's various commands also did not seem to matter.

I was shocked that the DSARC would approve the commitment of a large portion of money and resources to a weapon
that had received such bad reports from the testing and logistics
people, yet Secretary Weinberger signed off on the DSARC
approval and the Maverick is now being manufactured and
deployed. The engineers are still trying to correct its low accuracy, but it appears that no amount of fixing will improve the
Maverick because the flawed design demands that the pilot,
while he is trying to fly and avoid anti-aircraft fire, find a tank
through a sensor that sees such a small part of the landscape.

These are the problems that testing is supposed to weed out
of the system before weapons reach the battlefield, during the
time a weapon is envisioned and developed, but politics and
career advancement sometimes keep these weapons alive over
the objections of the testers. The testers in the Pentagon have
much less political clout than the procurement people who
develop the weapons. As mentioned earlier, the new 1983 law,
which Dr. DeLauer opposed, gives the main operational testers
in the DOD the same bureaucratic power level as the procurers
of the weapons, but the DOD has been extremely slow in imple-
menting it.

Warranties

It would appear that tight warranties in weapons contracts
would put pressure on a weapon contractor to make a reliable
weapon that could pass rigorous combat tests. Warranties on
cars, toasters, and televisions protect us from defective products. Shouldn't our soldiers expect the same protection from
weapons that they are expected to trust their lives to?

That was the sentiment of Senator Mark Andrews (R-North
Dakota) when he realized that the Pentagon was not consistently getting and enforcing warranties against defects in their
weapons purchases. He thought that, like a farmer who gets a

warranty on his tractor transmission, the Army ought to do the same on the troubled transmission of the M-1 tank. He wrote a bill in 1983 which stated that the government should not purchase a weapon system unless the contractor provides a written guarantee that the products are "free from all defects" in materials and workmanship. His bill further stipulated that if a weapon failed, the manufacturer would repair or replace all parts and if not, would reimburse the government for the cost of any repair.

The Pentagon reacted to this bill with wails of dissent, claiming that it would be very expensive for the government to get these guarantees from the defense contractors and the bill would unduly inhibit their flexibility in weapons purchases. I think their main fear was that the Congress was getting wise to their repeated assurances every year that all the failures of weapons that were coming out in the press had been corrected. Their excuses also did not hold water because Senator Andrews allowed in his bill for the Secretary of Defense to waive the guarantee if he felt it would not be in the national interest, if it would not be cost-effective, or if he explained to Congress why a guarantee was not sought on a particular weapon.

One of the Pentagon's stated objections to warranties is that they inhibit innovation: commercial products having warranties are made with limited application of high technology but DOD weapons must be state-of-the-art to meet the Soviet threat. As you have seen from the examples in this book, a fancy "state-of-the-art" weapon is useless unless it works. Warranties would help keep unreliable and unproven technology off the battlefield. Highly technical weapons that won't work consistently on the battlefield will become very expensive battlefield junk to a soldier who has lost confidence in their reliability.

The warranty proponents also pointed out that just as commerical state-of-the-art communications satellites and most European-produced NATO weapons receive warranties, we should expect the same from our own Pentagon. Even the former Deputy Secretary of Defense, Paul Thayer, claimed while he was working under Secretary Weinberger that "[m]ilitary contractors increase prices 10% to 30% to cover products that have to be remade because they are made improperly the first time." In other words, without warranties in defense procurement, the contractors actually have the monetary incentive to make the product incorrectly the first time and then get paid to fix their mistakes. Remember the $1.5 billion C-5A wing fix.

Despite intense pressure from Pentagon officials to kill it, the warranty bill passed in 1983. Secretary Weinberger publicly pledged to implement the law, but his underlings worked fervently in 1984 to undercut it. The next year, despite objections by the bill's sponsor in the House, Mel Levine (D-California), Senator Andrews agreed to a compromise in the bill that gave the Pentagon even more loopholes. The new provisions exempted many types of DOD purchases from warranties, including ammunition, jeeps, trucks, and shoulder-fired anti-tank missiles.

Despite this setback, sources in the Pentagon told me that the warranty law sent the message to the procurement community that Congress would not automatically take their word on weapons purchases. As our investigations and exposés had shown, the soldier and the taxpayer were not being well protected by the Pentagon from bad workmanship by the contractors.

Competition

Any critic of the current defense procurement system is, sooner or later, bound to hear from a defender of this system that our country needs a particular weapon system to protect the American way of life. The ultimate irony is that the procurement system these defenders claim is the arsenal of democracy and the protector of the free market economy is run in a very socialistic way.

According to the General Accounting Office (GAO), in 1981 only 6 percent of the Pentagon's procurement budget was competitively bid, according to the federal definition of competition—advertised proposals with sealed bids from two or more companies. The DOD claims that more than half of its procurement is competitive, but that misleading figure includes "negotiated procurement" by which the DOD and selected contractors sit down to work out terms of a contract together, away from other parties vying for a piece of the procurement pie. The DOD also counts in that figure contracts that were competitive, say, fifteen years ago, and the follow-on contracts for more units that went to the same contractor of the weapon without competition. Obviously the contractor, knowing that all he has to do is win the first competition, thereby capturing all the follow-on contracts, will not be encouraged to keep costs down.

Some members of the pro–free enterprise Reagan administration realized that the DOD procurement system is not competitive. Murray Weidenbaum, first chairman of President Reagan's Council of Economic Advisers, said, ". . . a first step can be made to control defense budgets by increasing the role of competition in military procurement. . . . The key to making defense contracting more efficient is an increased reliance on private enterprise. Actually we have not given it much of a chance. . . ."[9] Although Caspar Weinberger claims in his speeches and statements that his people are working to increase competition, the GAO reported that competition actually dropped from 6 percent in 1981 to 5.4 percent in 1983.[10] That lack of competition can have a very detrimental effect on the quality and price of our weapons.

The Congress and the DOD know that competition can drastically reduce weapon costs. In November 1973, in testimony before the Joint Economic Committee, Larry Yuspeh of the

Center for Defense Information presented the results of his review of twenty naval weapon systems that showed great reductions in price due to competition. One example was the RIM 66-A missile that cost $149,766 in 1970 dollars when it was purchased sole-source (with no competition from any other contractor) from General Dynamics. GD reduced its price to $61,039 per missile—a price reduction of 59 percent after the Navy opened up the contract for competition. I have heard many members of Congress compain about the lack of competition, yet the bills that are offered as a solution often just give the DOD more loopholes to avoid competition.

However, a change in the Pentagon's business-as-usual may come with a bill Senator Charles Grassley (R-Iowa) introduced in 1984. Taking one of the suggestions the underground had given the Project on competition, he wrote a bill that would force the Pentagon to raise the level of true competition every year by 5 percent until 70 percent of all Pentagon contracts are competitive. The switch to competition would be slow enough at that rate for the Pentagon to begin to undo its sole-source method of contracting. This inspired the senator to dub his bill the creeping capitalism bill. But one of the most important measures of the bill is the penalty to the Pentagon if they do not meet the 5 percent goal. Each year the Pentagon fails to meet its increased quota, its fund would be cut back by that percentage. Therefore, the Congress would not tell the Pentagon how to manage its competition but would exercise its control over our taxpayer investment—the power of the purse.

Besides wasting money, a lack of competition ensures that the Pentagon will spend so much money for each weapon unit that it will be able to afford fewer and fewer weapons, thus crippling true defense. And the high cost of sole-source contracting will also continue to consume the operations budget for items like spare parts, so there will not be enough stockpiled in case of a war. Another case of more bucks and less bang.

Readiness

The Pentagon is embarking on a massive weapons buildup supposedly to be more prepared for a war. Yet since the Pentagon has spent a higher and higher percentage of its budget on fewer weapons and an increasingly lower percentage on operations and maintenance (O&M) to sustain these new units, we are less prepared for war.

In February 1984, Secretary Weinberger went before the Congress to submit his annual report on the readiness of U.S. armed forces. He claimed that 39 percent more of the major military units are now categorized as fully or substantially ready for combat compared with the readiness status of those units in December 1980. However, numerous reports disagreed with his analysis, including one from his own Joint Chiefs of Staff that was leaked a month later. The Project compiled a list of the dissenting reports:

In July 1983, NBC News reported on a secret report issued by the House Appropriations Committee. The report concluded that America's armed forces are not equipped to sustain a conventional war with the Soviet Union for more than 10–14 days before we would have to resort to nuclear weapons. Both Congressmen Jack Edwards (R-Alabama) and Joseph Addabbo (D-New York) confirmed that conclusion. .

For example:

1) We have only about a week's supply of highly effective Sidewinder air-to-air missiles in Europe.
2) Spare parts for the F-16 have been so scarce that squadrons in the Far East keep two or three airplanes per squadron to cannibalize for spare parts.
3) The Navy had become too reliant on civilian technicians to keep weapons operational. Those civilians do not have to remain at their posts in times of military crisis.

4) There are critical shortages of medical supplies such as field hospitals, beds, X-ray machines, MEDEVAC units, and hospital ships.

5) The military is short of planes to fly troops and equipment overseas on short notice.

Finally, Congressmen Addabbo and Edwards acknowledged that the supply shortages could be blamed on funnelling too much money into weapon procurement accounts. They agreed that we are not now ready for war and hoped we would not have to fight one in the next year.

In 1983, CBS News broadcast a report on the spare parts budget of the M-1 tank. The report cited a secret 1981 study by the Army's Training and Doctrine Command which noted that the Department of Defense had only budgeted for 13% of the spare parts it needs to fight a 60-day war and it has no plans to build an adequate stockpile in the next decade. The report went on to state that the Army's M-1 spare parts budget is one half billion dollars short of what will be needed for peacetime operations alone over the next ten years. [Perhaps they are short of so many parts because the M-1 is continuing to break down at an unacceptable rate to sustain it in war.] Although the Army did not directly blame the shortfall on the high cost of spare parts, a senior Pentagon official told the CBS reporter that the Army is gambling there will not be a war and so would rather commit its resources elsewhere. That is a gamble that few soldiers in the battlefield would be willing to make.

At an August 1983 symposium held at Hill Air Force Base in Ogden, Utah, Dr. Lawrence Korb, Assistant Secretary of Defense for Manpower, Installations, and Logistics, claimed that the Reagan Administration's defense initiatives were taking effect. He said that in previous years, only 35% of our armed forces were considered combat ready. "The U.S. had gotten down in the active and reserve forces to dangerously low levels. . . . Amounts of spare parts were low, training was low and morale among the troops was low. . . . At Langley Air Force Base, where we're supposed to have the cream of the Air Force, they had a snap inspection and only 30% of the fighters could get off the ground." (*Ogden Standard Examiner* 8/21/84) At the time of his speech, Korb said armed forces readiness stood at about 50%. He was aiming for a peacetime goal of 75%, but even at that, he conceded, U.S. armed forces would have difficulty holding out in the event of the ultimate "scenario," a Soviet Warsaw Pact attack on Europe.

In March 1984, *The Washington Post* reported on an internal Defense Department readiness report prepared by the Joint Chiefs of Staff. It showed a 25% decline in Army readiness, a 15% decline in the number of combat-ready Air Force units, but a 100% increase in combat-ready Navy ships.

It also found that ammunition shortages were a critical problem and that there were not enough military transport vehicles (whether planes or ships) to move troops in time of war. Also inhibiting readiness were shortfalls in senior grade enlisted personnel, spare parts, training funds, adequate intelligence, and defense against chemical weapons.

In response to the leaked report, Chairman of the Joint Chiefs, Army General John Vessey, held a press conference to assure the American public that U.S. armed forces are readier and more capable than they were three years ago. He said the Pentagon's methods of analyzing readiness capability were "management tools" that did not reflect true military capability.

While the Joint Chiefs' report indicated that Navy capability had greatly improved, a March 1984 report released by a subcommittee of the House Government Operations Committee took issue with the way the Navy assesses the readiness of its fighter and bomber aircraft. The Congressional panel found that the Navy "overstates" its capability, which could lull Congress into believing that it could safely allocate more money to buy additional ships and planes and less to maintaining the existing fleet.

The report stated that audits by the General Accounting Office and the Naval Audit Service revealed inaccuracies and omissions and that Naval air readiness "is actually lower than what is reported to Congress." It said the Navy also tended to play down shortages of essential matériel such as munitions and spare parts.

The committee was concerned that the Navy will certify an aircraft mission capable if it is capable of flying at least one of its intended missions, even if it cannot perform most of them. They used as an example an A-6E medium attack aircraft which "would be considered mission capable even though unable to perform its primary mission of ground attack." The Navy also gives its seal of approval to aircraft that lack critical "subsystems," so long as the aircraft will eventually receive the needed equipment. The report also criticized the Navy for excluding from its computations aircraft that are not operational but are sitting in depots waiting to be repaired, which makes the overall readiness of the squadron look better than it is.

All these factors, coupled with shortages of support equipment and munitions, led the committee to conclude that "the Administration's planned expansion to a 600-ship Navy should not be at the expense of the existing fleet."

In April 1984, a secret memorandum by Adm. James Watkins, chief of Naval operations, was made public. Watkins said the Navy suffers a "serious shortfall in modern standoff weapons [which] must be corrected to maintain attack aircraft effectiveness and prevent excessive attrition against current enemy defenses."

The twelve page memo was sent to Navy planners who set guidelines for Navy spending in fiscal years 1986–1990.[11]

You might wonder what would possess a military man to go along with a system that buys units of hardware that cannot be supported in battle. Why are operations and maintenance so woefully neglected at budget time by seemingly intelligent people? There are currently few career rewards in the system for making sure that there are enough spare parts, fuel, and other items to keep these machines running.

Withholding Information

The Pentagon's withholding of information from the decision-makers in Congress and from the public continues to be one of the most manipulative and dishonest moves of the procurement bureaucracy. The officials rely on the fact that the Congress, the public, and sometimes even the press have a very short memory of what the Pentagon says a weapon will do and are easily distracted from any follow-up and oversight activity. I am constantly amazed by how little the Congress remembers (or wants to) of what the Pentagon claimed the year before. The Pentagon uses this to manipulate the Congress. It has been the Project's job to try to maintain a memory for the Congress and the press on past Pentagon promises of a weapon's performance or their pledges to clean up a troublesome procurement problem.

Every year when we on the Project staff attend congressional hearings on the Pentagon budget, we are disgusted by changes in the Pentagon's story of a weapon's performance and the apparent obliviousness of members of the congressional committee to the changes. In the summer of 1984 we had some student interns go back through past hearings on certain weapon systems to see how much the DOD changed its story from year to year. The results were surprising. Some examples that were compiled by Danielle Brian, a student at Smith College, were especially revealing.

The DIVAD (Divisional Air Defense) is a highly complex anti-aircraft gun that has had an especially notorious history of inaccuracy, cost overruns, and cover-up by the Army. It consists of two medium-sized cannons on top of a modified M-48 tank chassis. Its guns are aimed by two radars that originally were designed for an F-16 aircraft. The DIVAD tracks aircraft with its radar and shoots them down. The hardest targets for an anti-aircraft gun to shoot down are maneuvering aircraft, as opposed to aircraft that fly in a predictable line. One of the easier targets to hit with a traditional anti-aircraft gun is a hovering helicopter. Paul Hoven saw many helicopters in Vietnam shot down with just 50-caliber machine guns. With this in mind, watch how the Army changed its optimistic assessment of what the DIVAD could do as the Project and others began to uncover more and more of its failures. From Danielle Brian's report:

Statements on DIVAD's primary targets:

DOD REQUIRED OPERATION DRAFT, MAY 30, 1974
"Threat aircraft will include high performance, fixed wing close support fighter aircraft, at least half of which will have all-weather capability."

SENATE ARMED SERVICES COMMITTEE, MARCH 15, 1978
"The primary mission for the DIVAD gun is to provide effective air defense against attack by armed helicopters and high performance, fixed wing aircraft for armored, mechanized, and infantry divisions."
—Colonel Marrella

HOUSE ARMED SERVICES COMMITTEE, MARCH 17, 1983
"The primary air threat to the forward area has been and continue to be the attack helicopter."
—Brig. General Adsit

HOUSE ARMED SERVICES COMMITTEE, MARCH 23, 1984
"DIVAD is designed to cope with the hovering helicopter, the straight and level moving aircraft and any aircraft that

is maneuvering in a smooth curvilinear—at a smooth curvilinear rate, you know, a predictable curve."

—General Maloney

On March 21, 1984 the Project released a memorandum from
James Finsterle, the division director of land forces in the Office
of the Secretary of Defense's Program Analysis and Evaluation
(PA&E), which stated that the information the Army supplied
to the DSARC meeting overstated the lethality of the DIVAD
by as much as 300 percent and the reaction time by as much
as 400 percent. Yet the Army continued to express optimism
after that memorandum had been circulated. Again from Ms.
Brian's report:

Lethality and Reaction Time

HOUSE ARMED SERVICES COMMITTEE,
MARCH 28, 1979
"The DIVAD gun, with its all-weather capability and its
very quick reaction time, gives us the fire power to
counter the antitank guided missile armed helicopter."

—Maj. General Koehler

SENATE ARMED SERVICES COMMITTEE, MARCH 3, 1982
"The system has performed well against such measures as
probability of hit and probability of kill."

—Lt. General Merryman

LETTER FROM JAMES FINSTERLE, DIVISION OF LAND
FORCES, TO MR. DAVID CHU, DIRECTOR OF PA&E,
JANUARY 4, 1983
"Data released since the 'Buy' decision show that several
key effectiveness parameters were overstated in the information previously available to either you or Dr. DeLauer
or, presumably, to other DSARC members:

—Lethality by as much as 300%

—Reaction time by as much as 400%

[Note the continued optimism of the Army in light of this
disclosure.]

SENATE ARMED SERVICES COMMITTEE,
MARCH 10, 1983
"This also results in extremely fast reaction time from
target unmask, and although the exact value is classified,
I can inform you that it is sufficiently rapid to engage and
destroy a pop-up helicopter before it guides an antitank
missile to a target . . . DIVAD . . . has the rapid reaction
time and range to engage the threat."
— Dr. Sculley and Lt. General Merryman

SENATE ARMED SERVICES COMMITTEE,
FEBRUARY 2, 1984
"The DIVAD radar tracking here, lethal against helicop-
ters, lethal against fast movers, low altitude."
— General Wickham

* * *

After all these examples of weapons procurement illness, the
questions that beg to be answered are who are these men and
why do they perpetuate these outrageous polcies? What motivates them to put the procurement bureaucracy's wishes over
giving soldiers safe weapons? It would be easy for me to say, as
many have in the past, that these men are just bad and corrupt
characters, but that is not the answer. I have met many of them
and so have you . . . they are your neighbors, uncles, or even
husbands. Although some are just plain corrupt people, the
majority are pressured by the bureaucracy to go along with the
procurement system to advance their careers or even keep
their jobs.

Because of the high stakes created each year by a $100 billion
procurement budget, the system puts tremendous pressure on
each individual to not rock the boat and then places him in a
position to become very cozy with the contractor. Those who
see themselves as protectors of the tax investment and try to
save money are criticized. To understand the pressures that a
program manager (usually military personnel) has in promoting
his weapon through the system, one needs to see what his incentives are.

The power of a manager in the federal government is based not so much on his salary, which is standardized, but rather on the size of his budget and the number of people he has under him. Peers in the bureaucracy will judge him on whether his budget is increasing every year. If it does, he is on his way up; if his budget decreases, his power is waning. Since his boss is also judged by the amount of money in his umbrella of activity, the boss will not look kindly on any program manager who does not spend all of his appropriations or finds that he does not need all the personnel that was projected. The cardinal sin of a bureaucrat is to try to return any leftover money at the end of the year.

Therefore, the manager (in this case a program manager of a weapon system) has an incentive to spend his yearly allocation. It justifies spending more money next year and keeps as many people on the payroll as possible. There is no incentive to save money or try to do the job with less personnel.

Another way to guarantee that his weapon system is stable is to ensure that at the end of his watch (on the average only two years) he will be promoted to the next management level. To gain this stability, it is in his best interest to go along with a large and influential defense contractor who can help him in Congress and the administration if something should go wrong with a weapon system rather than to encourage competition for the weapon he is procuring. A large defense contractor with an army of lobbyists on Capitol Hill would probably be able to cover up or successfully "explain" to the Congress any cost overrun, test failure, or slip of delivery schedule that occurred. Besides, this program manager's superiors in the military and even in the top civilian positions in the Department of Defense have been telling program managers not to have an adversarial role with contractors but rather to look on them as part of the "team."

It is also important that no bad news about the weapon appear during the program manager's tenure. If there are problems, he should delay telling anyone in higher authority for as long as possible but write vague memorandums placing the blame for the failure somewhere else. A common practice in the bureaucracy is to develop a "Pearl Harbor" file that absolves the manager of all responsibility by showing that he did indeed inform his superiors and that they signed off on his actions. It is called a Pearl Harbor file because if "Pearl Harbor" happens and the problems are exposed to the Congress or the press, the manager can CYA (cover your ass).

If all goes well, the program manager will get through his two years with the bad news successfully covered up until his new orders are cut or he has a job lined up with the contractor he was working with. He can then dump the bad news on the incoming program manager, who will immediately feel the burden of protecting the program. If the bad news does get out, the new program manager can go to the Congress and say that he has been on the job for only a short time and has just begun to institute new fixes for the problem that will require only a slight amount of "get well" money. The successful program manager will always be able to convince the Armed Services committees in Congress that "prosperity is just around the corner," and another "slight" increase in the program budget will produce a weapon of outstanding effectiveness in meeting the "threat."

The young military officer or civilian coming into the system soon sees what the rules are and who gets ahead, and adjusts his behavior accordingly. Anyone who has entered a large organization can surely empathize with the new employee who is trying to fit in. The problem is that the incentive system is upside down and promotes waste and deception, so if the young employee complains too long he will not advance. Those who go along will. Quite a bit of my information in the Pentagon comes from a group of new employees who are butting up against the systgem for the first time. The bureaucracy has not yet gradually worn them down and dulled their senses to the waste and fraud.

Probably one of the most corrupting influences the civilians and especially the officers face is what has become known as the revolving door. At the Pentagon, this usually means that an employee of one of the armed services takes a job with the defense contractor he was overseeing while he was with the military. The Project has presented the problems of the revolving door in our issue papers:

> It is difficult to prove that the performance standards of a weapon have been compromised because, for instance, a program manager of a troubled weapon system has gone to work for the contractor. But it is reasonable to assume that the tough decisions about the future of that weapons program may not be made by the government official looking to the contractor for his post-government livelihood. The practice is not illegal. It is not prohibited under any existing conflict of interest statutes or regulations. There are conflict of interest laws, but they are too narrowly written to get at the "jobs as bribes" problem that can affect the military officers and civilian personnel who make key decisions about weapons programs.
> The Project on Military Procurement feels there are clear potential conflict of interest violations when a program manager, anyone involved in testing or overseeing a troubled weapons program, or anyone who awards or audits contracts, takes a job with the company manufacturing that weapon. In such a situation, there is little incentive for a program manager, auditor, test official, or anyone else involved in cost and quality control to vigorously represent the interests of the government when they conflict with those of the manufacturer. This is especially true when the pattern of the revolving door is well established and well known to the managers in both the government and the manufacturing communities.[12]

In February 1985 the Project released a 1982 trip report from the Federal Office of Government Ethics that contains an interview with the then Judge Advocate General, Colonel Jack

Finder at the Air Force Contract Management Division (CMD) in Albuquerque, New Mexico, who was in charge of the ethics program there. According to the report's author, Jack Covaleski, Colonel Finder stated in his interview that "there is a large turnover of CMD personnel, especially of the AFPRO [Air Force Plant Representative Office] office, who leave to work for contractors. For example, the head of AFPRO office at Northrop on Friday, could become the Northrop vice president for quality assurance on Monday, and immediately AFPRO morale is destroyed. Employees openly discuss what the former employee has done over the past few years for the contractor in order to obtain the new job and wonder why they themselves should be so ethical. AFPRO employees must deal with their former employees daily on many matters (the government seeking data from the contractor) and feel betrayed that the contractor now has all the inside knowledge on how the AFPRO operates.[11] Colonel Finder said these types of cases are devastating to the ethics program because of the 'appearance of conflict of interest alone.' "

The following are some examples of the revolving door, gathered by the staff of the Project from various news sources:

Lt. General Oren DeHaven/Lockheed

Before he retired in June 1983, Lt. General Oren DeHaven was the director of the Joint Chiefs of Staff's logistic branch. One of the last briefings he received at his request was by a group of junior officers who analyzed the results of a major Air Force study about the Air Force's need for cargo planes. The study concluded that the McDonnell Douglas C-17 was the best choice and that purchase of Lockheed's C-5's should be limited to the fifty already under contract.

According to [the *Boston Globe* and the Project's sources), DeHaven told the officers there that he wanted to hear the briefing because he would soon be retiring and going to work as a consultant for Lockheed. DeHaven did retire and is now consultant to Lockheed, presumably giving them the benefit of his knowledge for Lockheed's upcoming battle to try to convince the Air Force to buy more than the 50 C-5B's, rather than the C-17's.

Testing Personnel

Lt. Col. George F. Goodall was the Air Force test director of Hughes Aircraft's Maverick missile. He resigned in August 1982. Less than two weeks later, he was working for Hughes.

Lt. Col. Wayne O. Mattson was the Air Force systems project officer on the Maverick. He retired in January 1979 and went to work for Hughes. [Of 551 defense contractors, Hughes is the third highest employer of retired military personnel. It hired more than 200 high-ranking retiring officers and civilians in 1981 and 1982. Hughes has hired colonels who were the Maverick's project managers at Wright-Patterson Air Force Base in Dayton, Ohio, colonels in charge of testing the missile at bases around the world, and representatives of the Air Force at Hughes's Tucson plant. It also hired civilians who had worked for the Pentagon and the Air Force who were in charge of determining the quality of the missile and of auditing program finances.]

Col. James C. Crosby was president of the Army Defense Science Board which tested the poorly performing DIVAD anti-aircraft system. He retired in August 1981 to work for Ford Aerospace, the chief contractor on the DIVAD program.

Col. William E. Crouch Jr. was commander of Army Aviation Development Test Activity in Fort Rucker, Alabama. Five days after retiring in July 1981, he took a job with Hughes helicopter, working on the same equipment he was formerly in charge of testing.

Contract Negotiators

Maj. Walter D. Crafton was in the Air Force Plant Representative office overseeing contracts at TRW in Red Beach, California. He retired in May 1981 to a job as department manager on product assurance at the same TWR plant.

Defense Contract Audit Agency

Ernest R. Giardano was a DCAA auditor at a Boeing company plant. He retired December 31, 1979 and the next day went to work for Boeing.

Marvin Boodnick went to work for Hughes Aircraft two days after quitting his DCAA job as a price cost analyst at Hughes in March 1981.

Lt. General Hans Driessnack/United Technologies

Lt. General Driessnack was a member of the Air Force Financial Management Team when Pratt & Whitney's spare parts overcharging was the object of a major Air Force Study during the Fall of 1982 and the Winter of 1983. Pratt is a subsidiary of United Technologies. On July 1, 1983, Driessnack resigned to go work for United Technologies.

Col. Richard C. Goven/Rockwell

Col. Richard C. Goven was attached to the Air Force secretary's financial management team as an aerospace economic analyst and in that position had jurisdiction over Rockwell International's B-1 bomber. He retired in May 1983 to take a job as manager for pricing studies at a Rockwell subsidiary, North American Aircraft Corporation, in Segundo, California.

General William J. Maddox, Jr./Bell Helicopter

Ten years ago the Army discovered a potentially fatal flaw in the tilt rotor of some Bell helicopters, which under certain conditions causes the spinning rotor blades of the UH-1 and Cobra helicopters to teeter up and down to such an extent that they cut into the mast. If the mast breaks, the rotor blade may fly off and in some cases slice through the copter's passenger compartment. The design problem has killed 231 people in noncombat situations since 1967.

Ten years ago, the Army Safety Center concluded in a study that Bell had made an "error in design" when it built the helicopter and urged the military to stop buying it. The study was dismissed by the Director of Army Aviation, General William J. Maddox, Jr. Maddox was recently hired to run Bell's Asian operation.

There are hundreds of examples every year. The best explanation of why so many Pentagon employees, especially in the military, go through this seductive revolving door was given by Thomas Amlie in a 1983 memorandum. Dr. Amlie is a retired Navy engineer who helped develop the very successful Sidewinder air-to-air missile. He now works for Ernie Fitzgerald in the Financial Management Division of the Air Force. He helped put the military men's dilemma into focus by illustrating the pressures facing them at retirement:

The major problem with having a military officer in charge of procurement is his vulnerability. It turns out that not everyone can make general or admiral and our "up or out" policy forces people to retire. The average age of an officer at retirement is 43 years. Counting allowances, a colonel has more take home pay than a U.S. Senator. At the age of 43 he probably has kids in or ready for college and a big mortgage and can't afford a large cut in his income. Besides, he is at the peak of his intellectual powers, is emotionally involved, and doesn't want to quit. We throw him out anyway, no matter how good a job he is doing. Many of these officers, particularly the good ones who have spent most of their careers flying aircraft, operating ships, or leading troops, do not have the skills which are readily marketable in the civilian sector. This nice man then comes around and offers him a job at 50K–75K per year. If he stands up and makes a fuss about high cost and poor quality, no nice man will come see him when he retires. Even if he has no interest in a post-retirement job in the defense industry, he is taking a chance by making a fuss. The "system" will, likely as not, discover a newly open job in Tule, Greenland; Adak, Alaska; or some other

garden spot for which he, and only he, is uniquely qua-
lified. Thus, his family, as well as his career, suffers. To
their everlasting credit, many fine officers have made a
fuss anyway and suffered the consequences.[13]

In 1982 the Project suggested that the revolving door was a
dangerously corrupting influence on the procurement bureaucracy and that legislation was needed to stop the flow of Pentagon personnel to the contractors. Congresswoman Barbara
Boxer (D-California) and Senator David Pryor (D-Arkansas) introduced legislation in 1984 and 1985 that restricts the defense
companies from hiring Pentagon personnel for five years to
work on contracts that they were involved in while at the DOD.
The bill has a penalty for violation by the contractors.

Despite the assertions of many DOD officials, this proposed
law is not intended to penalize the honest government official.
It must, however, put a stop to situations that have even the
potential to create conflicts of interest. Even if none of the
officers I have listed did anything wrong by going through the
revolving door, the appearance of wrongdoing has a devastating effect on morale in the procurement bureaucracy and the
reputation of our officer corps. Conflict of interest laws have
traditionally been implemented to regulate evil before the fact
and to prevent the honest official from getting into a situation
that has even the appearance of wrongdoing. The revolving
door must be shut permanently if the taxpayer is to be assured
of honest procurement.

The damage to the reputation of the officer corps in the
revolving door system leads to another problem, the heavy
involvement of our officer corps in the procurement bureaucracy and its effect. I discovered that one of the reasons for this
military involvement in nonmilitary procurement tasks such as
contracting, lobbying, and auditing is that there are too many
officers in the Pentagon to fill the traditional slots of actual
military command.

While my husband, Thom, was working at the Project, he asked for a job that was more interesting than typing and filing. I gave him a chart from the Congressional Budget Office showing that a colonel has more take-home pay than a member of Congress. It inspired Thom to look into what salary officers make and how many officers are in the DOD. His report had some startling facts (Thom chose 1958 as a comparative year because although the United States was not at war, there was an arms buildup resulting from the Cold War with the Soviet Union, much as the situation is today)

—In 1939, before World War II, and in 1945, towards the end of World War II, there was 1 officer for each 12 enlisted personnel. In 1958 the ratio was 1 to 9, and by 1982 there was 1 officer for every 6.5 enlisted personnel.

—In 1945 the Army had 14 generals for each active division. In 1958 the figure was 33 generals per division. By 1982 it had declined to 24 per division.

—At the end of World War II the Navy had 1 admiral per 130 ships in service. In 1958 there was 1 admiral per 9 ships, while in 1982 it had 1 for every 2 ships (and this includes all categories of ships).

—The Air Force had 1 general for every 244 airplanes in 1945, 1 general for every 64 planes in 1958, and 1 general for every 30 planes in 1982 (which includes all categories of aircraft in the Air Force inventory).

This overabundance of officers not only caused too many to be in procurement, as well as costing the taxpayer an excessive amount to support them, but it has also hurt military effectiveness and leadership. The report concludes:

The damage of an excessive officer corps on the taxpayer's pocketbook is obvious and can be measured rather

accurately. However, a hidden casualty to this problem
may be our own military effectiveness. An overabundance
of officers often means an underabundance of commands.
This forces our military men into areas far removed from
military missions—often encouraging them to neglect
their original mission of leadership and strategy to win the
next war.

We need to re-examine what we want to require of our
officer corps. Do we want our officers to work on winning
wars, teaching leadership, creating new strategies, or do
we want them preparing budgets, lobbying for programs
on Capitol Hill, and wrangling with government contractors? Right now we must place our overabundance of Generals and officers in commands of dubious military value,
which threatens to make being an officer just another job.
Encouraging officers to get advanced managerial and business degrees to fill these slots could backfire if a real war
beckons. In a war, we need military men and warriors, not
business executives and public relations men. In the procurement process, we need our officer corps input as the
user of the equipment, not the manager. As we allow our
excess of officers to continue, we will find commands for
these men outside the traditional military areas, and inevi-
tably encourage a drift away from their original mission—
war.

Edward Luttwak, a well-known military analyst, states
the problem well:

> The military has become civilianized in the sense
> of emulating at higher cost, things the civilians can
> do better—but not concentrating on the things the
> civilians cannot do, which are to train combat lead-
> ers, to study tactics, and prepare strategies.

> Reduction of the current officer corps will encourage
> the right type of officer to emerge and be promoted—
> those intent on fighting and winning real battles, rather
> than bureaucratic, business, and political ones.[14]

The question remains why our politically appointed officials,
who are not in the system for a very long time, also feel the

pressure to go along with the current procurement situation. For a long time, these officials did not react to the Project's exposés because they did not really feel pressure for change from the average citizen.

Our sources discovered, however, an issue the public could identify with, and become outraged enough about, to demand change in the Pentagon's wasteful procurement policies. It was the issue of overpriced spare parts. The Project started out with the original releases and exposés on spare parts in the fall of 1982, and our investigation at Travis Air Force Base helped open the issue to a larger part of the American public and pressured the elected and appointed officials to take a stand one way or another on the wasteful Pentagon procurement practices.

In August 1984, I received a call from a Bob Greenstreet who lived in Kentfield, California. He was a captain in the Air Force at the nearby Travis Air Force Base and worked on the flight line as a mechanic for the C-5A and C-141 cargo planes. Over the past three years he had grown concerned about the excessive high costs of the spare parts for the planes and other wasteful practices he had seen on base. While I was in nearby El Cerrito, I made arrangements to meet him at a restaurant.

Bob had told me over the phone that he didn't have much information, but once I began to look at his information in the restaurant I saw that he had more documents than most whistle-blowers. Bob is an intense man of thirty-one, tall and rather slight. A certified Airframe and Powerplant (A&P) mechanic, he spent much of his time drawing pictures of items for which he had Air Force spare part ordering documents. He had also taken pictures of small items from the local stock which showed the parts numbers and prices.

The parts ranged from a mechanical aircraft clock that cost $591 to a cowling door for the sides of a C-5 engine that cost $166,000 apiece. I could not tell if the prices were too high because I had not seen the items and did not have a frame of reference for the correct cost of such matériel. But I could see Bob's anger with the system building with every example. I felt he was sincere and decided to check these items out. I told him to try to get more examples without jeopardizing his position and to see if any people he worked with were upset about the prices and wanted to give me more information.

I was excited about the information Bob had given me on spare parts costs because we were in the second year of a battle with the Pentagon on that same issue. The DOD was claiming that the problem had been solved because Secretary of Defense Caspar Weinberger had issued a ten-point plan to stop spare parts overpricing and the military services claimed that they had an awards system for grass-roots employees to turn in items of excessive cost. I had heard from the field that these "reforms" were not taken seriously or enforced, but I did not have any new evidence.

Bob called a few days later and told me that Airman Thomas Jonsson, who also worked on the flight line, was upset at the high cost of the spare parts he was working with and wanted to talk to me. I called Thomas, and he said he'd like to meet me to talk about his frustrations with the system. With my husband, I drove out to Travis Air Force Base and met Thomas at a donut shop.

Airman Jonsson, a blond athletic man of twenty-four, was quite shy when we first sat down to talk, but he soon began to open up and even become angry as he told us of the excessive prices he had seen on the flight line. We spent almost four hours poring over his documents as he explained each item. As with Bob's information, it was hard to tell to what extent some items were overpriced, but most costs seemed excessive. Two examples seemed especially absurd.

The first one was the ten-cup coffee brewer made for the C-5A crew and passenger area. According to Thomas's Air Force documents, it cost $4947 in 1980 and had risen to $7622 in 1984. In his previous job in the Air Force, he had repaired the coffee brewer and drew us pictures of its simple mechanics. He told us that on top of being overpriced, the coffee unit had a tendency to break down often and was not well made. I knew that this item had to be overpriced and made a note to check it out.

Thomas then pulled out an armrest pad from a seat on the C-5 and asked us to guess how much the Air Force paid for it. The armrest pad had an aluminum frame that clamped it onto the armrest, and was covered with about an inch and a half of foam with a rather cheap blue vinyl covering. I could not guess but figured silently that the Air Force would outrageously pay $100 for such an item. Both my husband and I nearly fell out of our chairs when he told us the price was $670.06 each.

Thomas proceeded to tell us how he found, through the head of manufacturing on the base, that the Travis Air Force Base had the facilities and the manpower to make the armrest pad for between $5 to $25. He submitted the suggestion that the base manufacture the armrest itself, and potentially save the Air Force up to $1.5 million a year, to the base suggestion program and the much-vaunted Air Force Zero Overpricing Program that was one of Secretary Weinberger's attempted "reforms" of the spare parts problem. Thomas did not hear back from the Zero Overpricing Program and was led through eight months of red tape with the base suggestion program.

He had a carefully documented paper trail. I was amazed by the lack of knowledge or pretended lack of knowledge shown by those who evaluated his suggestion: first they claimed that they could not tell if the part number of his suggestion pertained to an armrest or an ashtray in the armrest, so he sent them copies of the technical manual drawings with the armrest pad colored in. Then they said that they could not find the blueprints on the drawing, so he got the blueprints from the vendor for the evaluators. Then they thought Thomas was suggesting on-base repair instead of manufacture.

They turned down his first request because they claimed,

backing it up with a document, that since the base ordered only twenty-five armrest pads a year it would be "not in the best interests of the Air Force" to repair that few. Thomas gave me the document they used to justify turning down his request, which actually showed that the base bought 106 armrest pads in twenty-five *orders*. Also Thomas was talking about in-house manufacturing of the item, not repair. He did some more research and resubmitted his suggestion. When I met him they were about to turn it down again, and his eyes flashed with frustration as he told me about the system.

His story did not match what the Pentagon was claiming was happening at the grass-roots level. As my husband and I drove home, he remarked that Bob and Thomas were unique sources because they were actually using the equipment.

I spent the next few weeks talking with the underground in Washington and trying to verify Bob's and Thomas's documents. They all appeared to be in order, so I had to sit down and decide what to do with the material while trying to protect the sources. To my reluctant surprise, both men were willing to go public and testify. Concerned that they would be punished like so many other whistle-blowers I knew, I counseled them against going public. However, when they insisted, I told them to wait until I could provide them with diligent congressional protection. Bob was scheduled to get out of the Air Force within about a month, but Thomas had another year. At that time, neither was interested in an Air Force career because both were so disgusted by what they had seen during their first enlistment, and that made it easier to try to protect them. (Thomas Jonsson recently reenlisted for six more years.)

Since it was the fall of an election year, I thought it would be hard to find anyone right away who would be interested enough in their story to hold hearings. I expected to have to wait until the Congress geared up for the 1985 session. However, as luck would have it, Senator Charles Grassley's Senate Judiciary Subcommittee on Administrative Practices and Procedures had been closely following the spare parts problem and the Pentagon's administrative reaction to it, and they had an available hearing date on September 19.

It did not give me a lot of time to prepare, but I knew that I could not release any of this information without jeopardizing the sources. I wanted to give them as much protection as possible. I had decided early in the life of the Project that no information, no matter how important, was worth ruining anyone's career. I also knew that if the subcommittee announced ahead of time that these two men were coming to testify, the Air Force might try to block their testimony and intimidate them. So the subcommittee agreed with me that the two men should be secret witnesses, and the Project agreed to pay the expenses of bringing them to Washington from California. It was a financial hardship for the Project, but I felt that what these men had to say was important enough to sacrifice the money.

On one of my trips back to El Cerrito, Thomas Jonsson called me to ask if I wanted to come on the base and look at the items to verify his story. I jumped at the chance and asked Bernie Ward, a staff member of Congresswoman Barbara Boxer's office who had worked on spare parts reform legislation in the House of Representatives, if he would like to come along. Bernie was visiting his parents in nearby San Francisco and was excited about checking out Thomas's and Bob's claim. Coincidentally, Bob Greenstreet lived in Marin County in California and therefore was a constituent of Congresswoman Boxer.

Thomas told me that it was common for airmen to bring friends onto the base and even on the C-5 flight line to show them where they worked. As long as we were escorted by him, it was all aboveboard. I told him right off that I did not want to do anything illegal or look at any classified material, and he agreed with me. I could sense that he was nervous about having us visit, but determined to do it anyway.

We decided that the best time for us to come was during Thomas's shift on a Sunday afternoon, because we would be less noticeable. While Bernie and I drove to the base, we discussed what we would do if we were caught and decided that we would not misrepresent ourselves. I felt better with Bernie along because he had congressional credentials and the base was only a few miles from the edge of Congresswoman Boxer's district. I brought along two cameras, one with a zoom lens, but I decided not to use them unless Thomas felt that it was safe.

Thomas met us at the Travis Air Force Base gate and escorted us in without any problems. I was surprised that we were not required to sign anything. Then we went with him in his delivery truck to where he ordered and delivered parts for the C-5. As we approached the flight line where the planes were being serviced, Bernie and I held our breaths because the area was roped off and the entrance was guarded by a soldier wielding an M-16 rifle. But Thomas remained cool as he told the guard that we were friends of his who wanted to see the planes. He assured the guard that we would remain with him. After peering in at us, the guard, looking unconcerned, waved us on.

Suddenly I was before the huge C-5A cargo planes, the largest in the world. Although I had seen C-5s taking off at other bases, I had never been very close to one, let alone inside. As I craned my neck to see the top of the planes, I thought how ironic it was that I was about to do another exposé on the plane that contributed to Ernie's career problems and whose cracked wings had brought me my first military exposé. Now I was about to see it intimately, inside and out, while collecting data on its overpriced spare parts.

Bernie asked Thomas if there were any classified areas on the plane, but Thomas assured us that the classified instruments had been removed and locked in a secured area when the plane came in. I also knew that it was not unusual to have civilians tour the C-5 because my father and a friend had come to a public viewing day at the base and crawled all over the plane and taken pictures. But I continued to follow Thomas's wishes so he would be protected.

On slow periods between his runs for parts, Thomas took us outside the plane and pointed out parts that he felt were especially overpriced and showed us the documentation for them. It was a slow day on the flight line, but Thomas always had one ear tuned to his radio so that our visit would not interfere with his work. Then he took us inside and showed us many of the items that he thought were outrageously priced. Among them were the ten-cup coffee brewer that cost $7622, a 12-by-14-inch push-button metal drawer in the galley (kitchen) area that cost $656 to replace, the flight engineer seat that adjusts for height and swivels at $13,905, and a rechargeable emergency flashlight unit that cost $181 apiece and that Thomas claimed broke down often.

I was taking pictures as fast as I could while Bernie and Thomas fidgeted and eyed the maintenance workers who were milling in and around the airplane. But they did not seem to notice or care about the picture-taking; they probably just considered us another pair of tourists. Nevertheless, the entire process was nerve-racking and I had a hard time keeping the cameras steady in the low light.

We later went into a supply depot where Thomas once again asked the man in charge if he could show us around. The man agreed but after eyeing my cameras told us that we could not take pictures. Inside, we looked at many of the replacement parts, including the coffee brewer. Thom showed us the elements inside. It was not a complicated machine.

The new information was useful for me, but I knew that if Thomas and Bob had made even one mistake matching items to documents the Pentagon would seize upon that error to discredit them. Thomas took us inside his office, looked up the stock number of each item on the documents that they had previously given us, checked it against the microfiche data he used to order the parts from, and checked that the items we saw matched the stock number and technical drawings in the technical manual. Since we were looking at about twenty different items, it was a slow, painstaking process.

Bernie made sure the stock numbers that Thomas had given us matched the microfiche while I located the technical drawings in the manual to see if they matched what we had taken pictures of. I then took pictures of the drawings for verification. It was during this time that we were the most nervous. Although Thomas's office door was shut and he was not receiving any requests form the flight line, it would be hard to explain to anyone who came in why Thomas's friends were looking at microfiche and hunched over his desk taking pictures of technical drawings in the manuals. Even Thomas's usually cool demeanor began to crack and he turned whiter and whiter with each of our requests. Looking back, it resembled a scene from a spy movie spoof. We were definitely amateurs.

In the long run it was worth it. Not only did we absolutely verify around twenty parts, but we were also able to get price growth since 1980 on several items. In 1980 the ring cowl engine for the C-5 cost $94,730, yet four years later the price had jumped four times to $367,676. Also in 1980 the coffee brewer cost $4947 and in 1984 it had risen to $7622. This data was especially important considering the DOD claim that the Reagan administration had gotten the spare parts prices under control. In these cases at least, it was not so.

After six nerve-racking hours, we had enough evidence for a very tight case. I felt a lot better about having the two men testify because their claims had been verified by me and a congressional staff aide using the base's own microfiche prices. Thomas walked us to the car, and Bernie and I drove off the base. It was during these last few minutes that total paranoia gripped us. As we drove we expected that any minute a swarm of military police would appear and arrest us while ripping the film from my cameras that was our main evidence. But the guards at the front gate waved goodbye to us on this sleepy afternoon, as we sped toward San Francisco and civilian safety. We were elated by our success. It was one of my most thoroughly investigated cases.

But my job had just begun. Not only did I have to prepare these two men to testify before Congress for the first time, but we also planned to release some of the documentation a few days before the hearing. I had to pick out examples from the group that were fairly easy to identify as overpriced.

I called an acquaintance in the commercial airline business to get comparable prices on such items as the coffee brewer and the flashlight in a 727. Unfortunately, I was not able to reach him until after I released the items to the press. I made the mistake of trying to get prices on similar items from department stores. Although the C-5 rechargeable emergency flashlight is different from the rechargeable type at a department store, I included the price of a Montgomery Ward's rechargeable flashlight for reference in my release. It was a mistake because the Pentagon would later claim that I did not understand the function of the "emergency lighting system."

I prepared the release of some of the items and headed back to Washington with the developed film. I was quite pleased with the pictures, especially since I had taken them under such unfavorable conditions. Although the C-5 coffee brewer was one of the best examples I had, Congresswoman Boxer asked if I would hold back on releasing it so she could use it as an illustration at the Grassley Senate hearing. So I put together the best of the remaining examples and released the information to the press.

On the day I released the information, my airline source called me back with the needed prices to compare similar airline articles. The impact-resistant, rechargeable emergency flashlight unit on a 727 airliner cost the airline company $35 in contrast to the $181 the Air Force paid for their flashlight that did the same job. The 727 airliner's flight engineer seat was $5,065 compared to the $13,905 price the Air Force paid on the

C-5 seat. The coffee brewer on the 727 cost $2,125 versus $7622 the Air Force paid for the same size brewer on the C-5. The pilot wheel, which cost $2733 on the C-5, ran $2165 on the 727 —not much difference on that item. But the main point was that the Air Force was, in many cases, paying much more for these parts than the commercial airlines, which have to worry about a profit. I called the reporters who had received my information package and told them of the new numbers. I felt that since these items were compared to the counterparts in the commercial airline business, the Pentagon could not try to say that we were not comparing similar items.

But the Air Force immediately took the offensive against the released information. Before the stories came out, I received a call from the Air Force public affairs spokesman, who complained that they could not answer the reporters' questions or make comments because they did not know to what parts the reporters were referring. Since the hearing was only a few days away and I wanted to be as fair as possible, I broke my own rules and gave the officer all the Air Force item stock numbers and prices I had released. He thanked me profusely, and I felt that the public affairs people would now try to comment fairly on the parts.

I was wrong. When the stories hit the papers on September 12, 1984, the Air Force flew in General Dewey Lowe from McClellan Air Force Base to rebut the evidence that the prices were inflated and to insist that our research was unfounded. The general told *The Wall Street Journal* outright that "the items mentioned were reasonably priced in accordance with rules and regulations in existence." That had become a standard explanation for all the other spare parts stories in the past and, as I will illustrate later, that is a major element of the spare parts pricing problems in the Pentagon. I was surprised at the Air Force's extreme reaction to our material until I saw that at least eight major newspapers had carried the spare parts story on the same day. We had touched a nerve in the Pentagon and the hearings were just a few days away. The reporters called me for more material, so I hinted that they should be sure to attend the Grassley hearing on September 19, 1984.

Now I needed to turn all my attention to Bob and Thomas and their testimony. Before I left California, we had gotten together and written rough drafts of their statements. Since both of them could come in only one day before the hearing, I knew that we had to work fast to polish their testimony into a tight and convincing case. Neither Bob nor Thomas had ever testified before or even been to Washington, so it became the Project staff's responsibility to help guide them through the maze of reporters and senators who wanted to talk to them. I had earlier tried to warn them how tough it would be and also assured them that we would be with them every step of the way, but I knew from my own experience that no amount of advice would make their job any easier.

Shortly after Bob and Thomas arrived and I had a short meeting with them, we went to meet with a small group of reporters I thought might be interested in doing stories on them. Then we spent most of the evening and part of the early morning hours finishing their testimony.

The next morning when we walked into the hearing room even I blanched at the number of television cameras and press people milling about. As a group of reporters rushed up to us, I advised Bob and Thomas not to say anything until after they testified. It was strange for me not to respond to the reporters, but I wanted to protect my sources from Air Force accusations that they were merely seeking publicity. They had come to talk to the Congress first and foremost. Thomas had taken official leave for the days he was in Washington and Bob had coincidentally finished his last day in the Air Force the day before and was to begin work in the Air Force Reserve. The committee and I were determined that they testify as private citizens, do everything by the book, and not even wear their uniforms, so the Air Force would have no cause to discipline them. Still, Senator

Grassley, Congresswoman Boxer, and I realized the risk these two men were taking and that we would have to be diligent after the testimony to make sure that they did not suffer for their testimony to the committee. By public law 18 U.S.C. 1505, it is illegal for anyone to retaliate against a congressional witness for his testimony, but the law is rarely enforced.

Senator Grassley made it clear in his opening statement that he wanted to put the Air Force on notice that he would not tolerate any harassment of the witnesses. He also tried to make the men feel at ease by introducing Thomas's wife, Loretta, who was in the audience. Bob and Thomas were at the witness table with Congresswoman Boxer in between them, and I awkwardly shuttled back and forth between them as each one spoke. Congresswoman Boxer had a tough opening statement and held up a diagram of the coffee brewer while dozens of photographers took her picture. Then Thomas went first and for the first ten minutes his voice was strained. Senator Grassley worked hard to put him at ease and he began to relax until he held up his armrest and once again the hordes of photographers lunged forward to get the picture. He related how he had tried to go through the Air Force suggestion system to have the armrest made on base for $5 to $25 instead of buying them from a contractor for $670.06.

Bob's story was a bit more complicated because he had to describe why the supply system at the base was set up to encourage officers and airmen to throw brand-new but unused spare parts into the trash instead of returning them to the supply depot. He displayed some of the parts that he had retrieved from the dumpster, and he also took apart one of he $181 C-5 emergency flashlights to show the committee how uncomplicated their 1960s technology was when compared to some of his complicated stereo units that cost about the same amount in stores.

The hearing received quite a bit of news attention, including a front-page story in *The Washington Post*. The coffee brewer became the subject for a rash of jokes around the country, including some on the Johnny Carson show.

Thomas and Bob were asked to fly to New York to appear on the NBC *Today* show the next morning, and I accompanied them at their request. They had never been to New York and both were nervous about going on television. Both of them did extremely well at the hearing and on television, considering the tremendous pressure that was put on them. Any nervousness they showed actually endeared them to the press, which was used to slick politicians and officials in Washington who pretend they have all the answers. I think the natural side of these men also made them more credible to the public. They had little to gain by coming forward and a lot to lose, and they showed great strength under pressure. Their willingness to come forward focused great attention on the spare parts problem and helped make a start in solving the problem of overpricing weapons in general.

Their story was another verification that the Project was right in our long battle with the Pentagon on spare parts prices. Although the Pentagon claimed that they discovered the spare parts horror stories and their own people had rooted out this waste, the spare parts scandals that have appeared over the last few years started when someone leaked what has become known as the Hancock memo. In a memo dated July 12, 1982, Robert Hancock, the deputy chief of the Commodities Division at Tinker Air Force Base in Oklahoma, complained to the Air Force Plant Representative office at the Government Products Division in West Palm Beach, Florida, that Pratt & Whitney, a defense company that builds aircraft engines for the Air Force, had thirty-four spare parts for which prices had increased 300 percent in one calendar year. He was concerned that the company had gotten out of hand and, in unusually strong words for a bureaucrat, wrote that "Pratt & Whitney has never had to control prices and it will be difficult for them to learn."

I remember calling Hancock after releasing the memo to the

press to warn him that reporters were going to ask him for a statement, but I had no idea that the release would have such an impact. Of the twenty-two reporters I called, twenty wrote stories. My sources had realized that the public identified with the cost of a wrench or a screw because they had a frame of reference, but not with the cost of a fighter or a ship. The public knew how much a wrench should cost but were hard-pressed to tell if a B-1 bomber was overpriced. Several members of the underground understood that point and planned to use the spare parts issue to have the public eventually realize that weapons were just as overpriced as the spare parts.

The Air Force's initial reaction to the stories that followed the Hancock memo was that the prices paid to Pratt & Whitney for the thirty-four parts were justified. It so angered Ernie, who had looked into the matter and knew better, that he remarked to me that "generally the public relations people [in the Air Force] lie instinctively, even when the truth would serve them better." I thought that maybe he was exaggerating, but as I continued to follow and expose the spare parts scandals over the next few years, I was forced to admit that he was often right. The Air Force (as well as the other services) has continued to evade and deny the spare parts problem for several years and has tried to "fool all of the people all of the time."

I did not expect such great public interest in the spare parts issue. I was soon swamped with requests for stories on spare parts and with examples from the underground. I knew that in order to handle the workload that was pouring in with our increased publicity I could no longer do everything myself. So I assigned Donna Martin the subject and introduced her to the sources. She quickly picked up the subject from the sources and soon surpassed me in knowledge on how the spare parts system is failing to provide enough parts at a reasonable price. From that point on most of the successes that the Project has had in exposing this problem is due to her careful and relentless work.

She has shown an uncanny ability to judge the accuracy of the information we receive.

After the Hancock memo and the resultant stories, the Air Force and the other services started reacting to any spare parts stories by telling reporters that the prices paid for any spare parts items were either "fair and reasonable" or just isolated incidences of overpricing. It took the Project and other investigative sources many months of releasing more and more examples of overpriced spare parts to show that the problem was deeper than a few isolated incidences.

There was such an uproar over the high-priced spare parts in the Hancock memo that the Air Force set up an Ad Hoc Pricing Review Team in the fall of 1982.[15] They concluded that Pratt & Whitney had reaped "windfall profits" in the sale of those thirty-four parts listed in the Hancock memo. One reason they found for the increase in cost was that the prices for the spares were often "renegotiated" between the time of the Air Force order and the time of delivery. The team found that the price markup accounted for 67 percent of the increase. Pratt & Whitney's negotiated markup rate was 24 percent higher than it was fairly entitled if it had been limited to reimbursement for actual costs to make the part plus a negotiated profit. The review team found that by combining excess markup with its negotiated profit, P & W had received 32 percent more compensation than its expected costs. We released the leaked report to several reporters, who wrote stories on the ad hoc team's findings.

Yet even as late as March 1983, six months after the ad hoc team's report, the official Air Force response to press inquiries about the Pratt & Whitney spare parts price escalations was that they were "proper because growth could be attributed to changes in the materials or techniques used to fabricate the part. . . . The Air Force verified the contractor established 1981 prices on 33 of 34 items."[16]

The reasons the Air Force was able to make these carefully worded disclaimers became apparent after Colin Parfitt, an assistant for Air Force Financial Management in the office of Ernie Fitzgerald, went to Pratt & Whitney's offices in Connecticut to see why these prices were considered "reasonable" by the Air Force. The Parfitt report found that the Basic Ordering Agreement (BOA) Hancock had complained about (in his now famous memo) permitted P & W, in its spare parts orders from the government, to reprice parts between order and delivery and in some cases after delivery. The rate of markup of the parts cited in the Hancock memo alerted Parfitt to the possibility of general overpricing. But more importantly, after analyzing P & W's pricing formula, Parfitt found the same degree of inflated markup rate applying to the entire TF-30 engine. In other words, the spare parts he found were priced using the same formulas for buying the entire engine. It meant that the engine, having been bought with the same pricing formulas, was as overpriced as the individual spare parts.

The bottom line was that what the Air Force considered a "fair and reasonable" price for an item would not be considered reasonable by the public and any business person in the private sector. Since the DOD had legally agreed to these excessive pricing formulas and their unrealistic markups, they had actually institutionalized the high prices. Furthermore, these high prices then became the new standard for future negotiations. The implications of this institutional waste are hard to comprehend, but over the next few years the Project and investigating congressional committees found many other examples of this disturbing purchasing practice.

An example that best illustrates the absurdity of the pricing formulas the Pentagon and the contractors have agreed to is a simple claw hammer that Congressman Berkley Bedell (D-Iowa) gave to the House Armed Services Committee as an example of spare parts waste. The Navy bought this hammer for an astonishing $435 from the Gould Corporation as a backup tool for an electronic project. The outraged Bedell took the example to Navy auditors and asked them to check the records and find the waste or fraud responsible for the hammer's cost.

The Navy came back with the amazing statement that Gould had used "government approved purchasing and estimating systems"[17] based on the reviews by the Pentagon's audit agencies. Not only that, the Navy informed the congressman, according to their audit, the Navy had actually paid one dollar *less* than they should have. The chart on page 165 shows the pricing formula contractually agreed upon by the Navy and the Gould Corporation so that a $7 hammer cost $436, Pentagon style. (Remember, the time written off is for each individual hammer, though each was purchased from a Gould subcontractor.)

Notice that it supposedly took Gould one hour per hammer for program management and .9 hour for quality control. The hammer was just one item of an entire box of tools that the Navy had bought from Gould for a price of $10,168.56, using approved pricing formulas. Congressman Bedell's staff aide went to a hardware store and bought the same type of tools in the box for $119.23. Examples included:

TOOL	RETAIL	GOULD
Pliers, slip joint	$3.77	$ 449.00
Screwdriver, Sq.Blade, set	1.69	265.50
Crimping Tool	3.96	729.00
Superjust Wrenches	4.88	1150.00
Drill Set	1.69	599.00

It is hard to remember that these outrageous prices were approved in the pricing formulas that the Navy had signed with Gould.

On top of this insult, the Navy audit system agreed that the tools were overpriced in that contract by over $750,000 and that the money should be recovered. However, the Navy audit agency overruled the finding, stating that the costs were "exorbitant but legal." They then negotiated with Gould to return only 10 percent of the overcharge as determined by the original

Pricing Example: Gould, Simulated Systems Division

Purchased Item
Item—hammer, hand, sledge—Qty.—1 each

Direct Material	$	7.00
Material Packaging		1.00
Material Handling Overhead @ 19.8%		2.00

·Spares/ Repair Dept.	1. hr	
·Program Support/ Admin.	.4 hr	
·Program Management	1. hr	
·Secretarial	.2 hr	
	2.6 hrs Engr. support	37.00

Engr. O/H [Overhead] @ 110%		41.00

·Mechanical Sub-assembly	.3 hr	
·Quality Control	.9 hr	
·Operations Program Mgt.	1.5 hr	
·Program Planning	4. hr	
·Mfg. Project Engr.	1. hr	
·Q.A. [Quality Assurance]	.1 hr	
	7.8 hrs Mfg Support	93.00

Mfg O/H @ 110%	102.00
	$283.00
G & A @ 31.8%	90.00
	$373.00
Fee [profit]	56.00
Facilities Capital Cost of Money	7.00
TOTAL PRICE	$436.00[18]

auditors. Then the DOD had a "press event" with top officials of Gould handing back a refund check and the DOD claiming a big victory. This was certainly another case of trying to fool all of the people all of the time. The Project barely had time to keep ahead of the public relations maneuvers and make sure that the press had the real facts on the spare parts cases.

Another example was a small plastic stool cap that fits the end of the leg of the navigator's stool on the AWACS plane made by Boeing Aircraft. The cap was bought by the Air Force for $975.26:

Overhead (executive salaries, lights, etc.)	$459.00
Labor	204.00
Eight Hours of Inspection	34.00
Fringe Benefits	127.00
State and Local Taxes	32.00
Profit	119.00
Plastic Material	.26

After the cap was discovered by Air Force Sergeant Kessler, and exposed by Dr. Thomas Amlie, who works for Ernie Fitzgerald, a spokesman for the Defense Industrial Supply Center, which ordered the cap, defended Boeing in a statement to *The Washington Post* on September 21, 1983: "Rates contained in the Boeing cost breakdown were consistent with *approved* rates." [Emphasis added]

When I first saw the price breakdowns, I found a dark humor in discovering that each stool cap required eight hours of inspection: it must have been a dreadfully dull job. But the sad part is not only the obvious waste of money but that these parts are so expensive per unit that there will always be an institutional spare parts shortage that will affect the soldiers in a war.

By August 1983, there had been numerous congressional hearings and exposés of spare parts institutional waste, including statements by the General Accounting Office (GAO) and other investigatory agencies, that the spare parts controversy was not just a few isolated cases but revealed a fundamental procurement problem.

Partly because of all the negative publicity it had received, the Pentagon could no longer ignore the spare parts overpricing problem or dismiss it as a few isolated examples. In August 1983, Defense Secretary Weinberger issued a ten-point directive for reforming spare parts procurement. He vowed to eliminate excessive pricing, recover unjustified payments, and punish offending contractors and DOD employees who contribute to overpricing. One of the problems with these new initiatives was that, once again, the Secretary did not describe what action would be taken if the initiatives were ignored by the bureaucracy.

Early in the first term of the Reagan administration, Secretary Weinberger and his then Undersecretary of Defense, Frank Carlucci, issued a set of thirty-two procedurement reforms that became known as the Carlucci initiatives. The DOD made a big show of their implementation, but the entrenched bureaucracy, for the most part, chose to ignore the directives because there was no penalty for doing so. Even Weinberger and Carlucci admitted that the reforms in the thirty-two initiatives had not been successfully implemented. Yet the Secretary failed to change the situation when, with great fanfare, he issued his ten-point plan on spare parts reform. These so-called reforms were quickly dubbed the ten commandments by the underground. The procurement bureaucracy has seen DOD secretaries and their "reforms" come and go with little impact on business-as-usual. The underground describes the process of not letting any new directives change the system by giving the top civilians the "mushroom treatment"—keeping them in the dark and feeding them bull manure. This was humorously illustrated when a member of Congress, during the course of Weinberger's testimony, showed the secretary an official copy of his ten-point directive that a serviceman had sent to the congress-man with the word "bullshit" stamped in large letters across the front.

One of the best indications I had that the ten-point plan had not reached the people involved in reforms was when I found out that neither Bob Greenstreet nor Thomas Jonsson had heard of the plan, and that one of the Air Force savings pro-grams instituted in response to the plan, the Zero Overpricing Program, had never even responded to Airman Jonsson's sav-ings plan on the C-5A armrest. The DOD attacked these men and others who came forward with new spare parts horror stories instead of using the opportunity to crack down seriously on the bureaucrats who continued to waste money, so it is hard to believe that the Secretary and his deputies were really seri-ous about a true reform of the system. Ernie put it best when he remarked that Secretary of the Air Force Verne Orr had declared war on procurement waste only to discover that his soldiers (the procurement bureaucracy) were conscientious ob-jectors.

In December 1984 the DOD tried again to "reform" the system by appointing a spare parts czar, the Deputy Assistant Secretary of Defense, Spares Program Management, Maurice Shriber. Once again the DOD had a big press conference to introduce Shriber, but they were met by skeptical reporters who felt that this new attempt at reform was merely a further public relations effort.

As with most previous new officials appointed to high posi-tions in the DOD, I called and asked to meet with Shriber to let him know of our concerns on spare parts procurement. In the past, I had never received a call back, so Donna and I were pleasantly surprised when Shriber called personally to ask us to have lunch with him. It was one of the first signs that he might be serious about cleaning up the spare parts procurement prob-lems in the Pentagon.

Shriber listened carefully as we described many of our concerns and seemed open to having us work with him. He then told me that when his boss, Assistant Secretary of Defense Korb, was taking questions from reporters during the press conference announcing Scriber's appointment, one reporter asked Korb why he didn't hire Dina Rasor if he was serious about solving the problem. As a result, Shriber thought that he should hear what we had to say.

However, the frustrating truth about Shriber's mission to clean up the spare parts scandal is that the problems are merely a microcosm of the procurement morass in the entire DOD. Reforming the spare parts procurement problems would really mean reforming the entire entrenched procurement bureaucracy that has been building a base since World War II. Until the incentive systems change for the people responsible for buying our planes, ships, and tanks, business will continue as usual.

For such bureaucrats as the program managers of weapons, there is no incentive to provide a low-cost effective weapon and return money to the program office. What are the incentives to encourage the appointed officials in the Department of Defense, such as the service secretaries, to continue to go along with the gag? They, too, have the political pressures to not bring bad news about a weapon or an accounting system to the surface because of the backlash from the administration that appointed them and from angry members of Congress where the weapon is built, and pressure from powerful defense contractors to not rock the boat by insisting on tough contracting and testing.

I cannot pretend to know what goes through the minds of these appointed officials when they first come into office, but they are soon placed in a squeeze by the various entrenched factions to support the status quo. Ernie, who has seen many appointed officials come and go through both Democratic and

Republican administrations, summed up an appointed official's reaction in this way:

> . . . Top managers in the Pentagon bureaucracy were often walled off from harsh realities by the military bureaucracy's practice of "staffing" and "coordination." These processes filter, censor, and alter information as needed to protect boondoggling. The resulting top management ignorance is a phenomenon familiar to management writers. Professor C. Northcote Parkinson, author of *Parkinson's Law* and other studies in management, called it "the dark at the top of the stairs." He and other students of management usually assumed the obstructions to information flow were universally viewed as undesirable by top managers. They didn't study the Pentagon where "programmed ignorance" is often a sought after state. In the military bureaucracies you're innocent if you're ignorant. Woe be unto the bearer of bad news demanding actions unpleasant to big-spending political leaders.
>
> At the same time there were politically appointed officials in the Pentagon believed to be sympathetic to buying an adequate defense without bankrupting the country. The Pentagon's palace guard was polite and deferential to these individuals, but protected the status quo by giving them the "mushroom" treatment. In pungent but descriptive Pentagonese, this consisted of "feeding them horse manure and keeping them in the dark."[19]

The clue to maintaining the status quo that benefits the defense companies, the Pentagon procurement bureaucracy, and the pork barrel members of Congress is to make sure that everyone goes along with the gag. The secret to success is to intimidate and quash any honest person in the bureaucracy who comes forward to report waste and fraud in the system and tries to reform it. Because the Pentagon bureaucracy has been brutal to whistle-blowers, who have tried unsuccessfully for years to reform the system by going through legitimate channels, people have been more and more reluctant to come forward internally. And because I was in the right place at the right time, they turned to me in frustration to try to stop the Pentagon procurement spending machine from using all its clever and persistent dodges to fool all of the people all of the time.

6.

THE UNDERGROUND

In November 1983, I received a luncheon invitation from Richard Sauber, former lawyer in the Justice Department who had been appointed chief prosecutor in the new Defense Procurement Fraud Unit, set up in October 1982. The press reported that the unit would uncover evidence of criminal activity in the DOD and then turn it over to the Justice Department for prosecution.

Many people in the underground were skeptical that the unit would be effective because of the Justice Department's past reluctance to go after examples of major defense fraud and waste. One congressional investigator who had followed Sauber's career with Justice described him as ambitious and interested in keeping the highest echelons satisfied. However, since he wanted to meet with my associate Donna Martin and me, I decided we should see what he wanted from us. When we met, I was surprised that he appeared to be only in his early thirties. He seemed surprised, then a little amused, at our cramped and shabby office space.

At the Chinese restaurant, Sauber reiterated the information in the DOD's press release. He told us that he wanted to crack a "big case," and if we had any good tight documentation he would be willing to work with us.

I don't know why but I took an instant dislike to Sauber, so I let Donna do most of the talking about the Project and our policies in using documentation. But I jumped into the conversation when he said he wanted us to turn a "big case" over to him. I told him that many of my sources were skeptical of working with the Justice Department in any formal investigatory department in the Pentagon. These two departments have rarely gone after anyone involved in a politically powerful fraud case and any information that was given about the whistle-blower was sometimes used against him.

Sauber, appearing annoyed, told me that he could not be held responsible for the Justice Department's past activities. I replied that if he wanted to work with my sources he would have to understand their hesitations and convince them that his efforts were not the "business-as-usual" that they had experienced. At that point, he leaned forward and told me that he just wanted documents and didn't want to deal with the whistle-blowers themselves. He thought whistle-blowers were strange and a little off.

I sat back and glared at him as he continued to talk. I thought back to the pain that so many of the whistle-blowers had gone through trying to do the right thing without any benefit to themselves and the arrogance of the young man across the table who wanted to use these men for the "big case" that would undoubtedly help his fast track career. Now he was belittling them.

Poor Donna, who could see that I was about to unload my anger on this man, tried to salvage the conversation. I remember thinking that it was not worth my time to tell Sauber off, but I did tell him that there was no way I was going to hand over documentation to him that could be traced back to a whistle-blower without making sure that he would protect the

whistle-blower's anonymity and thus life and career. I told
Sauber that I could not have my sources work with him in
good faith as long as he had his antagonistic attitude toward
whistle-blowers. He took our information and left rather an-
grily.

I suppose I could have been more understanding since his
attitude about whistle-blowers and the underground was not
unusual in Washington and I had been leery of them at first
myself. But what angered me was that though his position in the
government required him to protect sources who came to him,
he seemed to have little understanding and little compassion
for these people.

Until the Project was founded, many of the disclosures of
wrongdoing in the Pentagon were made by whistle-blowers
who would come before the press and the Congress and make
a big splash with a news story, and then spend their time trying
to defend themselves. It was always difficult for them to prove
their case once they were out of the bureaucracy because they
could not keep track of what was going on inside to cover up
the mistakes or frauds.

So when Ernie Fitzgerald helped create the Project as a front
for the people in the underground he also came up with a new
name for the people who come forward. He calls them "closet
patriots" because they do not reveal themselves and can stay
inside the bureaucracy to continue to rebut official claims that
the problem has been solved. Also because they are known only
to the Project, they can concentrate on the problem they have
discovered rather than on protecting themselves from the bureaucracy. Last but certainly not least, the men on the inside
can expose waste and fraud without ruining their careers and
personal lives. As you will see, whistle-blowing can have a devastating effect on the life of the whistle-blower.

By the end of 1982, the Project began to gain credibility due
in large part to the hard work of the underground. I do not
know the size of the Pentagon underground and I certainly do

not know all the members. Many cannot make themselves known even to me because of the risk to their careers, so others must intervene on their behalf to bring the information to me. The underground is not unlike an organism of cells in which I see and deal only with the top layer and unexposed cells bring the information up to that layer. There is no reason for me to know more names than necessary—the documentation usually speaks for itself.

For obvious reasons, our system is designed to expose as few people as possible. For the same reasons, I cannot name or describe in detail the members of the Pentagon underground, but they fall into four character types. This group, like any other, has members of great moral strength, and some whose intellectual honesty is continually stretched by the demands of survival in the corrupting atmosphere of the Pentagon procurement system. But I sincerely believe that I work with the best, most honest, and most refreshing people in Washington—people who are unwilling to make compromises that would injure the defense of our country.

The groups that make up most of the Pentagon underground are:

Scientists and Weapon Designers

In personality, this group ranges from the sophisticated, highly educated weapon designers and analysts to backyard tinkerers turned Ph.D., but all of them rely heavily on empirical data rather than Pentagon briefings in reaching their conclusions of the effectiveness of major weapon systems. Generally speaking, these men are critical of the political and unscientific decision-making process used by the current Pentagon procurement management.

Most in this group are aware of how important it is for weapons not to be overly sophisticated to work reliably on the battlefield, but some still cling to the hope that technology can make highly computerized weapons to outsmart the enemy. However, these scientists, after conferring with men with battlefield experience, often must concede that no matter how advanced, their weapons can't match the inventiveness of the human mind.

These men of science have split with their "technocratic" friends in the Pentagon by trying to design weapons using the wisdom of the combat soldier and pilot rather than the new technology that may have been invented in a laboratory far away from any battlefield. To show how much opposition they face, consider an incident from journalist Gregg Easterbrook's *Atlantic Monthly* story on the DIVAD anti-aircraft gun. A project officer of the DIVAD gun spent a great deal of time and resources trying to get the complicated aiming computer in the DIVAD to hit a hovering helicopter. The task can usually be accomplished with an uncomplicated 50-caliber machine gun and the human eye. From the article:

> It was found . . . that radar could track a fast-moving helicopter high in the sky much more easily than it could a hovering helicopter low to the ground. (Radar waves traveling near the ground bounce off trees, rocks and other "clutter" to create distortion similar to the distortion that spoils FM radio transmission.) Maj. William Gardepe, a DIVAD project officer, explained how electronics engineers had labored to overcome this obstacle. I suggested that aiming at a stationary helicopter is so easy that almost anyone can do it—without the technical breakthroughs. He gave me a hurt look and said, "But that was the *technical challenge.*"[1]

These scientists and weapon designers struggle every day in the Pentagon to try to design weapons that will be truly effective for the combat soldier, and not to meet the newest technical challenge that may not work on a battlefield. This group has been invaluable in trying to explain to journalists and the public how some razzle-dazzle new technology is not suitable for the battlefield.

Former and Current Military Officers and Enlisted Personnel

This group ranges from junior officers and enlisted men who are first experiencing the corruption of the system to gruff and battlewise warriors who quit the military as majors or colonels because they refused to "go along with the gag." The military men who have seen combat are more adamant about the necessity of reforming the current procurement system than those who have not. For the most part, this group is the most independent and aggressive in the Pentagon.

I have to be exceptionally careful with the groups of young officers I work with because they are not savvy about the bureaucratic methods that will be used to put them down. Several of the young majors I have worked with are disillusioned with their senior officers but feel very guilty about going to the outside (nonmilitary) world through the Project to stop what they see as corruption.

I once worked with a group of junior officers and a well-known journalist to uncover a major procurement scandal. The officers had given me some documents to pass on to the journalist showing how the procurement under investigation was unduly influenced by the defense contractor that would build the weapon. I checked the document in my usual way and passed it on to the reporter. Later I received a frantic call from one of the sources, who told me that the senior officer had told the group that the reporter had been passed a classified document. When the reporter was confronted with that fact, he said he was going to print it anyway.

The source also told me that the senior officer was threaten-

ing to give all the officers lie detector tests because of the alleged breach of security. Whoever failed the test might be
discharged. I told the source that I was sure the document was
not classified because it bore no security markings and to sit
tight until I called the reporter. It was 11:30 at night and the
reporter was incredulous about what I told him. He had called
the senior officer and asked him to comment on the document.
The official refused but never said a word about the document
being classified, nor did he ask the reporter not to print the
story for security reasons.

I was angry with the senior officer for terrorizing his underlings but I was not nearly so upset as the young officers when
they realized that their senior officer was capable of lying to
them about such an important issue as a security breach. The
document was not classified, and the lie detector tests were
never given.

The incident demoralized the junior officers even more and
made them more determined to do something about the corruption in their office. I received more documentation from
them than before.

I often wonder how strong military discipline would be in
that office during a war if that senior officer needed the trust
and respect of his junior officers to carry out orders in a life or
death situation. The incident reminded me of what a corrupting influence can exist when military men in procurement are
pressured to compromise their integrity in order to advance.

My experiences with younger officers contrast with the experiences I've had with the older military officers. The older
men have not compromised themselves yet have managed to
stay in the system for many years. Most of them have advanced
because of their brilliant combat records only to find themselves in an unreal procurement bureaucracy. Savvy infighters,
they have reluctantly turned outside the system to prevent the
adoption of weapons they knew would be ineffective and potentially deadly to the soldier in the field.

By design, I have had very little direct contact with this group. Many of them have been labeled troublemakers in the system and are watched very closely, even in retirement. I have learned a lot from them about combat and the military that has proven to be invaluable when a new source comes to me about a weapon scandal.

The older officers very cleverly watch and predict the moves of the bureaucracy when the Pentagon is trying to discredit one of my document releases. They have come through with good inside information when the heat has been on the Project. I also hear from other less vulnerable sources that these men are silently cheering me on from the inside. In addition, they tell me the disparaging remarks that are said about me and my organization and the concern that the Project is causing on the inside. That has proven to be very important during times when the Pentagon seems to be ignoring or dismissing our work and that of the reporters. It has given me a boost when I have wondered if the Project has been worthwhile.

Because of their experience with the bureaucracy, the older officers for the most part do not have to be carefully protected by the Project. They can take care of themselves and have often helped me protect myself and other more inexperienced members of the Pentagon underground.

Cost Analysts (Industrial Engineers) and Auditors

Those in charge of watching the books on major weapon systems are in a very difficult position because if they raise a fuss over outrageous expenditures for weapons, they are punished for being spoilers of the gravy train and for being somehow unpatriotic. They are also not always involved in the major procurement process in the Pentagon and thus do not realize the nature of the politics surrounding a weapon. Some of them, however, have discovered, along with military officers, that if they do not raise a fuss, they might get a much higher-paying job with the defense company they are auditing or analyzing.

However, even when this group (especially auditors) tries hard to do the right thing within their own sphere, their efforts are often overturned by a weapon system's program manager. Most of these auditors are reluctant to go outside the system and will play along with the game until one of them is brave enough to stand his ground and gets away with it. Then the others begin to sharpen their pencils and look more closely at the various padded accounts that come across their desks. The brave ones are usually from the old school of auditing and retain an unyielding sense of right and wrong. It would be fair to say that Ernie Fitzgerald is considered the head industrial engineer in the Pentagon because so many auditors and cost analysts seek his advice on how to do the right thing and get away with it.

The Hangers-on

It is very hard for me to write about this type in the Pentagon underground because so many dedicated and unselfish men work long hours to expose corruption in the Pentagon. As in most groups there are individuals in the Pentagon underground who rarely take an active role. Some appease the resulting guilt by assisting in the discovery of documents for self-serving reasons; others fancy themselves "defense intellectuals" who believe that all the intellectuals should get together and solve our defense problems.

These members of the underground are often critical of me and the activities of the Project because we seek to inform the general public, not just the defense elite. They bicker among themselves over how the problem should have been solved and who should get the credit. Some of them seem to want to spend most of their time analyzing what it all means over a few beers or glasses of wine.

I do not like to write about this faction of the Pentagon underground, but I feel that it is important to know that this not-so-noble element exists. Part of my job as the director of the Project is to make sure that the "sour grapes" element does not expose or hinder the men who unselfishly give their time. I am also aware that as a group, we are far too small to bicker on the "purity" of each member's commitment to our goals.

The men in the Pentagon underground are from diverse political and social backgrounds and have differing opinions on the direction of the country, often conflicting with my own. But we all agree that something must be done about the Pentagon procurement system to provide a better and more reliable defense for less money. Many in the underground have been unwilling to give organized groups studying the Pentagon any information because they do not want their facts used to advance some hidden political agenda. That was one reason I was determined to keep foreign policy and politics out of the Project. I made a commitment to these men that I would pursue only the Project's five objectives.

Interestingly, the Pentagon underground tends to have two factions with different goals. One group, which I have dubbed the "less bang" underground, feels that the current procurement system is producing weapons that will be ineffective on the battlefield. They are also alarmed that because our planes, ships, and tanks are getting so high in per unit cost, we are buying fewer and fewer. For example, in the 1950s the United States bought over 6000 tanks per year but in fiscal year 1986 the Pentagon plans to procure only 840 tanks. The same is true of airplanes and ships. In the early 1950s the United States bought over 6000 fighter aircraft per year but will procure fewer than 370 in fiscal 1986. Finally, in the early 1960s the Navy bought around fifteen surface warships per year but have only three budgeted in fiscal 1986.[2] These men know, many from actual battlefield experience, that fewer planes and tanks could make the crucial difference in a war. But the fallout rate of weapons in a battle could be devastating to the troops because there will be no units to replace those that have been blown up or have failed.

When I first contacted this "less bang" faction, some of its members were reluctant to suggest that the defense budget needed cutting because they thought they might be labeled "soft on defense." They also feared that politicians would not cut the fat and waste in the budget but would instead go after the more vulnerable budgets of training, testing, and logistics (supplies). These were legitimate fears, but as they began to talk to the other major underground faction, it became clear to them that the excess money in the Pentagon was corrupting the system and was the major cause of higher and higher priced weapons and fewer and fewer weapons.

The other group that the Project works closely with is what I call the "more bucks" underground. Consisting mainly of auditors and industrial engineers, it is mainly concerned with the blatant waste of money in the Pentagon.

Oddly enough, until the Project was formed, these two groups rarely worked together. Like the reporters and the whistle-blowers, the two undergrounds often did not understand each other's motives and initially were unwilling to work together. But because of the patience and work of individuals within both groups, an unusual coalition has been formed in the underground to cut defense waste and unnecessary spending and to lower the per unit cost of the individual weapons so that enough units could be procured to make a difference in a war.

The "more bucks" underground has realized that if the weapon the Pentagon buys doesn't work, it is the ultimate waste of money and soldiers' lives—a very poor return on investment. And Ernest Fitzgerald was one of the individuals who helped the "less bang" underground see that much of the high unit-cost problem is waste and inefficiency, and that an unchecked and continued flow of money into this bad system will just produce fewer, more expensive ineffective weapons.

In the last four years, as these two undergrounds have been working more closely together, the common belief has been that if the Congress and the Pentagon had the political will to reform the system, it would be possible to get better defense for less money. It is a hard concept for many in the press, the Congress, and the public to accept, but after numerous exposés on how the system works, the list of people ascribing to this approach has grown. The Project and our underground explained this concept in a book (appropriately titled *More Bucks, Less Bang*) that we published in 1983:

> Excluding the Vietnam war years, the defense budget was surprisingly constant for the twenty-five years following the Korean War: roughly $195 billion measured in constant 1984 dollars. The Carter Administration, however, in a desperate attempt to bail out its sagging political fortunes and buy a second term, unlocked the defense coffers in fiscal 1979. Accelerating the Carter-initiated defense spending surge a bit, the Reagan Administration had now proposed a 1984 budget of $275 billion, about $80 billion above the stable peacetime level that prevailed throughout the Eisenhower, Kennedy, Nixon, and Ford Administrations.

What Does an Extra $80 Billion Buy?

> Conventional wisdom holds that such a large increase in spending—40% or so—has to buy at least *slightly* better weapons. Admittedly, there might be some extra waste in spending the extra money, but there is bound to be *some* overall improvement in the nation's defenses.

> Conventional wisdom could not be more wrong. Given what the military Services want to buy today, the larger budgets will have the effect of further shrinking our forces and of buying weapons that will needlessly waste the lives of our soldiers, sailors, and airmen. Such a mind-boggling

reversal of ordinary logic needs explanation. A few concrete examples will show what really happens when more money is poured into the Pentagon budget.

Example: Bigger Budgets Lead to Smaller Forces

First, let us turn to the Navy for an example that explains how more money shrinks the forces. Secretary of the Navy John Lehman has widely advertised that he wants to expand from a "400-ship Navy" to a "600-ship Navy." He has used that to justify and obtain a remarkable 80% increase in the shipbuilding budget since 1980. Looking only at surface fighting ships and ships to carry Marines, his 1983 budget bought six ships: three extraordinarily expensive CG-47 guided missile cruisers at over $1 billion each; two small but complex and unreliable FFG-7 guided missile frigates which represent the so-called cheap end of the ship menu at $400 million each; a one Marine landing dock and cargo ship, an LSD-41, for another $400 million. The $4.2 billion for these six ships sailed through fiscal 1983 Congressional approval without a hitch.

But in May of 1982, before Congress even had a chance to act on these ships, inflation forced the President to order the Pentagon to cut some fiscal 1983 outlays. The Navy, among other cuts, offered a $249 million reduction in ship operating fund to be achieved by decommissioning ships. The Secretary of Defense duly passed this proposed cut on to Congress, where the House Appropriations Committee approved it in August, but with the specific wording encouraging the Navy to use other funds to continue operating ships that the Navy had proposed for decommissioning. The Senate Appropriations Committee followed suit in December of 1982. But by then, the Navy had already started decommissioning good, sound ships that had not been programmed to retire for two to five years to come.

How many ships did the Navy have to mothball to save the $249 million in operating money? *Twenty-two* ships. Thirteen of these were Forrest Sherman class destroyers, over half of them modified with the most modern antisubmarine warfare weapons. Twelve of the thirteen had enjoyed $25 million overhauls within the last three years. These Forrest Shermans have long-range antisubmarine rocket launchers and three five-inch cannons. They are, in fact, more reliable and better armed for ASW convoy escort or for supporting Marine landings than the new FFG-7 guided missile frigates being bought in 1983, and two-thirds of the cost of only *one* of the new FFG-7s would have paid for operating all thirteen Forrest Shermans as well as the nine other ships decommissioned.

These other nine ships consisted of four Decatur-class guided missile destroyers and five LSD-28 Marine landing dock ships. The LSD-28s are so similar to the new $400 million LSD-41 landing dock ship in external silhouette and dimension that an expert would be hard pressed to tell them apart. Of all the ships cut, the fleet commanders complained most about the loss of the five LSD-28s—because of the extent to which this has crippled their ability to actually deliver Marine landing forces. Yet two-thirds of the cost of the one LSD-41 in the 1983 budget would have paid to operate the five LSD-28s and nineteen other useful ships!

One can hardly escape the conclusion that the Navy— and the Congress, the Administration, and the shipyards —would rather buy ships than have ships. How else can one explain moving towards a "600 ship Navy" by taking six steps forward and twenty-two steps back?[3]

With this "more bucks, less bang" underground working together under the Project, we have begun to raise serious questions in the minds of the press, the Congress, and the public about whether or not the Pentagon procurement system is working in the best interests of our national defense. For the most part, we have been able to do this without jeopardizing the careers of the people who supply us with information. Some people come to us with some kind of grudge rather than with a legitimate concern about the procurement problems in the Pentagon. It is up to the Project to sort out these people from those who have a fair and well-documented case against the

Pentagon. But curiously, the grudge-holders often do not have a well-documented case and are unwilling to put in the time and effort it takes to successfully expose a scandal.

Many people write and call us after I make public appearances. Many of them are first-time sources who are surprised that we are not shocked about their disclosures of a few million dollars of waste. They often do not realize that the scandal they report is just one symptom of a much larger procurement disease. Now when someone calls me about a new scandal or scam, I am often able to tell the source the end of his story, even though I don't know the details of his particular weapon system. I am not as good at it as Ernest Fitzgerald, but it is surprising how the Pentagon bureaucracy tends to act the same way whether they are buying a plane, a ship, or a tank.

It takes my staff and me a lot of time and effort to sort out all the documents and stories that come into our office to see which cases we can credibly prove to the reporters and the public, which do not have enough documentation, and which are matters of someone trying to get even with the bureaucracy. We almost always suggest strongly to our new sources that they not go public in order to protect their careers, and that the Project will front their information for them. I am proud to say that in the four years of our existence, to our knowledge, no one has ever lost his job due to information the Project has released.

However, sometimes we get involved with someone who feels it is necessary to go public or is forced into that situation by circumstances. When that happens, the Project checks out the claims and documentation of the whistle-blower, and then works closely with him to take the case to the Congress and the press. But most importantly, we continue to monitor the whistle-blower and alert the press and the Congress if he is being harassed, so that pressure can be brought to bear on the Pentagon. It is not easy to apply pressure on the Pentagon, but in the past many whistle-blowers have had their lives shattered by the bureaucracy because the Congress and the press have been too busy or distracted to continue to fight for the whistle-blower once the headlines have disappeared.

Although the Project does not encourage people to go public with their information because of the severe consequences, the few who have, with the Project's help, give the public a rare view of the personalities in the Pentagon underground. Because these people have gone public, I can tell their stories. Each one I describe here gives us a glimpse of the pressure cooker atmosphere of the military procurement system that the underground has to work in. Until these people went public, they were just government workers trying to do their job. Going public pushed them into the limelight, often unprepared, and they faced the wrath of a powerful and angry bureaucracy.[4]

George Spanton

Perhaps no whistle-blower has handled the shock and pressure of whistle-blowing in the past few years better than George Spanton, an auditor with the Defense Contract Audit Agency (DCAA). The DCAA is the audit arm of the DOD, the agency most responsible for protecting the taxpayer's investment in defense. Yet when Spanton tried to do his job in the spirit of the goals of the DCAA, he could not get the support of the agency or its director.

Spanton had been a military contract auditor for thirty years. In early 1982, as the DCAA chief in West Palm Beach, Florida, he began investigating and demanding access to records of wage rates at Pratt & Whitney Inc., which has a plant in the area. He also began to question travel and entertainment expenses incurred by Pratt & Whitney executives that the government was being asked to pay. These expenses included $10,000 parties in West Palm Beach and lavish overseas trips that included bills for visits to a Danish massage parlor. The total bill came to about $1 million. The excessive wages and salaries would also cost the government nearly $150 million more than should have been paid over three years.

Pratt & Whitney denied Spanton much of the data he requested. Like any good auditor, Spanton complained to his superiors in the Atlanta bureau and also threatened to hold up payments to Pratt & Whitney until they handed over the information necessary to finish the audit. He held out little hope that his superiors would back him up because his boss, DCAA regional audit manager Arlin Tueller, was pressuring him to retire. Then, after years of receiving outstanding ratings for his work, Spanton was ranked among the bottom three of the eighteen auditors in his region.

His fears were justified. His report to his boss sat in the Atlanta bureaucracy for four months. Tueller refused to back up Spanton's demands for the information and Spanton claimed he was told to finish the audit without the documents. He knew that he could not do this in good conscience and began to investigate Pratt & Whitney even further.

He claimed that the Air Force had paid Pratt & Whitney $1.4 million for spare parts that should have cost only $531,000. Spanton also turned in a report in March 1982 which found that companies with government contracts gave pay hikes to their employees that were far higher than the increases granted to federal government employees. According to his findings, the raises at one defense firm were 178 percent higher than federal employees received and 108 percent higher than those for employees in private industry. He estimated that the cost to the taxpayer could reach as high as $150 million over three years.

This deep investigation and audit proved to be too irritating to Spanton's superiors, especially since Pratt & Whitney began to complain bitterly about Spanton's work. But he was merely doing what any auditor should do to protect the taxpayer from the excesses of a defense contractor. I have worked with many whistle-blowers who have gotten in trouble with their superiors for merely doing their job when that job might not be viewed favorably by powerful political interests such as large defense contractors.

Spanton's report came to Ernie's attention because he was working on excessive labor cost in the Air Force at the request of Secretary of the Air Force Verne Orr. When Ernie contacted Spanton about his excessive wages report, Spanton informed Ernie that his superiors, Tueller and Tueller's boss Paul Evans, told him that he must accept a transfer to Los Angeles or resign because they did not agree with his report. This was an unusual ultimatum since Spanton was only a few months away from retirement and had made his home in the West Palm Beach area since 1978.

Washington Times reporter Clark Mollenhoff suggested that he file an appeal to the transfer order with the special counsel of the Merit Systems Protection Board, an agency in the civil service bureaucracy that is supposed to protect whistle-blowers in the government. The special counsel is generally mistrusted by most whistle-blowers because he really does not have enough power in the bureaucracy to truly protect the whistle-blower, but in this case Ernie thought the new special counsel, William O'Connor, might be receptive to George's case.

George filed an appeal with the special counsel's office in August 1982, claiming that the threat that he would be transferred or fired by September 15 was "illegal retaliation" for his candid audits. Ernie told me that the felt George had a good case: his studies and audits were credible. He thought the Project might want to get involved in helping George Spanton continue his good work and protect him from the bureaucracy, since George had gone through legitimate channels in the system to no avail. When I began looking into Spanton's case, I found that a lot of time and effort would be required to present it to the reporters and the Congress.

The case began to heat up during the fall when the head of the DCAA, Charles Starrett, got involved in the transfer argument and upheld his underlings' insistence that George be transferred. Veteran investigative reporter Mollenhoff began to investigate and write about the Spanton case. Secretary Weinberger then got involved: he accepted Starrett's explanation that George's transfer was part of the DCAA's normal five-year rotational process. Weinberger went on to say that no DOD employee who suggests cutting waste and saving money "would be penalized." However, in the same month the Secretary reversed himself after several Mollenhoff stories on the potentially illegal transfer appeared, and intervened on George's behalf with the DCAA. Reportedly, Secretary Weinberger decided that George "should not be removed until next March—the normal rotation period—if then." The DCAA reversed the decision to transfer. It was an impressive victory for George, but Ernie and I realized that the bureaucracy would soon spring back to life.

At that time, I could not give the Spanton case the attention it deserved, so I assigned Donna Martin to follow the case and cover whistle-blower cases in general. Donna is ideally suited for this role at the Project. Since she has been a reporter, she is very good at sorting out factual documentation from theories in evaluating a whistle-blower's case. She also has the compassion and patience to work closely with whistle-blowers who feel that the world is crashing in on them. The Spanton case was fast becoming a watershed case for whistle-blowers and Donna became an expert in it, helping George as events pushed him into the limelight with his studies and audits.

In July 1982, George had an unannounced visit from DOD investigator John Batson, who was assigned to investigate charges made in an anonymous letter that George *was showing favoritism to Pratt & Whitney.* It was the ultimate irony. Whoever had decided to harass George in this way saw his plan backfire because George wisely decided to cooperate fully with the investigator. Batson discovered much of the scandal George had been complaining about and more. The target of Batson's investigation changed from George Spanton to Pratt & Whitney, and at George's request the FBI and a grand jury became involved.

This turn of events caused George's superiors at DCAA to intensify their campaign against him. By January 1983, they were pressuring George to resign by February 1. George told the FBI investigators, who in turn informed the Merit Systems Protection Board that George's removal would greatly interfere with their criminal investigation of fraud allegations at Pratt & Whitney. The alleged fraud followed the lines of George's investigation—lavish entertainment and travel expenses by Pratt & Whitney employees that were charged to military contracts.

By March, Clark Mollenhoff was reporting in the *Washington Times* that government investigators had obtained audio tapes supporting George's contention that he was being pressured to retire. Conversations were taped in February involving George, DCAA Atlanta bureau head Paul Evans, and other DCAA officials. In the tapes, it was proposed to George that if he retired by February 28, Evans would approve twenty-three days of overtime. George suggested that if he retired by March 31 it would give him enough time to complete the FBI investigation. Evans replied that "March 31 won't be worth a tinker's damn" because the Pratt & Whitney investigation would not be completed for two years. At that point, George had had enough and decided to retire on December 1.

At this time, Charles Thompson and Don Thrasher of ABC's magazine show *20/20* were investigating the Spanton case. George, who by that time realized that he needed outside help against the DCAA bureaucracy, agreed to be interviewed. The show aired on the evening of March 10.

The day after the broadcast, Charles Starrett struck again. He ordered that George be transferred within sixty days or be fired. In his letter to George, Starrett stated that one of the reasons for the transfer was that "the contractor [Pratt & Whitney] has voiced an intention not to provide certain [financial] data to you, although they would provide the data to their supervisor."

The head of the DOD's audit agency was telling an auditor who had gotten tough on a contractor that he had insulted the company and had to be removed. George had sinned against the bureaucracy by diligently looking after the taxpayer's interest instead of getting cozy with the contractor and not rocking the boat. His act reminds me of a warning that Navy Admiral Hyman Rickover once gave to whistle-blowers: "If you must sin, sin against God, not the bureaucracy. God may forgive you but the bureaucracy never will."[5]

What George did not do is what Ernie has often called "going along with the gag," the gag being not to question the status quo in the Pentagon. They did not want George and others like him to interfere with the gravy train that defense procurement contracts offer to all those who promise to go along.

Because Clark Mollenhoff continued to write stinging stories in the *Washington Times* on what had gotten to be called the Spanton case, members of Congress began to get involved. Senator Orrin Hatch (R-Utah) called for an investigation by Secretary Weinberger into the case. His request came after Representative Jack Brooks (D-Texas), chairman of the House Government Operations Committee, wrote to Starrett expressing fear that George's transfer would "inhibit other auditors from being too aggressive. . . ." Both members of Congress said that the efforts to transfer George appeared to be punitive.

In a March 18 letter to Representative Charles Bennett (D-Florida), Secretary Weinberger stated that George was being transferred only because he had been at Pratt & Whitney for the maximum number of years. This statement did not match the reasons that Starrett gave George in his letter demanding the transfer. However, Secretary Weinberger admitted in the same letter that the Air Force withheld $25 million in payments to Pratt & Whitney which otherwise would have reimbursed the company for "extraordinary" expenses. The FBI probe, with the cooperation of George, was beginning to bite.

In March the Merit Systems Protection Board (MSPB) ordered the DOD not to transfer George for at least fifteen days. The special counsel, William O'Connor, stated that he had "reason to believe the reassignment was proposed in reprisal for Mr. Spanton's protected disclosures of information [to the press]." A spokesman for the board said that the request was a "radical action" taken only where there was "a possibility of an egregious wrong, like a termination or transfer." The MSPB had taken a bold step and their reputation was wrapped up in the Spanton case.

About the same time, DOD investigator Batson claimed, according to his sworn testimony, that he was told by Colonel John Roberts, the Air Force plant representative at Pratt & Whitney at West Palm Beach, that he should be less concerned about any corporate wrongdoing on the part of Pratt & Whitney and should instead do his part to "get Spanton fired."

In April, Senator Charles Grassley, a conservative Republican from Iowa, wrote a letter to Air Force Secretary Verne Orr warning that the DOD's treatment of George is "counterproductive" to the Pentagon's campaign to cut fraud and waste. He said that George had been getting shabby treatment from the DCAA. Senator Grassley then told the *Washington Times* that the Reagan administration "must do something affirmatively to demonstrate support for Spanton" and must take "some kind of action against his superiors to show that abuse of honest whistle-blowers will not be tolerated. . . . The reward should go to the honest whistle-blowers who are trying to expose the waste and fraud. Those bureaucrats who take retaliatory action or otherwise stand in the way of the fight against waste must see that they cannot get away with it."

Senator Grassley described in his letter how the system *should* work, but even presidential intervention would not help George against the wrath of the bureaucracy. Senator Grassley went with Secretary Weinberger to see President Reagan to discuss the senator's concern about waste in the Pentagon and whistle-blower rights. According to Senator Grassley, the President had seen the *20/20* program on George and was disgusted by the examples of Pratt & Whitney's huge increases in spare parts prices and the entertainment expenses charged to the government. The President told Grassley he had then called the Pentagon and was satisfied with their response that ABC had sensationalized the situation to make it appear worse than it was.

That supposedly sensationalized information was the Hancock memo that the Project had released earlier on the thirty-four spare parts, the prices of which Pratt & Whitney had inflated 300 percent in one calendar year. As discussed in Chapter 5, even an Air Force investigation of the matter concluded that Pratt & Whitney had sustained "windfall profits" in their spare parts purchases.

But the President went on to tell Senator Grassley that his administration was doing an effective job in eliminating waste and fraud in military contracts. Secretary Weinberger then assured Grassley that George's transfer order from the DCAA was "routine rotation and not a cover-up for Pratt & Whitney." After the meeting Grassley told the *Washington Times* that he was disappointed with the reaction of both men and that they were "badly misinformed" on the seriousness of the problems at DCAA.

In April the MSPB granted George a thirty-day stay on his transfer, ruling that there was cause for them to believe that George was the victim of illegal retaliation by the DCAA. Yet shortly afterward, a spokesman for Secretary Weinberger told the *Palm Beach Post* that it was "immaterial" to the Secretary whether George remained on his job. The comment was in response to a letter from Senator Grassley asking that the Secretary back up the promise he made Grassley at a Budget Committee hearing. The Secretary reportedly told the senator that if keeping George on the job was all it would take to satisfy him, George would be retained.

MSPB special counsel William O'Connor finally took the offensive on the Spanton case by declaring that George had been a victim of illegal harassment, discrimination, and retaliation by his superiors including Starrett. O'Connor claimed that Starrett relied on "half truths" in evaluating the Spanton case, and he wrote Secretary Weinberger strongly urging that he overrule Starrett and cancel the transfer. O'Connor cited George's excellent thirty-year record in contrast to the recent low ratings that he had received from the superiors who were trying to put him down. Secretary Weinberger backed down and ordered George to remain at his post in Florida until his retirement on December 1.

We considered the overturning of the transfer order a major victory for all the pro-Spanton forces, especially for future whistle-blowers. We got more from the bureaucracy than we had thought possible. But the DOD bureaucracy was not finished yet. DOD Comptroller Vincent Puritano, who supervises DCAA, wrote a memo to Starrett shortly after Weinberger's order stating the controversy surrounding George's transfer was "not in the best interest of the Department of Defense." Puritano instructed Starrett to remind his managers that they are prohibited from taking "personnel action in reprisal for an employee's protected activity." Yet he then let Starrett, perhaps the man most responsible for continuing the reprisals against George, off the hook by telling him that he "may be assured that I have the highest regard for the quality of the work performed by the Defense Contract Audit Agency and am confident that, *under your leadership*, the auditors will continue as they have in the past to look at all claims and question any they feel should be questioned [emphasis added]." Starrett then wrote George a letter urging him to "make every possible effort to work with the regional management to assure that the government's best interests are served." Bureaucratic translation: we won; stop rocking the boat.

So the battle lines had been drawn. The special counsel of the MSPB warned that he might seek disciplinary action against the DCAA officials involved in the Spanton case. He was also referring the matter to the Department of Defense Inspector General, Joseph Sherrick. Shortly after that the Justice Department, under instructions from Starrett, began to investigate allegations that George had divulged corporate secrets in going to the press with his complaints. Starrett's action was reportedly initiated by a complaint from Pratt & Whitney.

I have taken you through the details of the Spanton case to show how much time and effort a whistle-blower and his supporters must expend to survive the wrath of the offended bureaucracy. But what of George's original concerns that Pratt & Whitney overcharged the Air Force? About a year later, in July and August 1983, action was finally taken on George's complaints, but once again only on his initiative.

In July the DOD acted on George's recommendation that it withhold $28 million in contract payments to Pratt & Whitney until it made financial records available to the DCAA in West Palm Beach. Pratt & Whitney appealed to the Air Force to have the DOD ruling overturned by claiming that they had turned over the financial records on executive salaries George had requested. The Air Force, however, could find no record of the data. Pratt & Whitney then countered that it would turn over to George the employee identification numbers but not the names for fear that Spanton would turn those names over to the press and violate the "privacy" of its top executives.

It is ironic that the company caused itself so much grief because George would not have gone to the press and would have been most unwilling to if he'd had these records when he was trying to do his job a year before. He sought publicity only out of necessity. Pratt & Whitney's dirty laundry would be aired in the press. It was another classic case of the DOD and the contractors spending more time and effort covering up problems and harassing legitimate investigations than simply fixing the problem. It does not seem logical until you realize that protecting the gravy train is the most important thing, and two of the ways to do that are to never admit mistakes and improprieties and to never let a whistle-blower win because it might encourage others.

In August 1983, Clark Mollenhoff published several stories on George's original audits that found executive salaries paid to Pratt & Whitney "exceeded the norm for other defense contractors by 40%."

By September, the special counsel of the MSPB, William O'Connor, recommended to the board that disciplinary action be taken against four employees of the DCAA, including chief Charles Starrett, for illegal harassment and intimidation of George. O'Connor concluded that "the job of auditor is to root out problems within the government. Mr. Spanton did his job and for that he was punished." If found guilty by the MSPB, it could mean removal from office and a $1000 fine for each charge. This paved the way for an administrative law judge in the MSPB to decide if these men were guilty. O'Connor told George to begin to prepare for an administrative law trial. It was to begin December 6, just five days after George was scheduled to retire.

By October, special counsel O'Connor had to seek a protective order preventing Starrett and other DCAA officials from threatening or intimidating George. O'Connor had learned that George's new supervisor, Joseph Cali, had criticized George for damaging the reputation of the DCAA and that officials there were working hard to fight the charges the special counsel had brought against them. Cali advised George to withdraw the complaint from the MSPB and to stop talking to Clark Mollenhoff. Senator Grassley called Cali's actions "inexcusable abuse of authority."

Yet George's supporters in the DCAA bureaucracy continued

to leak his audit reports to the press. George did not leak the reports himself, but by this time many in the DOD bureaucracy and the Congress were legitimately asking for and receiving his audits from the DCAA. His audits were leaked to interested reporters because the supporters realized that they would disappear in the DCAA bureaucracy. In November reporter Bob Shaw of the Knight-Ridder newspapers published an account of a Spanton audit which showed that Pratt & Whitney made a $900,000 profit on maintenance tools sold to the Air Force— nearly triple what the items were worth. as a result, the Air Force paid $221 for a pair of needle-nose pliers and $269 for a socket wrench extension.

As Donna and George began to gear up for the administrative law hearing, I finally got to meet George. One would expect that anyone who had been through what George had would be tense, bitter, and paranoid about coming to Washington and going through a grueling administrative hearing in which he was to be the main witness. But George was a winsome, sixty-three-year-old grandfather who impressed everyone with his calm manner and enduring optimism about the good side of people. He is a slender, wiry man with a soft smile and a shock of thick gray hair. During a six-month hearing he never got discouraged and propped up everyone else's spirits.

However, the odds were stacked against him. The Merit Systems Protection Board was set up during the Carter administration to try to protect whistle-blowers, but the special counsel saw this case as a special "make or break" case on the effectiveness of the board to protect whistle-blowers. On top of that, of the three possible administrative judges to be chosen to hear this case, George had the unfortunate luck of getting a judge who was a retired Air Force colonel. In July 1984, Judge Reidy found that there was insufficient evidence to show that punitive actions were directed at George for his whistle-blowing activities. Under the current law, the special counsel cannot appeal the case to a federal law court.

In the closing days of the 98th Congress in the fall of 1984, Senator Grassley tried to pass a bill allowing these cases to be referred to federal court. The provision passed without objection in the Senate. But at the last minute it failed in the House, as the Reagan administration, through the Justice Department, found a congressman to object to the provision. Ironically, it was attached to an amendment that would have given whistle-blowers cash rewards for exposing waste. On June 13, 1985, the MSPB overruled Judge Reidy and, in a surprising move, ordered DCAA head Charles Ferret fired and fined $1,000. George's superiors Tueller and Evans were demoted to non-supervisory jobs and fined $500. The underground considered this ruling our biggest victory ever for whistle-blowers.

George is now retired and living in West Palm Beach. He would have stayed on and probably saved the government considerable money if he had been allowed to do his job. His case sent a message to many potential whistle-blowers in the bureaucracy that they could not be successful in exposing major waste within the system. After the Spanton case, special counsel O'Connor, the chief protector of whistle-blowers in the government, told them in a statement to the press, "Don't put your head up, because it will get blown off."[6] The only consolation for George is that he has been asked by an investigative subcommittee to work on the alleged massive General Dynamics kickback scheme. He still may save the taxpayers some money and remains optimistic about his work.

George Spanton's case is not an isolated one. The Project has had to scramble over the years to try to protect other whistle-blowers from retaliation by the bureaucracy. A few examples:

Franklin "Chuck" Spinney

Franklin Spinney is a budget analyst with the DOD's Office of Program Analysis and Evaluation (PA&E) who, by his studies, found that if the DOD continued to buy its weapons in the same wasteful way, they would underestimate the cost of these weapons in the future by as much as 30 percent. The DOD worked hard to keep his study under wraps because they didn't want the public and some members of Congress to find out that they have systematically and chronically underestimated how much these weapons will cost in the long run. The bureaucracy has operated this way in order to buy into the program and then wait until contracts are signed to admit the bad news.

Once Spinney's study became known, several members of Congress insisted that he brief them and the press. The DOD at first refused but lost. The Project helped convince *Time* magazine to do a major story on defense and put Spinney on the cover. The DOD won in the long run, however, because Spinney has not had many meaningful assignments since. Several members of Congress have intervened to prevent his superiors from giving him unacceptable ratings in retaliation for his "sin" against the bureaucracy. So far, these efforts have been able to prevent a downgrading, but I am sure the bureaucracy will keep trying.

Ompal Chauhan

Chauhan is an industrial engineer who was assigned to the Air Force contract management division in Albuquerque, New Mexico. In 1982 he was part of a fifteen-man team that went to a Hughes Aircraft plant in Tucson, Arizona, to check on the production of the Maverick anti-tank missile there. Chauhan was appalled to discover that it was taking the production line seventeen times longer to produce the missile than even Hughes's own engineers had predicted it would.

When he and others from the team wrote a damning report on conditions at the Hughes plant he was criticized by one of his superiors for being "impolite to the contractor" and was transferred to an Air Force job in the Boeing plant in Wichita, Kansas. There he continued his tough scrutiny and exposed waste, including the fact that the Air Force was paying $748 for a pair of pliers that he bought in a hardware store for $7.61.

After he was transferred to Kansas, Chauhan's work on Hughes caught the eye of people in the Air Force and Senator Grassley. Partly because of Chauhan's work, the Air Force, Navy, and Army suspended payments to Hughes Aircraft because of shoddy workmanship. Meanwhile, Senator Grassley asked Ompal to testify with Ernie Fitzgerald at a hearing on June 7, 1984. At the hearing, Ompal observed:

> Contractors get what they want. Negotiated pricing and fact finding are largely formalities for the sake of appearance. When it comes right down to it, negotiated prices are what the contractor will accept if the government wants to buy the product. They are not dictated by should cost analysis, but by the amount of money the government has to spend. Rarely is the government able to come up with a should cost figure and make it stick in negotiations. . . . I think we can buy [weapons] systems with one half the amount [of money] we're spending at this point in time.

Twice since Ompal testified to Congress he has been downgraded in his performance ratings. Pressure by the underground and some members of Congress has not been able to stop these downgradings. As a result, we fear not only that Chauhan's career advancement is in jeopardy but that he will lose his job altogether. "I am consistently turned down for promotions I have applied for," he said, "and I believe my professional career is stunted. The equation I have observed is as follows: Flexible loyalties + laxity = job offers. Toughness + accountability demanded of the contractor = job stagnation."

Loebe Julie

I was contacted by Loebe Julie when I was working at the National Taxpayers Union and I have been involved in his struggle with the Army ever since. Unlike most whistle-blowers I have worked with, Julie is a small businessman who is trying to sell a better product to the Army but is unable to break the monopoly several large companies have with the Pentagon. His story is a good example of why so many small businesses cannot win Pentagon contracts. Donna Martin wrote a good overview of Loebe's problems in an article in *Conservative Digest*. Excerpts from that article:

Nine years ago Julie began trying to sell the U.S. Army a better product at a lower cost. His automated calibration system detects and corrects inaccuracies in equipment that tests sophisticated electronic instruments such as the guidance system of missiles.

Julie claims that his equipment is better and less expensive than that of his competitors. He says it would save the Army over a hundred million dollars a year. Those claims have been largely substantiated by government agencies and independent evaluations including tests and evaluations by the White Sands Missile Range in New Mexico, private companies such as Grumman, the Army's own Harry Diamond laboratories, the General Accounting Office and the Office of the Secretary of Defense.

In July 1981, for example, White Sands compared Julie's calibrators against those of his two largest competitors, John Fluke and Hewlett-Packard. The tests found Julie's LOCOST 106 system calibrated twice as fast as the others, was more reliable, and less than half the cost to operate per year.

Calculations by the General Accounting Office indicate Julie's equipment could save the military $134 million a year. An Army Inspector General reported Julie's system was better than the Army gave it credit for.

But after nine years the Army is still reluctant to buy Julie's equipment. And Julie, backed now by a Senate committee, remains locked in a battle of wills with the Defense Department. . . .

. . . It began in 1974 when the Army requested bids for an automated calibration system. The 50-employee Julie Research Labs submitted the low bid of $910,000 for five systems. But the Army, without even testing the Julie system, declared it "technically unacceptable" and opted for the nearly $1.5 million bid of the larger John Fluke Company, a Pentagon favorite.

The U.S. military did not recognize a good deal, but the Russians did. In 1977 they invited Julie to the Soviet Union, checked out his equipment, and drew up an order. But when Julie returned home, he changed his mind about the deal. He just couldn't bring himself to cooperate with adversaries of the United States.

What he did decide to do was to fight the Defense Department bureaucracy. His chosen weapon, for better or worse, was ridicule. Julie published his story in a series of comic books, the first one entitled, "You're Not Supposed to Get Mugged by Your Own Army." Copies were distributed to the press, Congress, the Defense Secretary and the White House.

Julie's efforts to draw attention to himself and his product have begun to pay off. Government and independent agencies, as mentioned above, have tested and evaluated his calibrating equipment with favorable results. In 1981, the TV program "60 Minutes," produced by CBS, focused on Julie's story. CBS plans to update Julie's story on "60 Minutes" this fall. [NOTE: That update ran on CBS in June 1984.]

The "60 Minutes" program helped spur hearings on Julie's "battle" with the Army by the Senate Governmental Affairs Committee in November 1981. In the hearings, Army witnesses admitted they had violated the "spirit" of procurement regulations by ignoring Julie's equipment, triggering a sharp reply by committee chairman William Roth (R-Delaware).

"It would appear that one cannot do business in some Army procurements," said Senator Roth, "unless one is part of the 'old boy network.'" Roth said he wondered how many other small businesses had the same difficulties.

The Army admitted to the committee that it didn't really know what its calibration needs were. The committee directed them to find out and include all known test results and information on Julie's system in a report to the committee on March 15, 1982. . . .

. . . The Army subsequently carried out the first step in the procurement. But then it changed the rules of the game. It spent $1.5 million on a comparison of low-grade meter testers that excluded the full-performance calibrators such as Julie's. Julie protested, but the Army ignored him.

By May 1982, it was clear to the committee that the Army had no intention of supplying to the committee the data on their calibration needs or in using Julie equipment. Four Senators, including Roth, then wrote to President Reagan warning that the Julie situation "only reveals the tip of the iceberg." Ultimately, Congress amended the Defense Appropriations Act last fall [1982] to prohibit the Army from purchasing any calibration equipment without committee approval.

Early this year [1983] both the National Research Council (NRC) and the General Accounting Office (GAO) issued reports adding weight to Julie's protests. NRC concluded that buying any of the calibration meters tested by the Army not including Julie's would actually waste money. GAO also recommended not buying any until the Army could figure out what its calibration needs were.

Support also came from an unexpected source—the Department of Defense itself. The department surveyed companies already using Julie's equipment and found it was regarded as highly accurate, reliable and well designed with a potential for an "early return on investment if utilized frequently."

Furthermore, DOD concluded that Julie's company was essential to national security. It directed the Army to buy six of Julie's calibration systems for $840,000.

So the Army, under Defense Department and congressional pressure, finally closed the deal three days before a second hearing on the Julie case by the Senate Governmental Affairs Committee in June [1983]. The Army's decision under pressure to buy only six comes despite the Army having about 100 military sites worldwide that could use precision calibration equipment.[7]

The Loebe Julie case has been one of my biggest frustrations. I worked closely with him through the triumphs of the favorable government reports to the big success of the *60 Minutes* program. But I found out that it does not matter that almost everyone involved admits he is right. The Army is not to be conquered. The members of the Senate Governmental Affairs Committee have grown weary of the fight and it is very hard to get the press to write any more about Loebe's case.

Unfortunately, as with most whistle-blowers, the Army has made much of Loebe's so-called abrasive personality to try to draw attention away from the real issues. It is true that at times Loebe has appeared impatient with the system, but no one could blame him after fighting for ten years to prove himself right and then finding out it doesn't matter. Not many people could have gone through what Loebe did without going crazy.

Loebe Julie's case and the others I have outlined in this chapter illustrate clearly why a Pentagon underground must exist. It does not pay to be a whistle-blower in the Pentagon if your goal is to solve a problem of waste. The bureaucracy purposely focuses its attention on the individual, and his supporters must spend most of their time and money defending his right to blow the whistle. Even the whistle-blower's lawyer in the government, the special counsel of the Merit Systems Protection Board, does not believe he can successfully protect whistle-blowers and warns them not to stick their head up because "it will get blown off."

The Project has had much more success exposing waste when the would-be whistle-blower remains in the underground. I have found that much more attention is placed on the factual side of the disclosure when there is no personality for the Pentagon to use to distract the press and the public from the waste.

But more important, I am glad that the Project provides a place through which individuals can expose improper actions by the Pentagon that they cannot condone. Whistle-blowing should be held in high esteem in this country because of the great courage it takes to do it. Yet, from what I have seen over the past five years, it usually is not.

The Pentagon underground will continue to exist as long as there is no other means by which people can internally or externally expose waste and fraud in the bureaucracy without suffering severe retaliation for the action. The underground will also continue to exist as long as people of conscience inside the Pentagon insist on doing the right thing, even at great personal risk. My job is to try to get their information to the press, the Congress, and ultimately, the public.

7.

THE PRESS

THE PRESS (including television and radio) has been vital to the Project, as we have tried to get out the underground's message. If we had not been able to work very closely with the press, procurement scandals would never have made it out of the bowels of the Pentagon. Yet when I started the Project, many of the underground were skeptical and negative about the press, and were reluctant to go directly to reporters. One remarked to me that reporters, in his opinion, ranked lower than used-car salesmen and ambulance-chasing lawyers. On the other side, many reporters have negative impressions of whistle-blowers because the whistle-blower often comes to a reporter in a state of desperation and is very impatient if the reporter is unable to start immediately a media crusade for the whistle-blower.

The two groups, the press and the underground, do not understand each other's system and mores for the most part. It was a monumental task to try to bring these suspicious groups together, but I have three advantages. First, I understand reporters' need for independence and the restraints of their profession. I also tend to get along with most reporters since I am trained as a journalist. Second, by having Ernie as my guide and mentor, I slowly began to understand and recognize what whistle-blowers are up against. I could understand reactions that reporters found puzzling and excessively paranoid. Third, I was the one with internal DOD documents that often revealed the full story, so reporters did not have to feel burdened with the welfare of an underground member who did not need to become public as whistle-blowers did.

The Project has become in many cases a delicate go-between. I did not start the Project with a grand plan to bring these two groups together: I had to feel my way to a balance by trial and error. But because of the tremendous need, the working relationship between the press and the underground became very fruitful. In the four years of the Project's existence, we have been responsible for or influenced approximately 450 articles in the press and dozens of radio and television shows. When I reflect on the media success of the Project, I often wonder why someone else had not thought to tap the great resources of the underground before. Ernie had some past success with the press, but only with a few reporters who consistently covered waste and fraud in the Pentagon and felt they had the background knowledge to tackle an investigation of a weapon system.

When I started I knew that if I was going to educate the public about procurement problems successfully, I would need many stories. An occasional small item in the paper on waste would not be sufficient. While I was at NTU, I discovered that the Pentagon had its own clipping service called "Current News," a daily news article collection of major articles in the media on defense and national security matters. Every day I checked out "Current News" for articles on waste in weapon systems. I began to make a list of reporters who showed even a slight interest in questioning the status quo in the DOD. I then called each reporter to let him know about my fledgling organization and my investigation of the M-1 tank. Although a few reporters were condescending, the majority expressed interest in what I was doing and encouraged me to contact them if I came up with any documentation.

A few reporters wanted to find out more about what I was doing. They included Stephen Webbe of *The Christian Science Monitor*, Patrick Oster of the *Chicago Sun-Times*, and Morton Mintz of *The Washington Post*. After the first series of articles on the M-1 OT II tests came out in the press, I received more calls from reporters who wrote for out-of-town papers, including James Coates of the *Chicago Tribune* and Bob Adams of the *St. Louis Post-Dispatch*. Ironically, the Army's detailed rebuttal of our release on the OT II test results, which they left on all of the reporters' desks in the Pentagon press room, helped me meet many other reporters because of the interest it aroused.

I began to introduce these new reporters to some of my newfound sources with the understanding that anything the sources said would be off the record. As mentioned earlier, both the reporters and the sources were initially suspicious of each other. I defined my role as that of go-between and found myself empathizing with both parties. Occasionally a reporter would try to get a source to take too big a risk to get a document or to expose himself unnecessarily, and I would interject that the source could not be asked to go that far. According to Ernie and others in the underground, in the past the friendliness and sympathy of reporters had misled sources into blurting out more than they should have. Therefore some of my sources were bitter about reporters until I explained that drawing out a source was something a good reporter learned to do from day one of the job and they should not forget that being with a reporter is a business relationship. Several times in the past few years, some sources have tried to talk to reporters without me over a few drinks and it has turned out almost disastrously for the source. When I am with them, the source can say no to the reporter through me and not strain his relationship with the reporter.

On the flip side of the coin, I help reporters lower my sources' expectations of what reporters can do for them. In the past some of my sources have been angry at reporters for not following through on a story or not having the story on page one. Many of the sources do not realize that a reporter must convince his editor to let him do a story and, if it is a controversial story, the editor must convince his managing editor and even the publisher. In the fast pace of news in Washington, few reporters or news agencies have the luxury of allowing a reporter to continue to investigate one story over a long period of time. Most reporters assigned to the defense beat in Washington are the only ones assigned by their paper to that beat and must be responsible for all the news that a $300 billion a year bureaucracy can create. The Pentagon works hard to generate favorable news by creating events that many of the reporters are expected to attend.

Another area of concern between the sources and the reporters is the attitude on the part of reporters that sources are too zealous. The sources in turn are often miffed when a reporter is skeptical of their assertions. Hostility begins to build between the two groups. Although I find that my sources are for the most part correct in presenting the facts, sometimes they are so determined to convince a skeptical reporter (reporters should be naturally skeptical) that they tell 110 percent of the story. The reporter will then find out later that the last 10 percent was embellished and that will tarnish the other 100 percent. When I am with a source and a reporter, I try to temper any statement the source may slightly embellish by telling the reporter that the story is best told by the source's documents and that the Project can back up only what we have documentation on. That often brings the source back to earth by making him remember that his strongest case is with the DOD's own documents.

As described in the previous chapters, many of the stories

that the sources had to tell seemed excessive to me at first but were generally true. I have found through experience that it is better to give a reporter our solid documentation of the story and assist him with leads for information for which we do not have documentation. It is safer for the reputation of the source and the Project to stick to the documentable information. I have told some sources who have appeared to be overzealous that their material was damning and incredible enough that it did not need to be improved on. Many of the reporters I have given information to have gone on to find much more waste than even the sources or I knew about.

The bottom line in this relationship between sources and reporters is the internal documentation that the sources are able to give the reporters. The Project would be doomed if our sources and staff tried to put our experts against the DOD experts because the press would have a hard time determining the validity of our arguments. But the DOD's own internal documentation, bolstered by inside information from our sources, has helped many journalists get a handle on a weapons procurement story that they would be reluctant to tackle with only their limited technical knowledge on defense.

I also had to decide whether to work with one reporter at a time on certain unclassified documents I had received or to give them to a group of reporters who would rush to get the story out first instead of investigating it. When I received one of my best leaks, a potentially illegal computer printout of a Lockheed, Air Force, and DOD lobby plan to force the C-5B cargo plane purchase through the Congress (see Chapter 8), one source, acting on a request from one of the reporters who figured that he might not get the release, suggested that I release the document to four reporters with an embargo date of several days later for publication.

I was surprised because I thought the Project was not a big and prestigious enough organization to be able to convince reporters to honor an embargo. I picked four reporters and released the document along with a memorandum explaining the document and rules of the embargo, which was to last one week after the release. To my surprise the four reporters, Morton Mintz of *The Washington Post*, Fred Kaplan of the *Boston Globe*, Frank Greves of the Knight-Ridder newspapers, and Bruce Ingersoll of the *Chicago Sun-Times*, did not break the embargo, and their stories were carefully researched because they had time to work on them.

The four stories appeared on Tuesday, June 22, 1982, in several cases on the front page. The Pentagon reaction was immediate and loud, and I realized that it was much more eye-opening to the Pentagon to have several stories appear on the same subject on the same day. I then adapted the procedure of memorandum release with an embargo for the most important documents I receive and it has worked well. I am impressed that no reporter has ever broken any of my embargoes.

The successful memorandum release came at a very important time for the Project. It had lost its funding, and the sources, my husband Thom, and I were desperately trying to show the public, the press, and especially the Pentagon that the Project was still alive and well. The release of the C-5B lobby plan came while I was on a fundraising trip with Ernie on the West Coast, and to bring such a recent coup to potential funders was very impressive. But more importantly, it showed reporters at other major newspapers that my releases were significant and my embargoes were honored. I began to receive calls from other journalists who wanted to take me to lunch and get on my release list. It was a nice feeling after a year and a half of courting the reporters.

At that time my husband and I were running the Project from our own savings and we were getting very low on money. Every time a reporter called to meet with me, my husband would yell across the office to have the reporter take me to lunch so I wouldn't have to spend any money. I would go to lunch with the reporter, who was on an expense account, and order far more than I could eat so I could take a doggy bag back to my husband for lunch. Few reporters realized that their expense accounts helped my husband and me keep the Project afloat for four months on our own!

Undoubtedly, however, the biggest breakthrough for the Project in terms of its credibility with the press came when I received and released the test results of OT III. It took me a year and a half after receiving OT II, in October 1982, to get the OT III results because, according to my sources, the Army was watching every copy. A January 1982 General Accounting Office report on the M-1 verified that many of the M-1 problems that occurred in OT II were reoccurring in OT III, but the Army disputed this, and the GAO did not release the actual test results. According to my sources, the Army was especially concerned that the OT III test results were not leaked before the full production decision on the M-1 was made in September. They got their wish: the DOD approved full production on the M-1 in September 1982, based on all its tests. It was very frustrating for me and I badgered my sources for the test results before the decision date. But they just could not take the risk.

But it was well worth the wait in terms of credibility with the press. Because I had heard rumors over the past year and a half from the underground that the M-1 was doing poorly in this final set of tests, I was expecting the results to be poor. However, I was not ready for the magnitude of the failures when the OT III test results finally arrived.

As you may recall from Chapter 1, the Army's requirement for the power train of the M-1 (the engine, transmission, and final drive) was that 50 percent of the test vehicles should be able to go 4,000 miles without a power-train overhaul. In OT II the number reached only 22 percent, and the Army was telling the reporters and Congress that the rate was getting better. In reality, the number dropped to a miserable 15 percent. My original source and I took the failure logs in the back of the test and scored the results as we had the OT II test by using the test

director's scoring method. The mileage between serious failure
went from 34 miles to only 43 miles, which was still an unac-
ceptably low figure for a tank that was about to be deployed in
Europe.

The Army had been less than truthful to the press and the
Congress about many other failures in other areas. My husband, Thom, and I were so angry that the Army had been able
to get by for so long with such misstatements that we were
inspired to thoroughly rebut the Army's statements. While I
read through the test results (one set taken in Fort Knox, Kentucky; the other in Fort Hood, Texas) and prepared a detailed
explanation of the test reports by page number, Thom dug out
all of the Army rebuttals over the past year and a half and the
Army's congressional testimony, and matched their statements to what they knew was happening in the ongoing tests
at that time. It was very damning to see how much they had
misled the Congress and the press. Major General Richard
Lawrence, who supervised the OT III tests conducted at Fort
Hood, was especially bold in making claims contradicted by
the test he was conducting. Some examples that Thom compiled:

Public Statements Versus OT III Test Results

Major General Richard Lawrence, Commanding General,
1st Cavalry Division, Fort Hood, Texas

**ON THE GAO REPORT THAT SHOWED POWER-TRAIN
DURABILITY TO BE 0.15:**
July 21, 1981 before the Joint Economic Committee:
"I'm not saying they're totally wrong. I'm not saying
that they're totally irrational. But I'm saying that on the
basis of the statements they've made concerning the operational supportability of that system and fightability of that
system, they haven't got the facts from Ft. Hood, Texas."

OT Test Report IER-OT-058 [OT III] and GAO Report
MASAD-82-7 found:

GAO		OT III
p.6	power train durability probability of 0.15	p.39
p.12	maintenance manhr: operating hr	p.49
	2.67 : 1	
p.8	mean miles between failure	p.51
	32 Ft. Knox	
	36 Ft. Hood	

ENGINE FAILURES:
March 18, 1981 before the House Armed Services Committee:
"[Since receiving tanks in September 1980] we have not had a single transmission or engine failure in a tank in my division to date."

Test Report, OT III, Fort Hood, page 78:
"During Phase I, which was from September 15, 1980 to March 15, 1981, there were four power train replacements or repairs, one final drive replacement, and two solenoid replacements on 7 tanks at Ft. Hood."

MAINTENANCE OF M-1S:
July 21, 1981 before the Joint Economic Committee:
"Maintenance support is no different than that currently used for our other tank battalions. . . . We actively accomplished maintenance actions with the M1 battalion using 3 less tank mechanics than in the conventional M60 battalion."

Ft. Hood OT III Test Report, page 117, Table 2-74, dated 1/29/80; OT III Test Report IER-OT-058, page 57, Table 6-1:
"Both reports show the need to add 7 more mechanics to the battalion based upon testing experience."

OPERATIONAL RATING OF THE M-1:
July 21, 1981 before the Joint Economic Committee and November 5, 1981 before the House Armed Services Committee:

"We maintained an operational rate of over 80 percent."

OT III Test Report IER-OT-058, page 46:
"The combined operational availability rating at Ft. Hood was 46 percent."

MAINTENANCE OF THE M-1 BY ARMY PERSONNEL DURING OT III:
March 18, 1981 before the House Armed Services Committee:
"We've insisted from the outset of the operational evaluation that no contractor technicians be utilized to help us maintain the tank at organizational or direct-support level. They have not. So the crews and the unit mechanics are supporting the system as they would in combat."
July 21, 1981 before the Joint Economic Committee:
"With my division, during the entire evaluation period, all maintenance actions were performed by Army mechanics [with] commensurate skill levels."

OT III Test Report IER-OT-058 Executive Summary, page iii:
"*Maintenance.* Maintenance at the depot level was performed by Chrysler Defense Engineering technicians. Maintenance at the lower levels was performed by military personnel with contractor technical guidance and assistance."

As you can see from several of the examples, the General Accounting Office report in January accurately described the OT III test results. When that report appeared in December 1981, the GAO was harshly criticized by the Army. But what was even more curious to me was that the Army over the past year and a half was unable to keep its rebuttals consistent. Thom made a chart (shown on page 217) to illustrate the facts from the OT II and OT III tests and all the Army's claims in between the two tests.

Another disturbing reliability failure in the M-1 had serious implications for the battlefield. During a field exercise the test

The M-1 tank, a comparison of data about the M-1 Tank and how it Differs from the Data Compiled During OT III

Item	Goal	OT II Ft. Knox 1980	A 3/81	B 4/81	C 6/81	D 7/81	E 2/82	F 3/82	OT III 11/81
System Reliability	101 MMBF	94	91–125	111	111	98	126	126	129
Combat Mission Reliability	320 MMBF	286	319–333	326	326	278	350	350	304
Power-Train Durability	0.5 prob.	0.22	0.19–0.30	0.27–0.54	0.33	0.21	0.37	0.37	0.15
Track Life	2000 mi.	707	851	—	1090	982	—	1050	1058–1108
Tank Availability	—	—	52%	—	—	—	59%	—	44–47%
Man-Hour of Maintenance per Operational Hour	—	—	—	—	—	1.7	1.34	—	2.67

Notes: A 3/81: Statements of Major Generals Wagner and Ball before the House Armed Services Committee, March 18, 1981.
B 4/81: U.S. Army Information Paper rebuttal of *Wall Street Journal* and *Christian Science Monitor* articles, April 25, 1981.
C 6/81: General Vessey, Vice Chief of Staff, U.S. Army's rebuttal to Project on Military Procurement's testimony, June 24, 1981.
D 7/81: Statement of Major General Ball, U.S. Army, before the Joint Economic Committee, July 21, 1981.
E 2/82: U.S. Army Information Paper rebuttal of *Boston Globe* article, Feb. 7, 1982.
F 3/82: U.S. Army Information Paper comparing the effectiveness of current tanks, March 8, 1982.

M-1s were put on a 96-hour exercise that the Army claimed would "match or exceed the most stretchful and arduous mission" faced by the M-1 during combat. The Army started with 39 tanks at the beginning of the exercise. The second day of exercise, after they covered 70 miles, only 34 tanks were still operational. This deterioration continued until on the morning of fifth day, after 178 total miles in the test, only 21 tanks were left. This means that the Army lost almost half of their tanks after going only 178 miles without being under fire or incurring the battlefield damage inevitable in a real war. In five days the M-1 literally killed itself during a test that the Army was anxious for it to pass.

I found it hard to believe that the Army could seriously think this tank was ready for full production and deployment in Europe. Yet the Army and the DOD had this disturbing test data when they approved the tank for full production. I felt it was my job to reveal that fact so later, when the tank failed in Europe or in a war situation, they could not pretend they did not know about the problems.

I knew that this research would be very disturbing to many of the reporters who, because of their own lack of technical knowledge, had given the Army the benefit of the doubt. I, too, was surprised that the Army had so boldly denied any problems while having such poor OT III test results.

I carefully prepared a long release reviewing OT II, explaining the documents that I had enclosed and going back over some of the claims the Army had made. I realized that many of the reporters had not been involved in the first release of the OT II test results, and the Project played a useful role in having a corporate memory on the subject. It has become standard practice in the Project releases to review what the Pentagon has said about a weapon in the past. Because the press and the Congress cover an enormous array of subjects, they are unable to keep track of what the Pentagon has said. As you can see from the M-1 statements by Army officials, the Army public relations people count on Congress and the press to not remember what their previous excuse was. I have made it a point in my releases to hold them responsible for their past promises. I know that the DOD public relations people find that very irritating, especially because it is rarely done in Washington, not only in the DOD, but in almost all of the other bureaucracies.

In my memorandums to the press I separated information on which I had solid documentation from information told to me by my sources as inside scuttlebutt. I had no way of proving the validity of many of these inside stories to the reporters, although they usually turned out to be true. I wanted the reporters to know that the Project only claimed as facts information that was derived from inside documentation.

I always felt our documentation and exposés on a weapon were solid after five to fifteen top defense journalists took our material, checked it out with their sources, passed it through their editorial process, and then wrote a story that, for the most part, confirmed our assertions. Because the Project was trying to figure out a giant puzzle with just a few of the pieces, I knew it was only natural for us to make an occasional mistake. That is why I was so strict about using only information on which we had very good documentation.

I realized that at this point in the life of the Project, fall 1982, the Pentagon was just waiting for us to make a careless mistake. We were starting to get a high profile on certain subjects, and I knew that the Pentagon would like to damage our credibility with the press. After all, other than our sources, that is really the only thing the Project has going for it. We do not have a big budget or a slick public relations firm to pull us out of a major mistake. We could not force the press to do our stories, especially if they thought we were just trying to complain about and harass the DOD.

The Project was even more vulnerable to the Pentagon's

attempts to attack our credibility after I prepared written releases instead of just telling the reporters the facts over the
phone. Occasionally, the Pentagon gets hold of one of my releases from a reporter, so I have to write them as if the Pentagon were planning to go over them with a fine-tooth comb. I
had some experience seeing the types of mistakes or overstate-
ments the Army might want to reinterpret when I got their
point-by-point rebuttal of the original OT II press stories.

I knew the information I was about to release on the M-1 OT
III test could make or break the Project in terms of having the
majority of the press take us seriously. Since my only help on
the Project was Thom and one source who would check our
release for accuracy, I knew that we would have to be very
careful. Thom and I worked one whole weekend photocopying
the mountain of reports and test results we were giving to about
twenty reporters. It was exhausting work, but both of us were
driven by our anger over the Army's past condemnation of the
Project for having dated material on the OT II test results and
their untruthful claims to the Congress and the press that things
were getting better.

We released the materials to the reporters a week before the
embargo so they would have some time to digest the information. Several reporters called back after they received their
release packets to tell me that they were surprised by how
much damning material we had put together on the M-1.

On September 20, 1982, the stories came out in the press.
The Army was furious and I was elated because I scored what
I was later to call a press grand slam. The M-1 stories showed
up in *The Washington Post, The New York Times,* and *The Wall
Street Journal*—all on the same morning. With this release I had
broken into all of what are considered the "papers of record"
in this country. It was not the first time that I had gotten a story
in any of these three papers, but it was the first time I had
convinced all of them to write a story based on one of my

releases. *The Wall Street Journal*'s lead paragraph was especially tough. Reporter Amanda Bennett wrote:

> To test its costly new M-1 tank, the Army sent 41 of them on a tough six-day field exercise. By the fifth day only about half were working.
> No one was shooting at them; they just broke down.
> The tanks, which cost as much as $2.7 million each, were designed to be the world's finest defense against enemy forces. But one of the last Army tests before the tank went into full production in late 1981 shows that the tank's own worst enemy may have been itself.[1]

The reaction around the country was swift, and I spent the next few days giving radio talk show and television interviews as well as sending out more packages of the memorandum release to other news outlets. It was exciting to have this reaction but it was also frustrating because the Project had very little money for copying all of the material and no clerical help. We had grown beyond our current budget and capacity. Anne Zill, president of the Fund for Constitutional Government—which had just adopted the Project and given us a little "breather" money—worked very hard after that release to help solve the financial squeeze.

The Army's reaction was typical. They claimed that they had "made a lot of improvements" since the OT III tests were completed in the fall of 1981. They claimed the tanks were "running very well" in West Germany, where many of them had been deployed. When the reporters called me about the old "dated material" charge, I asked them if they thought it was realistic to believe that the Army had suddenly solved the power-train failure problem which they could not solve under extreme pressure from the Congress and the press between OT II and OT III. The Army did not offer any data to back up this claim, and most of the reporters were not buying the answer because of the lies the Army had told them after OT II. Some of the reporters appeared to be angry at the Army's arrogance in using the same excuses and providing no data or evidence.

The barrage of news on the M-1 continued in the press for several weeks, as other reporters picked up the stories and various papers wrote editorials condemning the Army's management of the tank. Another high point came on October 22, 1982, when *The New York Times* ran an editorial on the M-1 test results titled THE TROUBLED TANK. I had been talking to one of the *Times* editorial writers, Nicholas Wade, but I did not expect such a tough editorial. It ended by saying, "A simpler, cost-effective weapon should be shaped by users and tacticians instead of the bureaucratic process in which requirements are piled on, never deleted, until a fighting vehicle becomes a suffering behemoth."

The Army began to gear up for a major public relations drive on the M-1 to counter all the stories of the M-1 OT III release. They handed out rebuttals to the press, they wrote letters to the editors of several newspapers strongly denying the M-1 was having major problems, and according to a few journalists who had written an M-1 story, they called some of the major newspaper editors and publishers to complain of the coverage they had received.

But the Army's most extreme reaction by far was to conduct what I dubbed a "reporter airlift" by helicopter from the Pentagon to Aberdeen Proving Ground in Maryland to let the press "see, touch, and drive" a few M-1s. Bill Lynch of CBS News described the "airlift" to me. A group of reporters, dressed in casual clothes and helmets, scrambled onto several large military helicopters at the Pentagon. The helicopters dramatically lifted off over Washington, traveling the seventy miles to Aberdeen Proving Ground where a few of the tanks were. The reporters took turns driving the M-1 around a small oval dirt track, received briefing material on the M-1, and were flown back to the Pentagon.

I was amazed that the Army believed they could convince reporters driving the tank around a small track a few times to disregard all the damning test reports carried out by the Army's own testing agency and surprised by this extensive and expensive public relations drive. I felt that my release was costing taxpayers a lot of money with this fruitless exercise in trying to influence the press. A few of the Pentagon beat reporters did come back and write favorable stories without contacting the Project, but the majority I talked to considered the whole exercise a big joke.

I did not expect to counter this media show with another volley because the OT III was supposed to be the last test of the M-1 before the tanks were deployed in Europe. But as fate would have it, the underground came up with another surprise. Unknown to me and many others following the M-1's progress, the Army had decided after the OT III to take five M-1 tanks to Aberdeen Proving Ground for a special developmental test. This was an unusual move because the full production decision had already been made. I would like to believe that the Army was responding to our criticism and, although they would not admit it, felt that it was necessary to remedy the miserable power-train failures of the M-1.

I found out about the test in an unclassified Army information paper that was being quietly passed to supportive members of Congress. I received a copy of the paper from the M-1 underground, checked out its authenticity, and released it with an embargo of October 9, 1982, less than three weeks after the M-1 OT III release to the press.

The test, conducted in July 1982, included five tanks that had their power trains modified since the OT III test. The goal of the test was to show that close to 50 percent of these tanks with modified power trains were able to go 4000 miles without a power-train overhaul, which, by the way, was the Army's original requirement. Each tank was to be driven 6000 miles. Much to the Army's chagrin, the first of these five tanks' power trains failed after only 153 miles and the best of the five went only 1484 miles before failure. In other words, all the tanks fell far short of the 4000-mile requirement. Even more disturbing was that the results of this developmental test, run by engineers and contractor personnel, not average troops, should have been much better than those from actual battlefield use.

I was thoroughly disgusted at the inability of the M-1 to pass even this basic test, and evidently so was the M-1 program manager, Major General Duard Ball, because he suspended the test for ninety days after the fifth M-1 flunked. The Army blamed the failures on poor quality-control problems on the engine production line at Avco-Lycoming in Connecticut and claimed they were reassessing these failures with the manufacturer.

Yet the Army claimed, even in this private information paper to Congress, that they were confident of the M-1's ability because of its performance in an ongoing war game exercise in Europe called Reforger. They claimed that among the 174 M-1s in the test only nine engine failures had occurred in the eleven-day exercise. They did not produce any statistics on how far the tanks had traveled and offered no failure logs or backup documentation whatsoever to this claim. They also did not mention any transmission and final drive failures in the information paper they sent to Congress. When the reporters asked me about the claim that the tanks "got well" in the Reforger exercise, I told them to pressure the Army to explain how they suddenly fixed the problem so soon after the Aberdeen test failure and to ask to see the actual Reforger maintenance log failures. The Army, as expected, did not provide any such documentation to the press.

This second episode of the M-1, coming on the heels of our M-1 OT III release, really gave the Project a big boost in credibility with the reporters, especially with ones we had only marginally worked with before, such as reporters from *The New York Times*. Bruce Ingersoll of the *Chicago Sun-Times* did an

especially biting story headlined: ARMY TESTS 5 M-1 TANKS—
ALL FLUNK. He went on to drive the point home by writing:

> When every M-1 tank broke down less than halfway
> through a durability test in July, Army Maj. Gen. Duard
> Ball called the whole thing off.
> Tank No. 1 rambled only 153 miles around the Aber-
> deen [Md.] Proving Ground before dropping out, an inter-
> nal Army progress report said.
> The best of the five M-1 Abrams tanks being put through
> their paces conked out at 1,484 miles—far short of the
> 6,000 mile objective.
> For the Army brass, already weary of the bad press
> befalling their turbine-powered tank, the outcome was
> dismaying and daunting. How so? It contradicted all their
> claims about having solved the M-1's durability problems.[2]

The OT III release and the following Aberdeen release to the
press gave the Project a great moral victory on the M-1, but the
soldier and the taxpayer have lost because the tank continues
in full production and deployment in Europe. The Army has
never adequately proven that the tank has been fixed and the
Congress continues to vote for its funding every year. In the
two years since the OT III release, I have yet to receive any
documentation on the tank to see if it is getting better or worse.
According to my sources, the Army is not doing anything to find
out. Occasionally, the Army will state to the Congress and the
press that the M-1 is doing very well in Europe and is liked by
the troops. We have heard rumors from Europe that the M-1 is
turning out to be a logistics disaster to maintain because of its
failure rate and the unavailability of spare parts. I am disappointed by our inability to stop or modify this potential disaster
for the soldier, but I have learned to look at the experience with
the M-1 philosophically.
I believe the M-1 exposé gave the Project credibility and
taught me how to successfully fight the bureaucracy by showing

the public and the Congress the discrepancies between the Pentagon's actual weapons test results and their statements on our weapon systems. The battle over the M-1 made it possible for the Project to show successfully the public other scandals such as the DIVAD and spare parts scandals. We had only lost a small battle in a long war.

But I will not concede that we have exposed all the information on the M-1. I suspect that sometime in the near future, someone will come into my office with new horror stories on the inability of the M-1 to be supported in Europe. If given enough time, many of the rumors I hear at the Project may be documented. This point can be proven by Ernest Fitzgerald, who has seen many exposés on the C-5 since he blew the whistle in 1969.

Another event that I felt gave credibility to the Project's sources was when two newspapers won major awards for writing series on the defense procurement problems. I helped two reporters from the *Chicago Sun-Times,* Bruce Ingersoll and Patrick Oster, and two reporters from the *Chicago Tribune,* Bill Neikirk and James Coates, plan and research many of the topics in their successful series. After the *Chicago Sun-Times* team won the Worth Bingham award and the *Chicago Tribune* team won the Raymond Clapper award in 1982, I found that more and more reporters were more receptive to our information.

After the M-1 OT III release, the Project began to be taken seriously by the "papers of record"—that is, *The New York Times* and *The Washington Post.* I gradually learned why the defense beat reporters from those two papers, Richard Halloran of *The Times* and George Wilson of *The Post,* appeared reluctant to work with my material. To understand these reporters' constraints is to understand what the responsibilities of the papers of record mean.

The Times and *The Post,* along with the wire services such as United Press International and the Associated Press, are looked upon to cover all the official activities of the Pentagon and other government departments. But these papers also compete for the exclusive inside planned leaks of information that can come only from top-level decision-makers in the Pentagon. Examples of information that is purposely leaked to these reporters to influence public opinion include detailed battle information on fighting in Lebanon or secret weapons program information that will influence Congress to fund a program A classic case of such a leak occurred in the Carter administration when top people in the Pentagon leaked details about the DOD's plan for a new Stealth bomber to quiet political opponents' charges that the administration was weak on defense.

The defense reporters at these papers have been there for many years and have carefully cultivated their sources at the top so that they will be the recipient of the latest policy leak. Reporters from out-of-town newspapers, for the most part, know that they will not be chosen for such information leaks and can rely on the paper of record reporters to write the stories in that area. Therefore, other reporters can afford to write the embarrassing stories about the Pentagon based on the Project's documentation.

In the past, the reporters at *The Times, The Post,* and other major newspapers ran the risk of destroying their chances for inside top-level information and exclusive interviews with the top officials if they continued to write the probing stories of fraud and waste that the underground has to offer. Occasionally one of these reporters would write about fraud and waste but it was usually a story that was leaked from the top, because the DOD had already put in place some study group or initiative to "fix" the problem.

As you might imagine, these reporters have, for the most part, been cool to the Project. However, as our information emerged as important news stories, an interesting but informal solution has emerged with *The Post* and *The Times.* I have dubbed it the "good guy, bad guy" system by which those two newspapers use our information while keeping a reporter in good graces with the top-level people in the DOD.

Each newspaper has two reporters working on the defense beat, one who traditionally attends the major news conferences, travels with the officials on trips, and gets the official policy leaks. He is the "good guy" to the DOD. The other reporter on their staff does the stories that the Project releases, along with his own tough investigative stories on the ineffectiveness of the DOD management. He is the "bad guy" to the DOD and cannot be expected to be in line for inside information from the policymakers. If the "good guy" gets complaints from his close sources in the DOD about the "bad guy's" stories, he can just shrug his shoulders and say that he does not have any control over that reporter.

This system has worked well for both these newspapers and some of the television networks. When I started the Project, Morton Mintz played the bad guy for *The Post* and George Wilson the good guy. But Mintz was assigned to another section of the paper and for a while *The Post* did not have a steady reporter to do my stories. Only on a rare occasion would Wilson do a story on one of the Project's releases. Later, reporter Fred Hiatt started doing the bad guy stories for *The Post.*

When I started the Project there was no such system at *The Times* and I could not, at first, get Halloran, the main defense reporter, interested in our material. Another *Times* reporter, Charles Mohr, literally carved the bad guy beat out for himself. One day he asked me to lunch and explained that he had returned to *The Times* after an illness and his editors had told him he could decide what area he wanted to cover. I spent the next few weeks introducing him to the underground and giving him information on our previous stories. Ever since then he has worked almost exclusively on investigating military procurement and leadership scandals; and has earned a reputation from the DOD press relations people as a bad guy. Wayne Biddle, Jeff

Gerth, and Bill Keller of *The Times* have also done quite a few of the investigative stories that the Project works on.

Many members of the underground have criticized the good guy reporters for not covering our material, but I cannot blame the management of these two large papers. It is their obligation to the public to get the official statements from the top managers of the DOD, because many of the small papers depend on their wire services. I feel no personal ill will toward the good guy reporters, although I know that some of them are not happy with my organization and its work. Reporter George Wilson told the *Washington Weekly* on September 24, 1984 that "[s]he has an ax to grind and she's caught up in dissent. She thinks the Pentagon is wasteful and out of control." But he then grudgingly acknowledged that "[she] urges that you check out her stuff, which is sometimes less than advertised, sometimes OK." Any positive comments about the Project surprised me, considering the careful relationship he must cultivate with the top levels of the DOD. I hope both of these papers and the television networks continue to see the need for the "good guy, bad guy" system because the Project's information needs to be reported by these major news sources.

We are gaining more publicity with every release and are acquiring more and more sources who have heard about our stories through television or the newspapers. Most of the news organizations we have worked with credit the Project as the source of the leaked documents. That is an important point for two reasons. Obviously, it helps us raise funds so that we can have more staff to handle more cases that come to us. But it also brings new sources to the Project.

The underground is still occasionally disappointed with press reporting on waste, but I believe the press may be the most responsible group in that effort. Most of the reporters I have worked with have not let my sex or youth prevent them from looking at our documentation, and most of them have treated me as a peer in the area of investigation. I cannot say that of some of the staff members of Congress or even some members of the underground.

The press has been vital to the Project and the underground in getting our information to the public and the Congress. They will continue to play an important role in reforming the military system into something that works for the soldier and the taxpayer. But they cannot be expected to reform the system; it is not their job. The public and Congress must demand reform. Otherwise all the risks the underground has taken to bring the information to the public will just be used by political opponents to complain about the party in power.

Pentagon waste and ineffectiveness is a bipartisan problem. The press will continue to investigate scandals involving the public's money, but the Congress has the power of the purse over the Pentagon. As you will see, they do not use that power well.

8.

THE CONGRESS

IN JANUARY 1983 the Pentagon submitted a budget of $239 billion to the Congress, an increase of 14 percent over the previous year. Because programs outside defense were being cut under "Reaganomics" and stories about Pentagon waste began to shock the Congress and the public, there were many predictions in the press and the Congress that it was the Defense Department's turn to endure some serious trimming.

The year before, Caspar Weinberger, the Secretary of Defense, told the Senate Budget Committee that there "was not one ounce of fat" in the DOD budget. Congress appeared to be fed up with that unrealistic appraisal and ready to make some reforms and reduce the *increase* in the defense budget. However, Senator John Tower (R-Texas), the chairman of the Senate Armed Services Committee, who opposed any reduction in the budget increase, knew how to quickly silence the cries for any serious scaleback of the constant increase in the money flowing to the Pentagon.

He sent a letter in February 1983 to all his colleagues in the Senate telling them that he was under a lot of pressure to cut the increase in the defense budget and asking them to give him suggestions of things that should be cut *from their own state.* The senator understood the patronage "pork barrel" system of the Pentagon budget well and knew that he would get few responses. In fact, he received a couple of responses from the hundred senators. Senators Grassley and Pryor rose to the challenge, but none of the well-known liberals who were criticizing the size of the defense budget did.[1]

Senator Tower's exercise demonstrated major problems in trying to keep the defense budget under control and canceling weapons that don't work. Over the past twenty years, as the entitlement programs have taken more and more of the federal budget, the defense budget has become the best means of patronage spending—that is, federal money that can be spent on companies or military bases in the state or district of each member of Congress to help keep the voters happy. Members of Congress have become very protective of the large defense contractors in their state or district, mainly because of the jobs these companies provide. They will work very hard to make sure that their companies and the products made in their state and district are well represented in the Pentagon budget.

I have often heard from officials inside the DOD that part of the problem of procurement is that the Congress forces companies and weapons on the Pentagon that it does not want. Yet I have also found that these same procurement people are more than willing to use this pork barrel system to ensure funding of their weapon program, no matter how badly it is performing. In this three-ring circus of defense contractors, the Pentagon, and the Congress each uses the others to help spread the money around, but each is quick to blame another when a scandal is uncovered.

I was fortunate to receive from a source probably one of the best-documented cases of how the pork barrel circus works to the benefit of the parties involved but to the detriment of the taxpayer and national security. It was a computerized lobbying plan of the effort by the DOD, Air Force, and Lockheed to force through another run of the notorious C-5 cargo plane. As you may remember, in the late 1960s Ernie Fitzgerald was made to testify that the program was overrun by $2 billion and a year later he was fired for that testimony. And I fell into the defense investigating business when I investigated the C-5A wing fix at the National Taxpayers Union in 1980. So I found it hard to believe that Lockheed would be taken seriously in the fall of 1981 in the competition for a new cargo plane called the C-X.

Lockheed was offering an up-to-date version of the C-5, but the Air Force was looking for a smaller, more maneuverable cargo plane that could land on unimproved runways, would not take up as much space on the ground, and would still be able to carry outsized cargo such as tanks and heavy artillery. The Project and members of the underground who had been involved in airlift were concerned that the Air Force was once again asking their cargo planes to accomplish missions that were unrealistic, such as delivering tanks to the battlefield.

However, the Air Force held a competition for the C-X cargo plane and on August 26, 1981, McDonnell Douglas Corporation emerged the winner with their design. Lockheed did not take the loss lightly and on September 14 gave the Air Force an unsolicited proposal to update the C-5. All that fall, many memorandums written by the airlift community circulated in the Air Force, and the DOD insisted that the C-X (now called the C-17) was a better plane. I'd heard rumors at that time that the C-5 might be making a comeback, but I did not have any reliable sources in the airlift area then.

To my shock and surprise, on January 20, 1982, the DOD leaked to the press the news that they would buy Lockheed's new C-5, designated as the C-5B.[2] It did not seem logical that the Air Force, after heralding the C-17 so widely in the Congress, would want to have an updated version of one of its most embarrassing procurements. After discussing the matter with Ernie, who was as surprised as I was, we came to the conclusion that the decision must had been made at the DOD level as a political bailout for Lockheed.

Our hunch was right: the airlift community was not happy with the political decision to buy the C-5B, and soon a member of the airlift underground contacted me. He was uncertain what I could do and somewhat suspicious of my motivation, but after a few discussions we established a working relationship. He went back to his colleagues and I was deluged with documents. I received many of the memorandums that had been sent from the Air Force people to the airlift decision-makers pleading not to bring the C-5 back. One general wrote that the maintenance cost per flying hour of the C-5A was the highest in the Air Force and that although the C-5A was only one percent of the airlift capacity, it used up 14 percent of the spare parts budget. Another general reported that when a C-5 landed at his European air base it clogged the runway because there was no place to park it and it interfered with the *peacetime* operations of the base.[3]

But the most significant document was a briefing Air Force Secretary Verne Orr had given to DOD Deputy Secretary Frank Carlucci on January 8, 1982, which showed that the C-5A had a very bad maintenance record, that the new C-5 would have the same trouble on runways as the C-5A, and that Lockheed's proposal had "no enforceable reliability or maintainability warranties."[4] Orr urged Carlucci to stay with the C-17, yet *days later, after the DOD let it be known it was going with the C-5B*, the Air Force Secretary publicly pushed for the plane.

Several months after that I leaked the documents to various reporters. It stirred up a controversy in Congress, as various committees began to look to see if the C-5B decision was justified and really accepted by the airlift community.

About that time, another monkey wrench was thrown into the airlift debate. On March 17, 1982, the Boeing Company sent an unsolicited proposal to the DOD offering to sell either new or used 747 cargo planes to the government for a much lower price than the new C-5Bs. It was an unusual step for another defense contractor to challenge a DOD decision. So the debate shifted from whether we should buy C-5Bs or C-17s to the C-5B versus the 747 cargo plane. The high-ranking military men who were so upset at the prospect of the C-5 were even more upset with the idea of purchasing the 747s because of their traditional opposition to buying anything commercial for military use, and they publicly rallied around the C-5B. But my airlift underground, which was concerned with getting a reliable and supportable airlift capability, was not against the idea and continued to leak me documents showing that the 747 could do the job despite what the Air Force maintained.

I made a concerted effort with the underground to try to get this increasingly bitter political debate to focus on the real airlift issues by putting out a paper based on the leaked documents entitled "Assessment C-5N versus KC-10 versus 747F." But I soon found out that few people other than the press seemed to care about the facts, as the debate quickly formed around political and pork barrel lines.

Besides the attractive feature of being half the cost, the 747 had other advantages over the C-5B: it was far more reliable, could take off from shorter runways, and could carry around a third-larger payload. Also, under the pressure of a congressional debate on which plane was the best to choose, Boeing made the unprecedented offer of guaranteeing the twenty-year life cycle costs of the 747. This was a blow to the argument for the C-5B because of its extremely expensive and unreliable history of maintenance. Guaranteeing the life cycle costs was common in the commercial airplane business but unheard of in the military plane business because the Pentagon did not insist on it the way the free market does. But Boeing probably felt that they could make this attractive offer because they had been flying and maintaining the cargo version of the 747 all over the world for years and knew what the costs would be.

But the best friend the 747 had was powerful Senator Henry

Jackson (D) of Washington State, where Boeing has its national headquarters. The C-5 also had powerful members behind it, including Senator Sam Nunn (D) of Georgia, where the C-5B was to be built. However, Senator Jackson had the most political clout and, to the DOD's and Air Force's astonishment, the Senate voted on May 13, 1981, by a vote of 60 to 30, to buy the 747 instead of the C-5B. It was clearly a case where the right decision for the national defense and the taxpayer was made for the wrong reason—pork barrel politics. In any event, the Air Force and the DOD were in disarray because the vote in the House of Representatives was approaching and they did not know whether the 747-Jackson forces could win again.

In the middle of June, one of my sources called to tell me that he had heard the Air Force, the DOD, and Lockheed were meeting to plan strategy to see that the C-5B won the airlift vote in the House. It did not seem to me a proper activity for the Air Force and the DOD to be involved in, especially since they would be responsible for monitoring Lockheed to see that they got the best performance if Lockheed received the contract. It was at least a gross conflict of interest if not illegal.

I called Ernie, and he agreed with me that it was improper for the Air Force and the DOD to be involved with Lockheed in this manner. I called my source back and asked him if he could get me a list of who was attending these meetings. If I could prove that these types of meetings were going on, I could take the story to the Congress and the press. The source called back in a few days and told me to meet him on a street corner in a small town in suburban Virginia.

As my husband and I drove to the meeting spot, I had no idea of the magnitude of the document I was about to receive. The source appeared unusually nervous when we pulled up and I jumped out of the car. He pulled a three-inch-thick manila envelope out of his briefcase and handed it to me. I knew from the weight of the envelope that it was not just a list of people attending the meeting. He did not want me to look at it on the street or discuss it with him there, and he appeared anxious to move on. So I told him that I would call him later.

As we drove away, I quickly opened the envelope and began reading. I could hardly believe my eyes. "This is big," I told my husband as we wound our way back to Capitol Hill.

The computerized printout of the lobby plan that I received was ninety-six pages long and broken down into two sections. The first section consisted of an action/status report describing the various tasks that Lockheed, Air Force, and DOD personnel (called the C-5B group)—who met three or four times a week —were to carry out. This was the group that my airlift underground had told me about. The second section was a list of members of the House of Representatives broken down by military committees and another list of the rest of the representatives.

Before me was probably one of the best-documented cases of how the political procurement system inside the Pentagon works and what the Pentagon must do to get a controversial weapon through the Congress. As you will see, there was very little emphasis on the substantive issues of airlift, but rather material on how to use pork barrel and horse-trading to influence the Congress for the benefit of the contractor's program. In the plan the contractor, Lockheed, the DOD, and the Air Force worked hand in hand trading assets and connections they had in the Congress. It was a coordinated effort that planned to use such "heavy hitters" as four-star generals, Senate majority leader Howard Baker, the mayor of Atlanta, the Secretary of the Air Force, the Deputy Secretary of the DOD, and even President Reagan. This C-5B group was not about to lose this lucrative contract for Lockheed.

Examples of the first section of the lobby plan, dated June 14, 1982, include the following (explanations in italics and brackets supplied by author):

ACTION: 05/24 AF [Air Force]
Provide firm Sec Def [Secretary of Defense] position to 2 House Committees plus appropriate Key House leadership.
STATUS: 5/24 LK [Lockheed] draft provided.
6/2 AF [Air Force] draft sent to Sec Def for approval.
6/4 Sec Defense signed letter to Price, Dickinson, Whitten, Addabbo, Edwards, and Michel [all influential members of the House of Representatives]
6/7 Signed and released (Does not address 747)
COMPLETE

[*One of the most serious problems with this task is that the DOD is allowing a defense company to write the first draft of the Secretary of Defense's position on their weapon which will be given to the Congress as justification for this defense expenditure.*]

ACTION: 05/26 DOD
Work specific assignments and get member to member commitments in HAC [House Appropriations Committee], HASC [House Armed Services Committee] and other members.
STATUS:
ACTION: 05/26 LK [Lockheed]
Work specific assignments to get member to member commitments in HAC, HASC and other members.

ACTION: 05/26 AF DOD
Get non-Defense Committee Chairman [a chairman that has a committee not connected to defense] support (like on the B-1).
STATUS: 6/4 AF draft "soft sell" Dear Colleague letter

[*A Dear Colleague letter is a letter that members of Congress send to each other on important issues. Here the Air Force was going to write the letter and then try to peddle it to a non-Defense chairman on Capitol Hill.*]

6/8 Attempt to have non-Defense committee chairman sign letter.

6/9 Draft provided to House Liaison Office.

[*The House Liaison Office is an office in the DOD and the services located on Capitol Hill to "provide information" to members of Congress on request. They were doing much more than that here.*]

ACTION: 05/26 AF DOD
Energize all military associations & obtain leadership and "back home" support.
STATUS: Open
LL [Legislative Liaison]: Issue too split by contractors.

[*Here the AF and the DOD were planning to get military associations such as the American Legion and National Defense Council to lobby for the C-5B as necessary to the security of the country. Government agencies are not supposed to seek support from outside groups.*]

ACTION: 05/26 AF DOD
Prepare paper and witnesses to make clear C-5B has high priority and how it relates & fits the POM [Program Objective Memorandum] planning for C-5B and C-17 type aircraft.

[*This was the DOD's way of making sure that the Air Force did not fall back and say that the C-17 was better because the Air Force did not want the C-5B. They wanted all of the troops to fall in line.*]

STATUS: 6/4 OSD [Office of the Secretary of Defense] "Murder Board" to insure witnesses understand DOD position.
6/11 Q&A [Question and Answer] preparation underway for HASC [House Armed Services Committee] hearing by AF/DOD and LK.

[*A "murder board" is an exercise done in the DOD to have mock members of Congress question the DOD and AF*] *witnesses to make sure they are able to answer all the questions. Most of the witnesses were AF generals and the DOD wanted to make sure that they would all rally around the DOD position. Note that the AF, DOD, and Lockheed were also preparing questions and the answers to them for friendly members on the subcommittee. Besides the questionability of whether the DOD and the AF should be engaged in this activity, they once again involved the contractor in the process.]*

ACTION: 5/26 LK
- Have Andy Young work caucus.
- Have Tom Hartnett and McCurdy work freshman.
- Have Evans, Beard, & Gingrich work moderates.

STATUS:

[This entry is a good illustration of how Lockheed had members of Congress and other political figures "work" other members for votes to protect parochial interests. Andrew Young is the mayor of Atlanta, which is located near Marietta, Georgia, where most of the C-5B would be assembled. They were asking him to work the Black Congressional Caucus for votes on the C-5B because he was told that the C-5B contract would bring 8500 jobs into the area. On June 17 he traveled to Washington to "work the caucus." Although you may not think that the liberal Black Congressional Caucus would be a fertile place to woo this type of military vote, in some cases it worked.[5] Congresswoman Shirley Chisholm ended up voting for the C-5B. The other names are members of Congress who had influence with either the freshman members of Congress or moderates.]

ACTION: 06/01 AF DOD
Consider ways to obtain support of DOD position from prime contractors and subcontractors like E-Systems, Vought, Northrop, and P & W [Pratt & Whitney].

STATUS: 6/4 DOD & AF have under consideration.

[*As though Lockheed's lobbying influence was not enough, the DOD and the AF went looking for other contractors to rally behind the C-5B. Some of these companies were involved in the C-5B contract, some were not. Once again, the DOD went outside to lobby the Congress: all of these contractors have large contracts with the Pentagon —a captured lobby force for the DOD.*]

ACTION: 5/27 DOD AF/LK
Develop list of members that Sec Def [Secretary of Defense], Dep Sec Def [Deputy Secretary of Defense], Sec AF [Secretary of the Air Force], Chief of Staff AF, Lloyd [Lloyd Moseman, AF Deputy Assistant Secretary], Hecker [Major General Guy Hecker, head of the AF Legislative Liaison Office and the leader of the C-5B group] should see or call.
STATUS: Continuing.

[*At one point when the General Accounting Office was investigating this lobby plan, the AF and the DOD tried to appear as though they were acting separately from Lockheed and only Lockheed was keeping tally of what was going on. This entry clearly shows that the Air Force, DOD, and Lockheed, were all working together to make a list of members of Congress for the DOD and AF "big guns" to lobby for this aircraft.*]

ACTION: 06/04 AF
Provide to LOK [Lawrence O. Kitchens, president of Lockheed Corporation] composite pictures of C-5 with 3 Chinook helicopters and C-5 with 6 Blackhawk helicopters.
STATUS: Will do pictures at Andrews this week.

[*The Air Force provided these pictures taken with congressionally appropriated money to the president of Lockheed for full-page advertisements that Lockheed took out in major newspapers such as* The Washington Post.]

ACTION: GD [General Dynamics Corporation]
- Work on [Senator] Levin and ask him to work liberals. Also work Udall.
- Provide list and work all members (approx. 60) in their plant locations and areas.
- Also send note to same 60 AA's [Congressional Administrative Assistants for various members] regarding attendance at C-5 Demo [Demonstration].

STATUS:

[*General Dynamics, a major subcontractor for the C-5B, was also brought into the action. Carl Levin is senator from Michigan, where General Dynamics is building the M-1 tank, which represents a lot of jobs in that state. GD was being asked to get Levin to work liberal members of the House. Liberal members of Congress may complain about the size of the DOD budget, but they are willing to go to bat for defense contractors that have influence in their state or district. GD was asked to produce a vote from any member they thought they had influence over in the C-5B contract—which turned out to be about 60 members. Then the AF wanted to make sure that the administrative assistants of each of these members of Congress were invited to a demonstration of the C-5A.*]

ACTION: 6/14 LK [Lockheed]
Get picture of "off runway" tests of C-5 to witnesses prior to Thursday hearing. (Col. Paul Godfrey who ran tests will be in the audience. He can be called upon by a member.)

STATUS:

[*This action was in preparation for a June 15, 1982, hearing by the House Appropriations Subcommittee on Defense. One of the claims that Lockheed and the Air Force had made for the C-5B was that it would be able to unload off the runway so as not to hinder airport operations. As you may remember, that was just the opposite experience of one of the Air Force generals, who said in a letter to the Air Force that the C-5 could not go off the runway and*] *severely interfered with peacetime operations. The Air Force must have known that several members of Congress who were against the C-5B had pictures of a C-5A that had been taken off a runway and had promptly sunk to its belly in mud. They wanted to call on one of the colonels involved with the C-5A to dispute the pictures. In fact, during the actual hearing Col. Godfrey was called on to attest that the C-5B could successfully go off the runway. Once again, Lockheed was working with the Air Force and the DOD witnesses prior to the hearings to influence the congressional decision.]*

ACTION: 06/14 AF
Need Gen. Jim Allen's testimony to be strong on C-5 & no 747 (prepared statement doesn't cover).

STATUS:

[General Jim Allen was a four-star general who at that time headed the Military Airlift Command (MAC), the organization that would be responsible for receiving and maintaining the new C-5Bs. He was one of the major witnesses at the June 15, 1982, hearings and evidently his prepared testimony that he brought to Washington from MAC headquarters in St. Louis was not a strong enough line for the C-5B and against the 747. The Congress wanted to hear from this general because he was from the command that would be using this plane, yet when he arrived in town his statement had to be "purified"—being a four-star general apparently did not allow him to speak freely to the Congress. A few years later, after a speech I gave on the C-5B lobby plan, an AF major approached me and told me that he had been an aide to General Allen during the controversy and that the general was very bitter about the interference with his testimony.]

ACTION: 06/14 AF
Need heavy hitter to see Mel Price in addition to Jim Allen on it. Need to fix perception that AF not fighting for the C-5. If want it fight for it. He will support Air Force in what it wants.

THE PENTAGON UNDERGROUND

STATUS:

[*Representative Melvin Price was the chairman of the House Armed Services Committee. Evidentally the C-5B group felt that the committee leadership was not convinced that the AF really wanted the C-5B. This was a sign that the disclosures of my airlift underground were having an impact. Obviously whichever "heavy hitter" they sent was able to strike a deal, because the committee voted heavily in favor of the C-5B.*]

The second part of the lobby plan, which listed various members of Congress, was also revealing as to how the good old boy network works. Many have speculated on how the system really works, but rarely has the public been given a glimpse into the back-room maneuvering of the U.S. Congress when dealing with the military-industrial complex. As you can see, the position of each member of Congress is listed along with the subcontractors who do business in his district, other members of Congress favorable to Lockheed who might influence him, and further actions necessary to ensure this member's vote for the C-5B.

Even Ernie, who thought he had seen it all, was impressed with the scope of the lobby plan. Several of my underground advisors reinforced my belief that the lobby plan was a major find and one of them encouraged me to release it with an embargo. I gave the plan to the four reporters and sat back to see what the DOD and Air Force explanation would be. I suspected that many members of Congress would feign outrage at the plan, even though some of them were well aware that this type of activity was constantly going on in Congress. But I expected the Pentagon to face this release with silence.

However, the Air Force was unabashed in their efforts. Excerpts from the stories that appeared in *The Washington Post,* the *Boston Globe,* and the Knight-Ridder newspapers—starting on page 250—illustrate the lack of shame on the part of the Pentagon.

**Examples from the lobby plan include [author comments
in italics and brackets]:**

Member	Contr. Contacts	Pos	Further Actions
Addabbo, Joseph P. (D-NY) 2256R 225-3461 (AC-Def.S/C-Chairman)	LOK	u	Carlucci one on one Orr one on one. AGAINST C-5 in FY82 markup.
Gen. Dyn. (GELAC)	Black-shaw	u	More work to swing.
Colt Indust. (GELAC)	Bolles		Will contact
Gen. Dyn. (GELAC)	Stirk		'Buy both C-5s & 747s' RKC: see Seelmyer (A/A)

[LOK is Lawrence O. Kitchens, president of Lockheed Corporation, and RKC is Richard K. Cook, vice-president of Lockheed. They were planning to have Deputy Secretary of Defense Frank Carlucci and Secretary of the Air Force Verne Orr go one on one with him. Representative Addabbo received so much attention because he is the chairman of the House Appropriations Subcommittee on Defense and his vote would swing other members' votes.]

Member	Contr. Contacts	Pos	Further Actions
Anderson, Glenn (D-CA) 2329R 225-6676	LOK	u	Need subcontractor calls or wires from Wetzel (Garrett), Puckett (Hughes), Bannum (West. Gear) AF: see Coleman: see
AVNET (CALAC)	Odintz		Has contacted
Hi-Shear (LMSC)	Luth		Contacted by phone
VSI (CALAC)	Thomas		Letter

Examples from the lobby plan *(continued)*

Member	Contr. Contacts	Pos	Further Actions
[Note that each subcontractor reported to Lockheed that they had contacted this member, whether by phone or letter.]			
Badham, Robert E. (R-CA) 1108L 225-5611	LOK	u	Need high level DoD/AF one-one-one meeting on total airlift plan prior to Hearings. Member/member commit.
Sundstrand (GELAC)	Hills	u	'Favors C-17, against 747s'
HITCO (CALAC)	Cusic		Has contacted
Parker-Hann (CALAC)	Schloe-mer		Has contacted
Consultant (CORLAC)	Kendall	u	Has contacted

[The planners wanted a high-level briefing for this member so that he would be ready to go to bat for them at an airlift hearing.]

Member	Contr. Contacts	Pos	Further Actions
Brooks, Jack (D-TX) 2449R 225-6565	RKC	u	Marine or Army follow-up
Menasco (GELAC)	Hawthorne		Letter sent 5/24 LK PAC

[Note that the LK PAC (Lockheed Political Action Committee) was notified, possibly to give a contribution to this member's reelection campaign. Jack Brooks is the powerful chairman of the House Government Operations Committee.]

Examples from the lobby plan *(continued)*

Member	Contr. Con- tacts	Pos	Further Actions
Conyers, Jr., John (D-MI) 2313R 225-5126		o	

[*Evidently the planners had conceded this vote.*]

Member	Contr. Con- tacts	Pos	Further Actions
Daniel, Jr., Robert W. (R-VA) 2236R 225-6365	RBO	u	Arrange trip to GELAC in the near future.
Colt Indust. (GELAC)	Bolles		Will contact.
USAF	Battista		Will contact re: C-5 flight.
AVCO (GELAC)	Kelly	s	

[*Note that the Air Force was planning to give this member a flight in a C-5, much like the ride I took in the M-1 tank. Battista is Tony Battista, a staff aide on the House Armed Services Committee who was sympathetic to the C-5B.*]

Member	Contr. Con- tacts	Pos	Further Actions
Dornan, Robert K. (R-CA) 332C 225-6451	LOK	s	Follow-up on his effort with D. Smith of Oregon—JEK
Sterer PAC (CALAC)	Lein- berry		PAC committee wire
Hi-Shear (LMSC)	Luth		Contacted by phone
Avnet (CALAC)	Odintz		Has contacted
VSI (CALAC)	Thomas		Letter

[*Note that this member was to follow up with fellow conservative member Denny Smith to encourage a positive vote for the C-5B and that Sterer PAC had been notified of his work. It did not work, however; Smith voted against the C-5B.*]

Examples from the lobby plan *(continued)*

Member	Contr. Contacts	Pos	Further Actions
Duberstein, Kenneth (Asst. to the Pres.)	RKC	s	Wk of 6/1; Brinkley (GA delegation) re: budget. 1 pg 747 Q & A.

[*As assistant to President Reagan for congressional affairs, his influence was very important in this vote.*]

Member	Contr. Contacts	Pos	Further Actions
Goldwater, Jr., Barry M. (R-CA) 2240R 225-4461			
Sterer PAC (CALAC)	Leinberry		PAC wired
Gen. Design (LMSC)	Globic		Will contact

[*Note that he had a "PAC wired," too.*]

Member	Contr. Contacts	Pos	Further Actions
Hawkins, Augustus F. (D-CA) 2371R 225-2201			Andy Young call
LAS	Greene		

[*He is a member of the Black Congressional Caucus, which Atlanta mayor Andrew Young was assigned to lobby.*]

Member	Contr. Contacts	Pos	Further Actions
McDade, Joseph M. (R-PA) 2370R 225-3731	LOK	u	Need Ginn to work him.
AVCO (GELAC)	Tuttle	s	AF see.
AFL&L		s	Murtha/Daniel
AVCO (GELAC)	Kelly	s	
Gen. Dyn. (GELAC)	Stirk	u	

Examples from the lobby plan *(continued)*

Member	Contr. Contacts	Pos	Further Actions
	Sec. Coleman		Will contact
Consultant (CORLAC)	Kendall	u	

[*Note there were many subcontractors who were assigned to contact this member.*]

Member	Contr. Contacts	Pos	Further Actions
Michel, Robert H.	RKC	?	Call again after visiting floor leaders. AF/DoD should visit President call & Sen. Baker call

[*Michel is the House minority leader, and he ranked high enough for the architects of the lobby plan to want him to receive a call from President Reagan and Senator Howard Baker, the Senate majority leader at that time.*]

Member	Contr. Contacts	Pos	Further Actions
Moorhead, Carlos J. (R-CA) 2346R 225-4176	LOK	s	Prepare & provide Moorhead mat'l for floor debate. List of members to work (at proper time).
Sterer PAC (CALAC)	Leinberry		PAC wired
Dyna Metric (CALAC)	McFadden		Has contacted
H.L. Yoh (CALAC)	Shand		Has contacted

[*This member was evidentally going to be one of the main speakers for the C-5B during the debate on the House floor. He also had a "PAC wired."*]

Examples from the lobby plan *(continued)*

Member	Contr. Con- tacts	Pos	Further Actions
O'Neill, Jr., Thomas P. (D-MA) 2231R 225-5111	RKC	s	GF corp. level contact DoD AF see

[*O'Neill, the Speaker of the House, has great influence in this type of vote. According to the* Atlanta Journal, *he was told that this C-5B contract was important to his state, Massachusetts, because General Electric, which has a plant there, would be making the engines. He reportedly pulled out all the stops for the C-5B, but what he was not told was that the C-5B engines would not be made at the GE Massachusetts plant but at a plant in Ohio.*]

Member	Contr. Con- tacts	Pos	Further Actions
Vander Jagt, Guy (R-MI) 2409R 225-3511	RKC	u	White House & House GOP leader contacts
Consultant (CORLAC)	Kendall		Will contact

[*Once again, the planners hoped to use White House influence to sway this powerful member of Congress.*]

Excerpts from *The Post:*

Air Force Lt. Gen. Kelly H. Burke, who is responsible for the proposed C5 program, said yesterday: "You're just wrong if you think this is a highly unusual happening. Anytime you get competing views, it's customary for the government to work with those contractors whose views are congruent with the president's. . . .

I do not want to sound platitudinous, but all you're seeing is democracy in action. This is the way the system is supposed to work." . . .

. . . Lockheed said the printouts were "apparently obtained by opponents of the C5 in the hope that publication might undermine the efforts to secure congressional pas-

sage of the Defense Department's airlift enhancement
proposals. . . . These working papers reflect what we said
we would do and what the Air Force and the DOD said
they would do to make sure that congressmen and their
staffs have accurate information on the issues involved."

From the *Globe:*

Military officers are barred by law from lobbying, and by
law, no appropriated funds can be used "to influence in
any matter a member of Congress, to favor or oppose, by
vote or otherwise, any legislation or appropriation by Congress." That portion of the law, which carries a penalty of
$500 fine or a year's imprisonment or both, has not been
enforced since it passed in 1948.

Other actions listed in the computer printout have the
Air Force, the Pentagon, and Lockheed composing questions and answers—"Q & A preparation"—to be used by
friendly members in congressional hearings.

Asked about such incidents, an Air Force spokesman
responded, "The Air Force has a responsibility to provide
facts to support the Administration's decision. We selected
the C5 after a lot of study. A congressman asks for data and
we provide it to him. That's part of our responsibility."

From the Knight-Ridder newspapers:

Col. Larry Shreve, associate director of the Air Force's
Legislative Liaison Office, defended the energy of the lobbying effort. "If we didn't, the administration would have
some claim to say we weren't doing our job," said Shreve.
Similar campaigns are involved on all major procurements, he said.

The persuasion campaign on the C-5B, Shreve added,
came only after a "very objective analysis" by the Air
Force, which concluded that it was superior to the 747 for
airlift purposes. "Once that decision *was* made, we *are* not
objective. We make every effort to *sell* Congress *that* the
administration's decision is the right one," said Shreve.

According to Shreve, the service's Legislative Liaison

Office acts only in response to congressional inquiries. "We do not solicit them to my knowledge," he said. But the lobby plan shows otherwise: the Air Force initiated dozens of meetings with congressmen and key aides to "obtain support."

Wally Raabe, a spokesman for Lockheed's Washington office, said the C-5B effort deals with "a Defense Department program involving a Lockheed product and we are vigorously supporting it." The campaign is intended "to make sure that congressmen and their staffs have accurate information on the issues involved—particularly in view of the vast amount of misinformation and distortion which this issue has generated." [NOTE: That "distortion" was in direct reference to the dozens of Air Force documents that the airlift underground smuggled out of the Pentagon to me showing that according to several Air Force analyses, the 747 was not an unreasonable airlifter for the mission the Air Force had laid out and the C-5B had a disastrous record.][6]

The problem with the Pentagon's and Lockheed's explanations was that they were pretending that they had arrived at the C-5B solution only after careful scientific study of all the airlift choices. The documents that the airlift underground supplied showed just the opposite. As the memos revealed, Air Force Secretary Verne Orr strongly urged DOD Deputy Secretary Frank Carlucci on January 8 not to go with the C-5B and the decision was made to go with that plane a few days later. The Air Force gave the task of coming up with a justification for the C-5B decision to Air Force Assistant Secretary Lloyd Moseman. The underground gave me his draft justification for the program, dated January 21—a couple of weeks after the decision. His draft had gaps in the text. He sent it to various commands asking for revisions or additions—in other words, asking them to try to find facts to justify the political decision.

Several examples of the blanks included:

The outsize requirement is driven by the increasing size and complexity of the Army and Marine Corps mobility equipment. For example, the NATO scenario requires — million ton miles per day of outsize airlift, or —% of the total airlift requirement for that scenario. This compares to an existing capability ratio of outsize to all other airlift of only —%. This airlift acquisition program, considering the acquisition of both KC-10 and C-5 aircraft, will change this ratio to —%. Whereas existing C-5 capability can satisfy —% of the NATO outsize requirement, procurement of 50 additional C-5s will satisfy —% of the requirement.

Two other versions of that same document supplied to me by the underground showed that the Air Force did not have the justification completed for Secretary Orr to sign until February 15, approximately one month after the political decision was made by the DOD. (After the C-5B finally won, Lloyd Moseman received a $10,000 federal bonus for his work that year.) So it was very inaccurate to say that the C-5B group was merely acting on a carefully thought-out decision by Air Force airlift professionals.

But beyond that rationalization, it shocked me and others in the underground that the people involved in the lobby effort did not see anything wrong with it and felt their work was "democracy in action" and business-as-usual. It was a good illustration of how the contractor's and the Pentagon's priorities became the same—to give Lockheed more work for their idle plant in Georgia. The national security consideration of getting the most effective airlift or sealift for the least money to make sure our troops were well supplied fell by the wayside.

But the even more frustrating end to this story is that the lobby plan worked. After all the disclosures about the C-5 and the release of documents leaked by the underground showing that the Pentagon and the contractor were manipulating Congress through an elaborate political pork barrel scheme, the

House voted on July 21, 1981, 289 to 127, for the C-5B. The House and Senate had to hammer out their differences on which plane to choose on August 18.

I had been hearing rumors that an internal Air Force study had estimated the cost of the C-5B to be higher than Congress had been told and that the delivery schedule for the aircraft had slipped more than a year, but I couldn't obtain any documents. I later received documents showing that the Air Force Systems Command was told on February 23, 1982 by their cost estimators that the program cost estimates for the C-5B has risen from $8.1 billion to $8.8 billion. On April 8 they were again told that the program had risen another $979 million. It was also estimated about this time that the scheduled delivery date had slipped a year.[7] However, the Air Force chose not to inform the Congress of these new developments.

Several House-Senate conference committee members also had heard of these rumors and asked the Air Force Legislative Liaison Office if it was true that the cost had risen and the schedule slipped. They also requested data on how the C-5B compared to the 747 in reliability and maintainability (the 747 beat the C-5B hands down). The Legislative Liaison Office, which had so piously portrayed itself as existing only to supply the Congress with vital information, was not willing to supply the conference committee with this vital information, which the Air Force had in February and April, until August 19—one day after the conference committee decision was made. They also did not supply the reliability and maintainability data until August 24.

But Congress has only itself to blame for allowing this deception by the Pentagon and voting for a $10 billion program based on pork barrel influences instead of examining the real need for national defense at the best price. In doing so, they completed the third ring of this three-ring circus process that should create a national defense.

Several members of Congress, some of whom were on the

other side of the C-5B debate, were upset by the lobby plan. Congressman Jack Brooks (D-Texas), chairman of the House Government Operations Committee, called for an investigation by the General Accounting Office (GAO). I had been disappointed with some past GAO investigations and impressed with others. It really depended on the main investigator, and whether he had the internal clout and perseverance to bring forward all the facts he uncovered in the investigation despite the political pressure. Whoever would investigate the lobby plan would be walking into a political minefield because of the high-ranking individuals involved.

As luck would have it, a tough and fair investigator was assigned to head the team. Dr. Carl Palmer of the GAO called to tell me of his assignment and the types of information that he was looking for. He was very reserved and skeptical of what I told him about the lobby plan uncovered by the airlift underground, so I invited him to come over to look at the documentation himself.

He and another investigator came and spent several hours going over the mounds of leaked documents from the airlift underground, including some of the documents that I had not yet given the press because I had so many. Although he did not say much as I showed him the evidence, he took careful notes. By the end of the first hour I could tell that he was alarmed by just how deep and high this lobby effort went and how closely and blatantly the individuals involved continued to brush against the law prohibiting lobbying by an executive agency.[8]

By the end of the conversation he was still noncommittal as I told him of my outrage, but he emphasized that what I had given them was valuable and that he would keep in touch to clarify some points. After he explained to me the scope of the law and the importance of showing that appropriated funds went improperly into the lobbying, I began to dig further into the mounds of documentation I had received and was able for the first time to concentrate on the lobbying rather than the issues. As the pieces began to fall together, I could see that the effort was even more insidious than the lobby plan itself showed.

One such incident that surfaced during the GAO investigation concerned commercial airlines' contracts with the Pentagon. Fred Kaplan explained the threat to these contracts in an article for *The Washington Monthly:*

> On June 4, Lockheed chairman Roy Anderson wrote several airlines—a copy of a letter to World Airways has been obtained—pointing out, in a not-so-subtle fashion, "Forced acquisition of commercial aircraft that the Military Airlift Command would be obliged to use . . . could adversely impact airline revenues from government contracts."
>
> On June 8, according to *Armed Forces Journal International,* undersecretary of defense Richard DeLauer called Boeing chairman T. Wilson and told him, "We're going to fight you tooth and nail," threatening to "pull the pursestrings" on Boeing's role in the Civil Reserve Air Fleet program. Wilson asked DeLauer whether his campaign would be executed "legally and ethically."
>
> DeLauer responded: "It'll certainly be legal. Ethically? I can't comment."
>
> Other airlines reportedly told Boeing officials that the Air Force—mainly its deputy assistant Lloyd Moseman . . .—had threatened to cancel their contracts with the Military Airlift Command if they lobbied on behalf of Boeing's B-747.[9]

The House Armed Services Subcommittee on Investigations announced that they would be holding hearings on the legality of the lobby plan in September 1982. I was very leery that this subcommittee would be willing to dig out all the controversial issues connected to the lobby plan. Congressional staff members and members of the underground informed me that the investigating staff was very much in favor of protecting the status quo in the Pentagon and was sympathetic to Lockheed and the C-5B.

During these hearings the Air Force and Lockheed officials once again proclaimed they had done nothing illegal or improper. They admitted that they had worked together and compared notes on their congressional contacts, but their actions were not wrong. Their denials were similar to those reported in the papers after the lobby plan became public. However, it was revealed in the hearings that the lobby plan was the brainchild of Lawrence O. Kitchens, the president of Lockheed, who was present at many of the C-5B group hearings.

The GAO made their report public on September 30, and even I was surprised by the intensity with which the GAO investigators criticized the efforts of Lockheed and the Pentagon. The report called for the Justice Department to investigate four top-ranking officials in the Air Force and DOD for possible criminal violation of the anti-lobbying law. They were the director of the Air Force Office of Legislative Liaison, Major General Guy Hecker; Assistant Secretary of Defense for Legislative Affairs Russell Rourke; Deputy Secretary of Defense Frank Carlucci (who was the number two person in the Office of the Secretary of Defense); and Verne Orr, Secretary of the Air Force. I was surprised that the GAO investigators and especially their bosses would go so far as to point the finger at such high-ranking officials, especially since Rourke, Carlucci, and Orr were presidential appointees. Usually controversial investigations implicate only the lowest-ranking people in the bureaucracy to avoid the political heat of naming high officials. But the GAO powers-that-be maintained a surprisingly tough stand on their report in the face of severe criticism by the Pentagon and the subcommittee chaired by Richard White. During one of the hearings by the White subcommittee, the chairman and other members of the subcommittee, trying to get the GAO to waver on their hard-hitting conclusions, strongly attacked the officials of the GAO and Carl Palmer for their report, but it did not work.

Bob Adams, a reporter for the *St. Louis Post-Dispatch,* who had done excellent reporting on the legality of the lobby plan, was able to get the usually elusive Carl Palmer to comment about his hard-hitting report:

> Pentagon officials violated federal lobbying laws in their joint campaign with the Lockheed Corp. to win congressional approval for the purchase of 50 Lockheed C-5B Galaxy cargo planes, congressional investigators say.
>
> The findings are contained in a report by the General Accounting Office, the investigative arm of Congress. The report is being made public today.
>
> The report says potential violations of a 1913 criminal law against lobbying by officials in the executive branch are being referred to the Department of Justice. Violators can get a year in prison and a $500 fine. But the report notes that apparently no one has ever been successfully prosecuted under that law.
>
> Another law that prohibits the spending of federal money also appears to have been violated, the report said.
>
> According to the report, officials of the Air Force and the secretary of defense office "violated federal anti-lobbying laws by using contractors to do things that they could not do themselves." But in connection with specific laws, the report states only that violations apparently occurred.
>
> Carl Palmer headed the GAO's investigating team that wrote the 22 page report. He said in an interview that information on potential violations of other federal laws also would be turned over to the Department of Justice. Palmer said this information dealt with allegations of threats.
>
> . . . Hecker, Rourke, Carlucci and several other Pentagon officials admitted before the House panel that they had known about, or taken part in, the meetings. But all said they had seen nothing improper or illegal about it.
>
> Carlucci cited rulings from the White House legal coun-

cil and the Justice Department to show that members of the executive branch had the right to promote the president's program among members of Congress.

But the GAO report cites legislative history and case law, saying that officials are not allowed to enlist federal grantees or contractors in such efforts. It says the laws were designed to prevent the organizing of such grassroots lobbying campaigns with federal money.

"Since the Air Force is prohibited by appropriation restrictions from directly mounting a grass-roots lobbying campaign . . . it follows that it may not engage in a network of defense contractors to accomplish the same thing."

It says the salaries paid to the Air Force and Defense Department officials during the joint lobbying constituted an improper expenditure of federal money.[10]

I was very pleased with the report and that Chairman Brooks had turned it over to the Justice Department, but when I called Ernie to tell him about it, he did not share in my enthusiasm. He felt that the investigation would come to an abrupt end at the Justice Department because we were "asking the King's attorney to prosecute the King's men for doing the King's business." He went on to explain that the Justice Department was very political because the Attorney General was usually the President's close friend or even his brother and we were expecting him to prosecute presidential appointees for successfully pushing through the President's program, regardless of the method.

I did not want to believe that Ernie was right, but I had to admit he was usually correct in calling the moves of the government. He then claimed that the only way to get a fair review of the charges against these high officials was for the federal courts to appoint a special prosecutor for the case. He felt Congress would not push for that because too many members were dependent on such a lobbying system for their patronage politics. He told me that he had seen it happen before. Congress would express outrage at some member or a governmental organization that had been caught playing the same game as everyone else, call for an investigation, and then let any possible follow-up die a lingering death in the Justice Department while they "found no evidence."

To my frustration, along with Carl Palmer's and members' of the airlift underground, that was almost exactly what happened. The Justice Department let the case sit until the end of February 1983 before they decided to close it. A Justice Department spokesman told Bob Adams of the *St. Louis Post-Dispatch* that "the decision had been made because 'no prosecutable violation' of the federal anti-lobbying statutes had been found."

Evidently the Justice Department did not try very hard to find any evidence. Carl Palmer told Bob Adams that the Justice Department did not ask to see any of the GAO's backup documents or call anyone on the investigation team. Palmer told the *Post-Dispatch* his reaction to the decision: " 'I'm really disappointed that they've decided not to prosecute,' Palmer said in a telephone interview. 'I think they should have gone further than they did. . . . Nobody has contacted us.' He said he remained convinced that the GAO's evidence of violations was strong."[11]

By then Congress and, for the most part, the press had moved on to new investigations and scandals. With the Justice Department's announcement, several members of Congress promised reform and new legislation. Secretary Weinberger had written new guidelines for the legislative people in the Pentagon to avoid any "appearance" of improper cooperation with contractors, but my underground reported back to me that people involved in the lobby plan were telling everyone that they were "vindicated" and that it was back to business-as-usual.

Needless to say, the people who had worked so hard and taken so many risks to get the real airlift story to the public were extremely disillusioned. However, I can't help believing that the public disclosure of these practices made the officials more careful about such business-as-usual activities and also made the public more aware of how and why our weapons are procured.

Although it is hard to get Congress to admit to the taxpaying public, this case was a larger illustration of the congressional role in the procurement process. It happens every year with other weapons in a similar but much quieter way. Every year the Pentagon sends a budget to the Congress that is passed first to the House and Senate Armed Services committees, which authorize the amount of money to be spent, and then to the House and Senate Appropriations committees, which appropriate the money for the Pentagon to spend for the next year.

While this process is going on, a horde of industry lobbyists descend upon members of Congress, especially those in these crucial committees. It is not by accident that many of the largest defense companies are located in the states of the prominent members of the Armed Services and Appropriations committees. In many cases, the member of Congress, because of his influence, has brought various defense plants or bases to his state, or he has lobbied to be on these defense committees to help protect the defense economy on which so many of his constituents' jobs are based. This system has been building since World War II, and the constituents of a district or state have continued to reward members of Congress who "bring home the bacon" of defense contracts.

So it should not be surprising to the taxpayers when well-known liberals who denounce the evils of a large defense budget and the resulting defense-based economy, fight like wildcats for the defense plant in their state. A good example of this paradox is the vote for the controversial and expensive F-18 Navy fighter aircraft. In 1982 the plane was bathed in controversy because of its severe development problems and its rising cost, and there was a move in the Congress to cancel the plane before it went into full production. Yet among its biggest supporters were Senator Edward Kennedy and Representative Tip O'Neill of Massachusetts and Senator Alan Cranston of California—all well-known Democratic liberals who criticize large amounts of spending on defense. The F-18 engines are made in a plant in Lynn, Massachusetts, and the main airframe is built in southern California. On the other side, some conservatives in Congress play the same game by proclaiming that they are for a strong national defense, but throw in all their chits to save a defense contractor in their state that has been caught making a defective weapon that may fail on the battlefield.

The contractors and Pentagon weapons program managers are well aware of how powerful this pork barrel system is, and it is not by accident that the B-1 bomber program has subcontractors in forty-eight states and the M-1 tank has subcontractors in forty states. The C-5B lobby plan documented what has been widely known for years in the defense business—spread your contracts around to as many states as possible to capture as much support in Congress as possible.

The loser in this system is our national defense because we are not getting the most effective product for the lowest price. On several occasions after I have shown a staff person or member of Congress evidence of a failed weapon system, they expressed outrage that such a scandal could happen. But they dropped their investigation and interest in my documents like a hot potato after they discovered a prominent subcontractor of that weapon system in their state or district, or they got a visit from a lobbyist for the prime contractor who made sure they knew their district depended on the program.

Probably the best pork barreling of the year occurs when the Armed Services committees and the Appropriations committees finally get down to brass tacks and make final decisions about the defense money in sessions known as markups. These sessions are almost always closed, and, according to staff aides who have attended them, a free-for-all horse-trading atmosphere exists that bears no resemblance to an endeavor that furthers national security. Members fight for weapons appropriations that affect their district and state, and zealously guard any military bases, even ones that the DOD would like to close.

Many would agree with Lt. General Kelly Burke that this "is the way the system works" and it is "democracy in action," but in matters of defense and national security, this system promotes weapons program managers with political connections. This system brings us such weapon calamities as the DIVAD, the C-5B, and the M-1 tank, as well as numerous horror stories regarding spare parts and wasted matériel.

However, the good news is that the underground and the Project see this system and its relationship to the Pentagon changing ever so slowly. A new breed of congressmen, albeit a small number, are beginning to see how damaging this business-as-usual system is to the national defense and economy. Several of these members of Congress have dared to go eyeball-to-eyeball with the Pentagon and sometimes have not blinked first.

Some of them are part of a newly formed, loosely organized Military Reform Caucus that has taken on the Pentagon on its own turf by looking at how to buy more effective weapons at a better price. The stated goal of the Reform Caucus, made up of liberals and conservatives, is to have a bipartisan approach to reforming the military procurement and planning systems. Not everyone in the Reform Caucus has shown a willingness to go to the mat with the Pentagon, but a few stars have been pressing the Pentagon, especially in light of some of the Project's exposures.

One of the Pentagon's most common reactions to the probing inquiries has been to refuse requests for accurate information or drag their feet in responding. Such a confrontation has proven to be a quick way to see which members are serious about their investigations and attempts at reform, and which members are probably looking into scandals for the press attention and political mileage. The publicity seekers tend to back off or not follow up on their investigation when they hit powerful roadblocks from the Pentagon and their defenders in Congress.

Confronting the Pentagon in a sincere and effective investigation is a tough business and is not for the fainthearted who are worried about making political enemies among the congressional leadership. This challenge to a business-as-usual method of weapons procurement directly threatens the profitable system of pork barrel that has built up over many years.

One of the best and most consistent challengers of the status quo is Republican Senator Charles Grassley of Iowa. On first appearance he would seem an unlikely choice to lead a charge against our ineffective defense spending. A freshman senator, he was elected in 1980 in what became known as the Reagan sweep. Before his election he was in the Iowa House of Representatives and the U.S. House of Representatives, and he is a hog farmer. The participation in his campaign of the right-wing political action committee NCPAC helped him defeat Democrat John Culver. Many in Washington assumed that he would take the standard conservative line that more money means more defense and would wholeheartedly endorse the large increases of the Reagan defense budget.

One of the incidents that first piqued Senator Grassley's interest in the waste of defense money was when a woman in a crowd in Iowa gave him Ernie Fitzgerald's 1973 book, *The High Priests of Waste.* After reading the book, Grassley called Ernie at the Pentagon to confirm that what he had read was true. Grassley then asked if things had gotten better or worse. Ernie replied that they were worse, so Grassley invited Ernie to visit him on Capitol Hill.

Then in 1982, Ernie was reinstated in his financial management job in the Air Force from which he had been illegally fired in 1969. It had taken him thirteen years in court to get his job back: he now had a federal court order instructing the reluctant Air Force to accept a job description giving him direct access to documents to allow him to monitor costs of Air Force weapon systems. Ernie had given up quite a bit of settlement money to get that specific job description and he was looking forward to trying to save the government some money instead of fighting them in the courts.

As an industrial engineer, he was appalled at how low the efficiency standards for Air Force contractors had dropped. In 1973, for a congressional committee, Ernie figured out, using the worst contractor efficiency ratings he could find, how much it would cost for that contractor to make a color television set that sold on the free market for $400. He found that the contractor would have to charge $8000 for the television. In 1983, after he returned to his old job and had access to the needed data, he took the worst efficiency ratings he could find and recalculated how much it would cost to make the $400 television (which, despite inflation, still cost $400). To his astonishment, he found that it would take the 1983 inefficient contractor over *$100,000* to make the same set. When he told Senator Grassley that, the senator wanted to do something about it.

One management system that Ernie had been trying to install in the Air Force since he began to work there in 1966 was the "should cost" method of pricing weapons. To understand how and why the Pentagon has paid too much for each generation of weapons, one must understand how the price of weapons has traditionally been estimated. Under the current system, Pentagon managers' estimates are based on historical costs. In other words, they estimate how much a weapon "will cost" based on the price of the weapon it is replacing, plus additions for any new innovations.

As a result, an increasingly unrealistic baseline for pricing our weapons incorporates into the system as "legitimate cost" any waste, fraud, and mismanagement of the previous weapon. So if a fighter plane cost the taxpayer $30 million, even though the price reflects a program full of waste and cost overruns, that price becomes the new baseline, justifying the new generation of fighter planes with additions that cost $40 million a copy.

Often the Pentagon says that the prices of their weapons are "reasonable" because they paid the bill. The waste from this method of deciding how much a weapon "will cost" is, there-fore, institutionalized. It is not difficult to see that if one extrapo-lates that method over several generations of weapons, you will get increasingly fewer weapons for more money—"less bang for the buck." This trend in weapons procurement has alarmed many in the Pentagon underground because they see that we will soon not be able to buy enough weapons to make a differ-ence in a war: the unit cost has become prohibitive even with a large increase in the defense budget. Of course, the defense contractors are not compláining about the system because it guarantees an ever-increasing amount of money for their weap-ons.

Ernie has spent his career pushing for a better way—a man-agement method for estimating costs that is, for the most part, standard for private industry. In simple terms, the should cost method of pricing estimates the price of a weapon based not on the weapon it is replacing, but by using industrial engineering formulas to find out how much it "should cost" the manufac-turer to make the item plus a reasonable profit. Donna Martin described what goes into a should cost formula in a series of issue papers the Project produced for the Congress:

> There are many elements that go into deriving an appro-priate should-cost formula. For example, industrial engi-neers can judge the efficiency of factory labor by using the concept of "work measurement" and calculating the cost of what is called a "standard hour of output." A standard hour of output is the amount of work that can be reason-ably expected to be performed by an experienced worker in an hour's time. It should be emphasized that the stan-dard hour is a measure of work output and has no neces-sary relationship to time actually expended in doing a job. It is used as a standard for comparing what should reason-ably be accomplished in an hour, versus what is actually accomplished.
> A dollars and cents charge for a standard hour of output is determined by an industrial engineering formula and

those charges may vary from task to task and contractor to contractor. Fitzgerald and his associates have found that the charges the government pays for the standard hour of output for defense contracts are considerably higher that what is charged in the private sector. For example, Dr. Thomas Amlie, one of Fitzgerald's deputies, . . . found that companies in the electronics field charge an average $25 to $35 per standard hour of output. In contrast, the government pays anywhere from $99 to $3300 to defense contractors for comparable output. . . .[12]

It is easy to see why the defense contractors and the status quo in the Pentagon are so vehemently against should cost accounting being implemented as a management tool to see that weapons are priced appropriately. Just as the spare parts scandals illustrate the Pentagon's practice of buying overpriced items, using work measurement and should cost estimating gives management a way of checking that the contractor and the weapons program manager he is working with are charging realistic prices for the weapon. Under the current system it is easy for the contractor and the program manager to say that whatever costs have been incurred are "reasonable."

One of the worst cases Ernie found in his review of contractor plant management involved the Hughes Aircraft Company, which manufactures the Maverick air-to-ground missile for the Air Force. Their standard hour of output was over $3300, and Ernie used that efficiency rating in calculating that it would cost them over $100,000 to make a $400 color television. He found that the plant was taking *seventeen times* longer to build the Maverick than Hughes's *own industrial engineers* had estimated.

Fitzgerald reported these disturbing findings to his superiors, including Secretary of the Air Force Verne Orr, and they initially urged him to continue his investigation on contractor plant efficiency and expand the review to include other defense companies. Senator Grassley, who sits on the Senate Budget

Committee, was also closely following Fitzgerald's work. Grassley saw that work measurement and should cost studies could give members of Congress a gauge by which to judge whether or not the prices the Pentagon was paying were reasonable. If they were, money could be saved without hurting the defense buildup he favors.

As Fitzgerald's analysis began to catch the attention of top-level people in the Air Force management and the Congress, his troubles escalated dramatically. He started to have problems getting access to records to continue his studies, especially at Hughes. Ironically, at first it was not Hughes that was resisting giving him the information he needed; it was the Air Staff and the AFSC (Air Force System Command), the military side of the procurement process, and DCAA. The Air Staff generals began insisting that all Fitzgerald's requests come through them, despite the wording in his court-approved settlement with the Air Force. They, in turn, would delay filling the request until it was too late for the information to be effective or refuse outright to supply it. These actions were a direct challenge to the legislated civilian control of the procurement process since, in this area, Fitzgerald was supposed to have the authority to provide guidance and direction to the Air Staff. This put Fitzgerald in an awkward position: if he insisted that the court order be honored and threatened to go back to court, he would alienate himself from his civilian bosses who would be targeted in a court probe of compliance.

Because Fitzgerald was increasingly being cut off from needed information, the should cost studies lay idle. This concerned Senator Grassley, who wanted to use the information to study procurement problems in the Pentagon, and he began contacting the Secretary of the Air Force and others to see if a satisfactory solution could be found without sending Fitzgerald back to court. Ernie, after years of court battles with the bureaucracy, only wanted to try to implement more effective management of Air Force weapons procurement.

The situation came to a head from an unexpected source. Republican Senator William Roth of Delaware, chairman of the Senate Governmental Affairs Committee, was concerned about the lack of access to records of the Defense Contract Audit Agency (DCAA) because of the highly publicized case of George Spanton's problems as a DCAA auditor. Fitzgerald was also having trouble getting records from DCAA since they were working closely with the Air Staff, so Senator Roth requested that Fitzgerald appear before the committee to tell how, as a civilian productivity manager, he had difficulty with getting cooperation with the DCAA for his investigations.

As with most officials in the Pentagon, Fitzgerald's statement had to go through a security review at the Air Force. Since his testimony did not contain any national security issues, there should have been no problems. But a faction in the Air Force was angry with Fitzgerald's statement because it criticized the DCAA and they refused to clear it. Ernie spent several days negotiating with the faction and thought that he had amended the statement to everyone's satisfaction.

However, on March 1, 1984, ten minutes before the hearing was to begin, the Air Force sent Ernie a note saying that his statement was not approved for release and that he could not testify in his official capacity. He could testify as a private citizen, but the committee wanted him to testify on his lack of access to DCAA records in his official capacity. The Air Force statement defied his court-ordered job description that allowed him to testify to Congress in his official capacity.

Chairman Roth and other members of the committee expressed outrage at the Air Force's suppression of a congressional witness, and the chairman vowed to get to the bottom of the situation. He released the written portion of Fitzgerald's testimony. In the long run, however, Senator Roth did not win. After "negotiations" with the Air Force, he decided that Fitzgerald could testify as a private citizen. Ernie declined to testify because he knew that agreeing to those terms would weaken the credibility of his court-ordered job description. A week later the committee took testimony from General Bernie Weiss, the head of the Air Staff contracting office, who told the committee that he was generally satisfied with the DCAA's performance. The Air Force was able to defy the will of a powerful congressional committee. It was not a good precedent for the members of Congress who were trying to reform the system because the Air Force and the other services would be more likely to ignore or subvert unpalatable congressional requests.

It was the freshman senator from Iowa who finally went eyeball-to-eyeball with the Air Force over Fitzgerald. Realizing that neither the Secretary of the Air Force nor even officials at the White House were going to help Fitzgerald get the needed information, Grassley, as chairman of a small Judiciary Subcommittee on Administrative Practices and Procedures, called for a hearing on the matter. His subcommittee charter allowed him to look at the information flow in the bureaucracy, so the hearings were arranged to investigate information access problems Fitzgerald and Air Force contract manager Ompal Chauhan were having in the Hughes case and others.

The first date on which Fitzgerald was to testify was June 19, 1984. True to form, at the last minute, the Air Force once again refused to clear his statement. A grim and angry Senator Grassley vowed to the packed hearing room and the press that he would see that Fitzgerald testified in his official capacity with his full statement, if he had to resort to a congressional subpoena.

I don't think that the Air Force and the press believed the senator would carry out his threat because of the Roth committee episode. But that same day, Grassley got the votes he needed to subpoena Fitzgerald to testify, got into his orange Chevette with his staff aides Kris Kolesnik and Lisa Hovelson, and drove to the Pentagon to deliver the subpoena himself. The Pentagon press corps got wind that he was arriving to serve the subpoena, so he was met at the Pentagon entrance by a gaggle of about twenty reporters and several television camera crews. With this strange entourage in tow Senator Grassley showed up at Fitzgerald's office to deliver the subpoena to a bemused Ernie.

When the senator and his staff aides returned to the Pentagon parking lot, they found that the Chevette was blocked by another car. This gave the press a chance to corner Grassley for an impromptu news conference while his staff drove the car over the lawn to escape.

Several reporters called me later in the day to express surprise at the gutsy and serious side of this senator they had so underestimated. Many of them in the past had characterized Grassley to me as a bumbling yokel because of his farmer background and his lack of Washington sophistication. I chided them because they had taken a lack of so-called Washington sophistication to be a lack of intelligence and character. Grassley is a true fiscal conservative who, in this instance, could put aside his traditional political allies to make the Pentagon respond as they were constitutionally required to do. I believe in this case he had a refreshing attitude of right and wrong that overshadowed any "Washington sophistication" that I had seen in other politicians. I told the reporters that the so-called sophisticated members of Congress would probably have taken a dive on this issue, and several admitted that I was probably right.

When Ernie finally testified on June 29, 1984, to a packed hearing room, he told a sordid tale of manipulation of the Air Staff and others to prevent any serious examination of the Hughes situation. Every attempt Fitzgerald and his associates made to obtain records was blocked and forced "through channels" until after nearly a year of bureaucratic obfuscation he was told that he could not have a document.

Ernie has a civil service GS-18 rating that puts his civilian authority in the Air Force on the same level as a three-star general, but he was often denied information from colonels and below. Moreover, the final authority of the Pentagon is supposed to be civilian. The worst part was the reluctance and indifference that his civilian superiors showed in getting the military side of the procurement system to cooperate with him. The only way much of the should cost information reached Congress was through Senator Grassley, who instructed his aide to insist that the Air Staff release the information or Grassley would call Secretary Orr or Vice-President Bush. Much to the surprise of the media and other members of Congress, it often worked.

Excerpts from Fitzgerald's testimony:

It had become clear to me that the equivalent cost information, including quantification of efficiency losses, which we obtained routinely on some programs more than 20 years ago, was not going to be brought back to life solely through the efforts of my office. Had it not been for your persistence, Mr. Chairman, and that of your staff, I doubt very much that we would have available to us the enlightening information you now have in your possession. Taken at face value, this information should be viewed as an opportunity to acquire more real defense readiness without bankrupting those taxpayers who remain solvent. We can save billions.[13]

Senator Grassley has held quite a few hearings on whistleblowers and their problems of getting information and action in the bureaucracy, and to his credit, his follow-up has been excellent. His persistence in seeing that the problem is being solved and that his witnesses are not harassed because of their testimony to his committee has shown the difference between a real reformer and a publicity seeker. It has also made the Pentagon realize that he will not accept its runaround about releasing information. He has been more successful than most in obtaining the information necessary to ensure that our defense investment is being used wisely.

The close follow-up is also very important in encouraging

people to come forward with honest testimony. I would have been extremely reluctant to let Airman Thomas Jonsson and Captain Bob Greenstreet testify before a committee that I thought would be interested in only one or two days of publicity. I knew Grassley would do everything possible to make sure these men's charges were followed up and would see that the bureaucracy did not punish them for their testimony.

Ernie, who has experienced Congress's lack of follow-through for years, expressed this sentiment well in his testimony to the Grassley subcommittee:

> In addition to the personal cost involved, a major reason federal government employees are reluctant to reveal embarrassing facts is that it generally does no good. I have seen too many cases of well-meaning government bureaucrats "setting their hair afire," having the news media and the Congress give the matter big play, then after the sensationalism had died down, find that nothing has changed.
>
> In dealing with your subcommittee and its staff, I have found them unusually good at follow-up. I believe that if you persist in your present lines of inquiry, that persistence alone will cause federal government employees to do the right thing more often.[14]

Another congressman who has been willing to demand that the Pentagon show him material that was his right to see is Representative Denny Smith (R-Oregon), who became interested in the effectiveness of the Navy AEGIS battle cruiser. An AEGIS radar-equipped cruiser is supposed to be the "shield of the fleet" in an aircraft carrier group, able to shoot down all incoming missiles and planes. The underground doubts that the AEGIS will ever be effective because of its complicated radar. According to the accounts of several of my sources, Smith had read in *The Wall Street Journal* that the AEGIS had hit thirteen of thirteen targets that shot at it during its most recent tests.[15] As a former Air Force fighter pilot who saw combat in Vietnam,

Smith was impressed by these figures and called the Navy to learn more.

He wrote the appropriate Navy personnel about the AEGIS and received glowing letters about its effectiveness. Then he asked an unforgivable question: to see the actual OPEVAL (operational evaluation) test documents. According to sources, "total panic" broke out among the program personnel of the AEGIS. After stonewalling for a few days, the Navy informed a bewildered Smith that he could not receive the test reports. When he pushed them for an explanation, they knew that they could not cite security reasons since Smith was cleared to see classified documents, so they told him that they were afraid that he might "interpret" the test data in the wrong way.

For the next ten days or so, Smith had an angry exchange of letters "from the bottom to the top" of the Navy. They finally relented and were willing to bring the document over if they also could give him a briefing on the AEGIS. Smith got a full-blown briefing laden with charts and graphs on what a wonderful weapon the AEGIS had become and how successfully it had passed its last set of tests. By this time, our underground had advised a now-suspicious Smith what to specifically ask about the test and which data chart had the information he was looking for. When he asked for that chart during the briefing, one of the briefers blurted out the page number as the other Navy men reacted with horror. It turned out that this damning page was missing from the copy of the test results that the Navy had given Smith. One of the briefers quickly recovered from his shock and assured Smith that there must have been a reproduction mistake.

When Smith finally saw the real test results showing that the AEGIS had really hit only six of twenty-one targets, he went on a rampage to get the truth out.[16] His fellow hawks in Congress tried to dissuade him, but he was extremely angry that the Navy would so blatantly lie and deceive a member of Congress. Although Smith's revelations did not cancel this expensive program, through his public outrage he was able to educate the public and uninitiated members of Congress about how serious the Pentagon's deception of the Congress can be.

Probably the Pentagon's most arrogant reaction to the will of the Congress was not in its refusal to give the Congress needed information but rather in its contempt for the law. It started when I wrote an article for the April 1982 edition of *Reason* magazine on the problems of operational testing in the Pentagon based on my experiences with the M-1 and other weapons. Although the article was not widely publicized, many copies floated around the Pentagon. One day shortly after publication, I received a lunch invitation from Democratic Senator David Pryor of Arkansas. He was concerned about the failures of weapons such as the M-1 battle tank, the M-2 infantry fighting vehicle, and the Maverick anti-tank missile. In the senator's dining room with several of his aides we talked about the Project and the goals of the underground. Near the end of the meal, the senator looked me directly in the eyes and proclaimed, "Dina, I want to *do* something about this! What do you suggest?"

I pulled out a copy of the *Reason* article and told him to read it and think about devising legislation making the operational testing of weapons independent from the developers of the weapons in the Pentagon. He promised to read the article and get back to me. I had asked him to do a rather controversial and difficult task, so I was not sure I would hear from him at all.

To my surprise, he called me a few days later and asked me to suggest how such an office for operational testing should be set up in the DOD and what jurisdiction the head of the office would need to prevent defective weapons from reaching the battlefield. This was one of the first times a member of Congress asked the Project's advice on legislation, and I went back to members of the underground who had urged me to write the testing article and told them that they now had the chance to design an office that would help ease the weapon failure problem. The proposed legislation had to be written as tightly as possible because the underground knew that the Pentagon would try to slip through any loophole we might accidentally put in.

After the initial legislation was written, I had the members of the underground work directly with Senator Pryor and his staff with the understanding that they would remain anonymous. It took almost a year for the draft legislation to wind its way through the system, but during that time it picked up some powerful cosponsors such as Republican Senator William Roth of Delaware and the then cochair of the Military Reform Caucus, Republican Senator Nancy Kassebaum of Kansas. The Pentagon vehemently denounced the bill, but to our amazement it passed both houses of Congress by an overwhelming margin in the late summer of 1983.

The testing law called for the DOD to set up the new Operational Testing Office and appoint an Assistant Secretary of Defense as director by November 1, 1983. The DOD delayed implementation of the law by pleading that they were writing a charter for the new office and looking for suitable candidates to head the office. The sponsors of the bill, especially Senator Kassebaum, urged that the interested members of Congress work with the Pentagon to implement the legislation and to give the system a chance to work. The sponsors wrote congenial letters urging the Secretary of Defense to make sure the law was complied with as soon as possible.

The Pentagon soon gave this spirit of cooperation a slap in the face. Hoping their activity would not be noticed, the budget writers of the DOD did not request any operating funds for the new testing office for fiscal 1985 in their January 1984 budget request to Congress. Instead they gave the developmental testing section, which was left under the developers of the weapons, the money that should have gone for the new operational office. In other words, the office would exist legislatively but would not receive any appropriated funds to run it and pay salaries. Lost in the enormous process of trying to pass around a $300 billion defense budget, the cut might have gone through unnoticed if not for the sharp eyes of a couple of congressional aides.

The bill's sponsors were furious and declared war on the Pentagon for so blatantly trying to subvert a law. The Pentagon, after a few false starts, insisted that the office's lack of funding was just an oversight. The funds were restored by the Congress, yet on November 1, *1984,* one year after the office was supposed to be in operation, the DOD had hired only half the people mandated and had appointed a military officer to temporarily head the office. (The law called for the office to be headed by a civilian. The DOD sent a nomination for the head of the office to the Congress in early 1985, yet the concept of an independent test office had been languishing for over a year after its congressionally mandated startup.) Finally, in March 1985, the DOD nominated and the Senate accepted John Krings, a former McDonnell Douglas test pilot, as the Director of the Independent Operational Test and Evaluation Office.

The U.S. Constitution calls for the Congress "To raise and support Armies, but no Appropriation of Money to that Use shall be for a longer Term than two Years; To provide and maintain a Navy; To make Rules for the Government and Regulation of the land and naval Forces." What the American public has to decide is how they want their elected representatives to "raise and support" a military to provide national defense and how much control the Congress should exercise over this powerful defense bureaucracy.

Procedural reforms passed by the Congress to change the way the Pentagon does business can have a positive effect. But every reform that the bureaucracy "deforms" for its own self-protection hurts the credibility of the Congress to enforce its will on the Pentagon. These reforms must be backed up by a tough, no-nonsense attitude accompanied by a power that only the Congress has over the Pentagon—the power of the purse.

If Congress is serious about reducing the overspending habits of defense and the resultant inferior weapons, they must be prepared to make the politically hard decisions to withhold or eliminate funds to pet Pentagon programs that are wasteful or ineffective. The careful control of the flow of the money for a program is what convinces a program manager and his service secretary that Congress is to be reckoned with. Congress can "fence" (withhold a certain portion of a program budget) until the Pentagon either proves that a defective weapon has been fixed or that a program whose costs are out of control has been brought under good management.

But Congress must also be willing to cancel programs that are failing or are ill conceived, no matter what the pork barrel politics are, and use management controls to find what a program should reasonably cost and refuse to pay any higher price or overruns. The Pentagon can no longer be trusted with the simple plea to trust them, as the examples in this book have shown.

The Congress must have the political will to cut the overall defense budget and reject the argument that the budget must go up every year for national security reasons. As I have tried to show, more money does not necessarily provide more defense. Ernie has likened giving more and more unchecked money to the Pentagon to "prescribing the financial equivalent of more booze for an alcoholic with the shakes on a fifth a day."[17] However, this political will cannot be achieved without the public's involvement.

In the past, the public has generally rewarded their member of Congress for "bringing home the bacon" in the form of defense pork barrel for their state or district. But that attitude is changing slightly as exposés show how damaging that system is to military effectiveness. Ironically, according to a study done by the Employment Research Associates in Lansing, Michigan, 320 of 435 congressional districts actually pay more in taxes for this defense than they get back in defense contracts. The states that have more money than they pay out are a few large states such as Virginia and California. So the pork-barrel-based defense system is really not an economic bargain for most. It hurts the national security and increases the debt unnecessarily.

This pork barrel system must change. The task is enormous because it has been many years in the making and it is hard to get any one member of the three-ring circus to be the first to stop. Congress will not begin to change unless the public is informed enough about the damaging effects of the current weapons procurement system to pressure it to try another way.

The Project was founded on the idea of making that type of information available to the public, and it is one of my most important yet personally difficult responsibilities.

9.

BEYOND THE BELTWAY

THERE IS A POPULAR ADVERTISEMENT in Washington, D.C., for the Riggs Bank. It begins with a tuneful melody and shows scenes of Washington interspersed with pictures of professional people arriving by plane and helicopter. It ends with the slogan, "Riggs, the most important bank in the most important city of the world."

This advertisement has been so popular that even the local television news have done features on its effect on local Washingtonians. To me, it also symbolizes how many people who work in Washington see themselves—as the most important people of the most important city of the world. Many in Washington believe the rest of the people in the country, "beyond the beltway" (the freeway that surrounds metropolitan Washington), need the people in Washington to help run their lives and guide the country. In fact, bureaucrats in Washington sometimes feel that what the country doesn't know won't hurt it, that the population beyond the beltway is incapable of understanding the complexities of government and should leave the decision-making to the "professionals."

Unfortunately this prejudice has even infected some of the self-appointed "intellectuals" in the Pentagon underground. One of them cornered me once at a party and chided me for trying to take some of the military reform issues to a public that could not understand them. He told me that it was much more important for the "defense intellectuals" in the Washington inner circle to solve the procurement and tactic problems of the Pentagon.

I reminded him that many defense intellectuals were the ones who had contributed to this defense procurement mess in the first place, and most of the defense problems could be solved with plain common sense and a clear perspective of right and wrong. I remarked that I had not seen a lot of that in Washington. I also told him that I hoped that I was still considered part of the "great unwashed" public who believe in citizen participation and democracy. Needless to say, he and others in that faction of the underground are still disturbed that I am informing the public on how and why we procure our defense.

For the most part, however, the Pentagon underground understands the great importance of the public's comprehension of where their defense tax money goes and how it affects their national security. Reaching the public in an effective and comprehensible way has been the Project's hardest and most important challenge. Luckily, my staff members Joe Burniece, Paul Hoven, Marsha Cunningham, Tim McCune, and Juli Carter all feel strongly about the public's right to know this information and the ability of the average citizen to decide for him- or herself.

There have been several methods and strategies for getting this information to the public. Our biggest challenge was for me to convince myself, the reporters, and eventually the public that the procurement racket in Washington is not too difficult to understand, and that it is the Pentagon and its protectors who purposely try to make the issues appear too complicated. The "less bang" underground and my staffers Joe and Paul convinced me that I could understand how tanks perform on the battlefield and other concepts. I was skeptical at first since I had no background in the area, but I soon found that much strategy is based on common sense and instinct, not complicated scientific and logical explanations. It made sense because much of warfare is fought by the common man and war is an emotional and intuitive endeavor.

The "more bucks" underground, especially Ernie Fitzgerald, helped me understand the seemingly complicated procurement process and convinced me that most people should be able to understand overspending if it is compared to something they can understand, such as spare parts. This underground showed me that although the procurement people can sit down with spreadsheets and economic formulas that will glaze the eyes of the uninitiated, they cannot answer some basic questions if the program is in economic trouble.

Shortly after the first exposés of the M-1 tank and the cruise missiles in late 1981, I received a call from Stephen Webbe of *The Christian Science Monitor.* I had worked with him on several projects over the previous months, but his request took me by surprise. He wanted to do a personal profile on me and my work at the Project. My first reaction was negative, and I told him that I would have to think about it and call him back.

I knew the positive aspects of having the Project profiled: it would definitely help us raise money to continue the Project and it would let other underground people who have no place to turn know we exist. But even with those positive aspects, I was extremely reluctant to allow a personal profile to be published. I felt that it was an invasion of my privacy and would focus attention on me rather than the issues.

I called Ernie at the Pentagon and asked him what he thought I should do. "Dina," he said, "you're the classic dog-playing-chess story, you'd better decide what you want to do because you are going to get more and more requests for this type of story." As a journalist I knew he was right: I am a journalistically attractive story because I am a young woman in a field of older men. Still, the idea of having people read about me hit a very negative chord.

In the end, after talking it over with my husband, I decided to put aside my personal feelings and do everything I could to get the underground's message to the public. If that meant attracting the reader to the subject of military reform through curiosity about my unusual profession, I would have to consider that part of my job. I reasoned that since my sources had to live with the distasteful task of putting their careers on the line every time they released a document to me, the least I could do was to put up with the invasion of my privacy. I had purposely put myself in the role of the front for these people; it was part of my responsibilities.

That decision has been very good for the cause of the underground, and I am glad I've learned to live with the consequences, despite my fear of appearing in public and on national television.

The biggest thrill since I started the Project had to be the filming of Bill Moyers's CBS show on the Pentagon underground. In early 1983, I was approached by Leslie Cockburn, a producer for Bill Moyers, about my ideas for questions and the focus for an interview that Moyers had secured with Caspar Weinberger, the Secretary of Defense. I gave her a few ideas over lunch and thought that would be the end of my involvement in the show. But a few weeks later, Leslie called and asked me out to lunch again to tell me that she, Bill Moyers, and his executive producer, Andrew Lack, wanted to contrast how Caspar Weinberger gets his information on defense procurement matters with how Dina Rasor gets her information on procurement from the underground.

I could hardly believe what she was saying. I was possibly doing a show on the Project with *60 Minutes*. Although reporter Ed Bradley was committed to doing a segment pitting me against the DOD Inspector General Joseph Sherrick, the producer of the segment, Monika Jensen, had told me that she could not make me credible on television against Sherrick. Now Leslie was telling me that Bill Moyers wanted to pit me against the Secretary of Defense!

I had to decide which show to do and whether I wanted to be put up against the Secretary of Defense (a terrifying prospect). I went with the Moyers show for several reasons. I knew the Moyers show would have thirty minutes instead of ten to seventeen minutes on *60 Minutes* to tell the underground's story, and the underground's information would be challenging the Secretary of Defense's word instead of the DOD Inspector General's. The only drawback with the Moyers show was that it was not watched by as many people as *60 Minutes*. But my gut feeling was that the underground's message needed the extra airtime to be told correctly.

Of course, doing either show was a risk because I did not have any control over the outcome and the editing of my interviews. But even though some members of the underground were naturally skeptical of what the television producers might do, I felt we had to take this risk to try to bring the underground's message to as many people as possible.

In late March 1983, Bill Moyers and his production crew spent three days in our office observing how the Project works with the underground. His producer, Leslie Cockburn, and her assistant had already spent several months poring over our documentation and gathering information from the DOD. Although my staff and I were nervous the first day he arrived, I was impressed with Moyers and his unpretentious manner as he observed our operations. Our small two-room office was swallowed up quickly with camera gear, cameramen, and sound men, but Moyers did his best to make us feel comfortable during the interviews. Having been exposed to some egotistical "star" type reporters at ABC when I worked there, it was nice to see a television personality act more like a normal reporter. Shortly before my interview, he asked to use one of our typewriters and proceeded to type out his own questions.

His interviews were tough and exhausting. He interviewed Paul Hoven and me for several hours and then finished his three days with a three-hour interview with me. He told me ahead of time, just as he had Caspar Weinberger, that he would ask me about five specific weapon systems. I was glad that both sides had the same information before we sat down to the interview. I did not want the Pentagon personnel to accuse us of helping CBS ambush an unsuspecting Secretary of Defense. I knew that Weinberger could not have an intimate knowledge of all the weapon systems he oversees, and I thought it was fair that he knew specifically what areas would be covered so that his staff could prepare him.

I felt that I had done well in the interview, but because I was so nervous, the whole interview remains foggy in my memory. The show was taped at the end of March and aired July 19, 1983. That three-month wait was one of the few times that I allowed myself to succumb to extreme nervousness. I was very concerned about my remarks being pitted against those of the Secretary of Defense and his advisors. I know that my staff was frustrated by my preoccupation with the show, and my husband had to keep reminding me that I had the Pentagon's own documentation to back up my claims. That thought helped me a little, but I felt that Weinberger would be articulate and convincing.

To my astonishment, the Secretary of Defense fared rather poorly on the show. When confronted with facts from the Army's own documents, he appeared confused and his defensive statements did not make much sense. Although the Project's supporters, the underground, and I were pleased that the program fairly reported the Pentagon underground's information, it was disconcerting to me to see the Secretary of Defense so uninformed on these military subjects. It bothered me even more when I realized that he and his staff had adequate time to master them. His reaction really matched

Ernie's description of the top officials being "the dark at the top of the stairs."

Excerpts from the show include:

MOYERS: So no weapon can be cut. Or should be—

WEINBERGER: Well there may be—may well be some and when you get your evaluation test in if you find that they're not up to specification then you cancel them.

MOYERS: Do you trust your evaluation tests?

WEINBERGER: Yes, we trust it—

MOYERS: Do you think you're getting the information from the bottom up?

WEINBERGER: We certainly do and particularly when you get as many ahh triangulations on it by having various other groups look at it and give you these tests . . . the M-1 tank. That took twenty years to develop. I couldn't possibly defend that. I think that's a—that is absolutely wrong.

MOYERS: You don't like the M-1 tank?

WEINBERGER: The tank is fine. But it shouldn't have taken twenty years to develop it and it shouldn't have cost as much to do that.

MOYERS: I'm told that this is a tank that only gets about five and one half gallons to the mile and that sometimes to change the oil you literally lift the engine out. If the Soviets were to strike, wouldn't that be a problem for the fighting man in the field?

WEINBERGER: No, we have, your—actually one of the things that makes the tank expensive and took so long is to get greater speed and a greater ability to operate in all kinds of terrain and also at night and as far as the oil change is concerned there are all kinds of maintenance vehicles and maintenance procedures that go along with it that keep this tank in service a great many more days and more hours than its predecessor as certainly should be the case—

MOYERS: But with all due respect isn't that one of the things where the critics deserve to be heard when they say that yes, you develop a tank like this but you then have to multiply the number of support vehicles until you have in the field a detriment instead of an offensive advantage?

WEINBERGER: They certainly should be heard to make that point and they certainly are heard to make that point. In fact sometimes I think that's all that is heard.[1]

In the end, the work on the Moyers show was worthwhile because an estimated 20 million Americans saw it, many more people than we could have reached through newspapers. The show was a heady experience for me—and one of the few times I allowed myself to be very satisfied with what the Project had accomplished on very small operating budgets. That experience was short-lived as the deluge of documents continued, showing us how much work there was left to do.

Over the past four years, I have noticed a distinct change in the public's knowledge and attitude toward waste in the Pentagon and ineffective weapons. When I began to do radio talk shows about four years ago, most of the listeners couldn't believe what I was telling them about military procurement and weapons and seemed more comfortable talking about foreign policy.

Now, most of my audience at these talk shows understand that the Pentagon is as capable of waste as any other government agency and they are usually outraged about some spare parts scandal they read about in the paper. The Thomas Jonsson $7622 ten-cup coffee brewer on the C-5A has been one of the most common examples given by the listeners. They understand that military spending does not necessarily reflect a foreign threat or a legitimate national security need.

The most effective exposés the Project has done to help

change public attitudes are the spare parts scandals. The members of the underground, who decided that the spares scandal would be effective because it gave the public a reference point by which they could measure prices for themselves, read the situation perfectly.

Now the Project's job is to show the news media and the public that the impressive fighter that they see flying overhead is just as overpriced as the nut or bolt that outraged them, because the same pricing formulas were used. The Pentagon is trying hard to tell the public that that is not true, but the evidence shows that it is.

I have heard from congressional aides that the waste exposés generated by the Project and elsewhere have started a public movement to pressure the Congress into changing the business-as-usual procurement policies. On December 16, 1984, a *The Washington Post* reported a Senate aide's assessment of the changing attitude in the Congress toward defense spending:

> As deficits mushroom, Congress pulled in the reins over the last two years. "The bloom has been off the rose for some time." said a key Senate Republican aide. "In 1982, when there was a move afoot to cut defense spending, there were no repercussions in the electorate.
>
> "Public sentiment has changed dramatically," said this official, who asked not to be identified. "Defense spending was not an issue in the [congressional] campaigns this year. Nobody cared how you voted on defense. They asked, 'Are you throwing money down a rathole?'
>
> "No one I knew was defeated on how many F-18's we should buy, how many nuclear aircraft carriers we should build," he said. "People are now persuaded that there is so much waste, they are putting pressure on their congressmen—that's what you are seeing now."

The underground has been encouraged by the public's reaction to their stories, but we all realize that the exposés must continue to show that the procurement system is not working toward a better defense. That is the main purpose of the Project —to be a place where the underground can come with good, solid documentation to have their stories told.

The ideal goal of the Project is to go out of business because the system has reformed itself enough internally, and the underground can expose a scandal within the Pentagon and have it heal itself. That attitude helps us focus on our mission rather than just trying to preserve a job.

Reforming the Pentagon will take more than the Congress passing procedural reforms because the bureaucracy will immediately try to "deform" them. But Congress can institute reforms to begin to change the incentive system now used by the Pentagon procurement people. In 1983 the Project listed in *More Bucks, Less Bang* the most realistic reforms that the underground believed could bring meaningful change if properly implemented:

—Mandate that the present 6% competitive procurement in DOD be slowly increased each year by say, one-quarter, until 70% of all procurement is based on competitive bids. As an incentive, non-competitive procurement would be cut back proportionally in any year that the Pentagon fails to write enough competitive contracts to reach the mandated percentage. [Senator Grassley has introduced similar legislation in the Senate.]

—To go along with the increased competition among suppliers, maximize constructive bureaucratic competition within the Department. Organize the Pentagon so that the military services compete openly and directly for as many missions as possible (for example, infantry, close air support, naval air patrolling and mining, etc.). Make sure that at least two research centers or arsenals are competing in the development of every major class of weapons.

—Legislate an independent operational testing office, reporting *directly* to the Secretary of Defense instead of reporting through the official in charge of all development programs. [As you know, a similar bill was introduced by Senator Pryor and was passed.]

—Pass a law to forbid any form of employment, including consultancies, of retired general officers by any defense contractor and permanently strip rank and retirement pay from any general officer financially involved with a defense contractor. [NOTE: Congresswoman Barbara Boxer has introduced similar legislation in the Congress, but her bill places the penalties on the contractors if they hire retired officers for a period of five years. The penalties would include, among others, the loss of government contracts.]

—Recognize the very special status and responsibilities of companies selling weapons to the U.S. government by forbidding them to use taxpayer money to influence their government—under pain of mandatory cancellation of all their defense contracts. Specifically, make it illegal for defense contractors to contribute, directly or indirectly, to any political campaign or any non-profit organization involved in national security.

—Recognize that adding money to the defense budget makes it impossible to cure these fundamental problems and therefore makes it impossible to achieve even minimally adequate defense. Adding 5% to last year's defense budget, even though the Administration demands 10%, is still an increase, not a cut—despite all the political rhetoric by a Congressional opposition pretending to be tough on the defense budget.

—In bringing the defense budget under some modicum of control, under no circumstances should the Congress follow the easy road of shaving away at training and ammunition accounts or of stretching procurement programs—as was done by the Congress in fiscal 1983 and by the Administration in its proposed fiscal 1984 budget.

—Nothing is as important as eliminating the grossly excessive numbers of senior officer positions as well as the cancerous growth in headquarter personnel—at least one out of every three people in the Defense Department are in a headquarters or in direct support of a headquarters.[2]

The Pentagon must be willing to cut weapons that are not working, however painful that may be. The attitude that bad test results don't count and more money will fix a fundamentally flawed weapon means that inferior weapons will continue to be sent to our troops in the field. The Pentagon must also adopt realistic pricing policies for weapons by submitting the programs for cost studies that will show an acceptable price. The service secretaries must be willing to cut the budget to a more realistic level for each weapon, no matter what the program manager says. This is an extremely hard request for a bureaucracy because the system is set up to promote the program manager who obtains the largest budget for his program and has the largest staff.

To truly change the current procurement system, the Pentagon has to change internally its employee incentive system. One way would be to publicly reward and promote program managers who find innovative and competitive ways to save money. I believe the only way the Pentagon will change this system is by extreme congressional and public pressure supplemented by realistic budget cuts.

The Pentagon and members of the executive branch must be convinced that Congress is serious about reform. Congress has to clean up the way it appropriates money for the national defense. The first job of Congress is to make blatant pork barrel politics in weapons buying a shameful thing rather than something to boast about to constituents back home. And that will not happen until the voters stop electing politicians who "bring home the bacon" in lucrative but corrupt defense contracts.

Congress must also back up its members who go one-on-one with the Pentagon bureaucracy and demand vital decision-making information, and those members who protect whistle-blowers. The public is already beginning to reward these brave politicians. The Congressmen I've mentioned who fought the Pentagon were all reelected in 1984. Senator Grassley was not up for reelection, but according to his staff, during his most controversial showdowns with the Pentagon, the senator's approval rating in the polls went from 40 percent to 70 percent.

Congress must acquire the political strength to cancel weapon systems that are proving to be duds, even if the Pentagon is unwilling to do so. It must be willing to prevent a bad weapon from reaching the battlefield, no matter what pork barrel politics are involved. It must cut the budget, not just reduce the increase in the defense budget to force the Pentagon into a cost-efficient system instead of continuing to throw good money into a bad system. Perhaps the enormous federal deficit will encourage congressional action in this area.

However, none of these needed reforms has a chance unless the public remains informed on the subject and demands accountability from their government. For in the end, the responsibility for the effective procurement of our national defense lies not only with the Pentagon and the Congress but with the public as well. The procurement system is sick, and the public must be willing to ensure that the necessary reforms are carried out.

Whenever I make a speech, one of the most common questions is, "What can we as citizens do about this problem?" Although the Project does not actively lobby Congress, I give these few suggestions:

—Be informed on the subject. There are now many stories on spare parts scandals, failed weapon systems, and contractor kickback schemes in the major newspapers and wire services in the country. If you see these stories on television or in news magazines and your local paper does not carry them often, call up the editor and ask him why not. Most small papers get the wire services from the major city papers.

—If you are angry after reading one of these stories, cut the story out of your paper and send it to your congressman and senator with a thoughtful letter on why this concerns you. End the letter by asking what *he* is going to try to do about the problem. Don't accept a vague form letter back. If you receive one, write again and tell him that you want a direct answer. If you are unsatisfied with that response, call the local office and set up an appointment with the member until he gives you a straight answer. Don't assume that sending an article and a letter doesn't work. I have gotten this advice from congressional staff aides who maintain that the member of Congress is concerned when a constituent writes in about something he or she has read in the local paper and just a few of these letters will get the congressman's attention.

—Don't vote for any politician who brags about the defense dollars that he brings into your state or district. As long as members of Congress think that pork barrel is an effective way to get votes, regardless of whether or not the money is spent efficiently, we will continue to see the type of back-room deals that surfaced in the C-5 lobby plan. It would be naïve to think that pork barrel politics will disappear, but the public should become more aware of its harmful side effects on national defense and discourage it.

For over four years the Pentagon underground through the Project on Military Procurement has tried to inform the press, members of Congress, and the public about how the American military procurement system is not working to the benefit of the country. All in all, our effort has been fairly successful and we will continue to bring the underground's message out in the open.

But that is only half the job. The American people and their government, armed with this information, must decide whether they have the political will to change a very entrenched system or whether they will allow the system to continue to spend more of their money while providing less true defense.

NOTES

MOST of the following documentation is in the Project's files and is available upon request—except to foreign governments.

1. Breakthrough

1. "For official use only" is an administrative restriction that has no criminal liabilities for its release.
2. This OT II test was an extension of the original OT II test to try to see if the reliability problems were fixed after the original OT II.
3. Scoring conference, OT II, p. 2-14. At the time of the OT II test, the evaluation of the test numbers was done by a group of various commands called a scoring conference. The Army has since changed the name. Numbers of the scoring conference are from the OT II test results document named in Chapter 1.
4. 50 percent power train requirement, OT II, p. 1-8. That 22 percent number was based upon the Army's own generous scoring method, which has been described earlier.
5. Leaking hydraulic fluid, OT II, pp. 2-26, 2-93, A-119, and A-122; commander machine gun, OT II, pp. A-37 and A-112; track life and problems, OT II, pp. 1-8, 1-9, 2-26, and 2-93; bad ventilation, OT II, pp. A-119 and A-122; air filter problems, OT II, pp. 1-8 and A-105; flammable hydraulic fluid: An Israeli tank commander who

had fought in the 1967 and 1973 Mideast wars told my source and
me in 1981 that he thought that 300 of the 800 tank crew mem-
bers killed in tanks died because of burning hydraulic fluid. There
are alternatives to the flammable type of hydraulic fluid that the
Army uses, as outlined in a Jan. 8, 1981, story in *The Christian
Science Monitor* by Stephen Webbe, blind spot, OT II, p. A-36; fuel
consumption, OT II, p. 1-7; hand-hold problem, OT II, pp. A-36,
A-116, and A-122. ABC News *20/20*, Jan. 10, 1980, produced by
Andrew Cockburn. During World War II, tank battles in North
Africa, the Ardennes, and the Heurtgen Forest were lost due to
fuel shortages.

6. First operational test of the M-1 was called Independent Evaluation Report: XM-1, 1978.
7. According to the *Baltimore Sun*, Nov. 6, 1981, the M-1 was deployed in Europe in October–November 1981.
8. Information on the M-1 scheduling problems was compiled by
   Senator Mark Hatfield's staff on the Senate Appropriations Committee, among others. Available upon request.
9. The Army rebuttal package was given out to reporters at the
   Pentagon. The main rebuttal paper was titled "DAMA-WSW April
   25, 1981."
10. I have never been able to track down how the Army came to that
    54 percent figure in light of the OT II test document figure of 22
    percent and the Charles Murphy report figure of 19 percent. On
    page 2 of the Army rebuttal, they peg the optimistic number to
    their "analysis" of the Fort Knox test results. We stuck to the test
    director's scoring of the actual failures.
11. Army Dept. Chief of Staff for Logistics, "Army Logistics Report on
    XM-1," 1979.
12. *Ibid.*
13. *Ibid.*, p. 19; *Ibid.*, p. 26.
14. When released, the report title was "Logistics Planning for the
    XM-1 Tank: Implications for Reduced Readiness and Increased
    Support Costs" PLRD-81-33, July 1, 1981.
15. Statements taken from Senate Appropriations Subcommittee on
    Defense hearings June 17, 1981.
16. OT II had pictures of the M-1 instrument panel, highlighting some
    of its problems, OT II, pp. A-35, A-5, and A-120.
17. Track problems, OT II, pp. 1-8, 1-9, 2-26, and 2-93.
18. Problems of height of driver and driving M-1, OT II, pp. A-36 and
    A-119; stabilization switch, OT II, p. A-37; also ABC News *20/20*,
    Jan. 10, 1980.
19. Ammunition door problems, OT II, pp. A-36, A-117, and A-122.
20. George Forty, *Chieftain* (New York: Charles Scribner's Sons,
    1979), p. 20.

21. Loader machine gun mount, OT II, p. A-116. OT II had many other incidences of poor-quality metal and material in the M-1 tank. Hand holds, OT II, pp. A-36, A-116, and A-122.
22. *Defense Week*, June 29, 1981, p. 10.
23. Maintenance manuals, OT II, p. 2-42. Several of my sources had also reported back to me that the maintenance manuals were too complex and had to be rewritten.
24. Asbestos mittens, OT II, pp. A-38, A-105, and A-123. In OT II the crew complained that even asbestos mittens did not work well on the hot engine and they worried about working on the hot engine in an emergency situation.
25. I have a notarized memorandum for the record on Mr. Tatarintev's visit.

2. Background

1. My many thanks to Mary Faux of ABC for getting me past the receptionist there.
2. Coal Commission book is The President's Commission on Coal, John D. Rockefeller IV, Chairman, *The American Coal Miner: A Report on Community and Living Conditions in the Coalfields.* (Washington, D.C., 1980).

3. The Mentor

1. GAO, LCD-75-204, "Airlift Operations of the Military Airlift Command During the 1973 Middle East War." April 16, 1975.
2. GAO, PSAD-76-148, "Information on the Requirement for Strategic Airlift." June 8, 1976.
3. The APEX report was an internal engineering report for the Air Force. C-5A report by the House Appropriations Survey and Investigations Staff, January 1980.
4. For details on the 1971 engineering report, see Jack Anderson's column in *The Washington Post,* July 27, 1979.
5. Statement taken from House Armed Services Committee testimony, March 14, 1980.
6. Senator Nunn's remark taken from *NBC Magazine* show broadcast, March 29, 1980.
7. Competition Feasibility Study—C-5A Plan "H" Modification, U.S. Air Force, Headquarters Aeronautical Systems Division, Wright-Patterson Air Force Base (Dayton, Ohio), February 15, 1975, 29 pp.
8. Taken from statement of Dr. Paul Paris, Joint Economic Committee hearing on August 25, 1980.

9. Statement taken from Joint Economic Committee hearing on Aug. 25, 1980.
10. Dina Rasor, ed., *More Bucks, Less Bang: How the Pentagon Buys Ineffective Weapons.* (Washington, D.C.: Fund for Constitutional Government, 1983), p. 301.
11. Ernest Fitzgerald's statements at Taxpayers Foundation conference taken from conference tapes.
12. Statement of Ernest Fitzgerald taken from Senate Judiciary Subcommittee on Administrative Practices and Procedures, June 19, 1984.

4. The Experiment

1. The Project had the GAO "sanitize" five reports on the cruise missile in 1981 and 1982. Their titles are:
C-PSAD-80-19, "Cruise Missile: Status and Issues as They Near Production." Feb. 28, 1980.
C-MASAD-81-11, "Issues Affecting the Navy's Anti-Ship Cruise Missiles." Feb. 28, 1981.
C-MASAD-81-9, "Some Land Attack Cruise Missile Acquisition Programs Need to Be Slowed Down." Feb. 28, 1981.
C-MASAD-82-13, "Air Launched Cruise Missile Shows Promise But Problems Could Result in Operational Limitations." Feb. 26, 1982.
C-MASAD-82-15, "Defense Plans to Deploy Some Cruise Missiles Before They Are Ready." Feb. 26, 1982.
2. Pierre Sprey quotation taken from conference transcript.
3. Dina Rasor, ed., *More Bucks, Less Bang* (Washington, D.C.: Fund for Constitutional Government, 1983), p. 302.
4. Stories on the Project appeared in the *Chicago Sun-Times,* March 24, 1982, *The Washington Monthly,* May 1982, and *Human Events,* May 22, 1982.

5. Fooling All of the People All of the Time

1. John Fialka, "Embattled Weapon," *The Wall Street Journal,* Feb. 17, 1982.
2. Procurement process quotation taken from Dina Rasor, "Fighting with Failures," *Reason* magazine, April 1982.
3. Battista quote taken from "The Maverick Missile: If at First You Don't Succeed . . .," in Dina Rasor, ed., *More Bucks, Less Bang* (Washington, D.C.: Fund for Constitutional Government, 1983) p. 157.

4. Murray statement from testimony to Senate Governmental Affairs Committee, October 1981.
5. Note that the 1979 Copperhead test results quoted were the Army's last *operational* test on the Copperhead. Points on Copperhead problems taken from the Project on Military Procurement's analysis based on test documents and literature on northern Europe cloud cover released to the press on April 6, 1983.
6. Background on Copperhead's past problems based upon numerous news accounts.
7. "The Maverick Missile," *op. cit.* The Project on Military Procurement also had congressional testimony and internal DOD documents on which this article is based.
8. *Ibid.*
9. GAO, PLRD-82-45, "Reporting Competition in Defense Procurements—Recent Changes Are Misleading." March 8, 1982. Murray Weidenbaum, *The Christian Science Monitor*, March 23, 1984.
10. GAO report.
11. Defense Procurement Information Paper, prepared by Donna Martin, Project on Military Procurement, August 1984.
12. *Ibid.*
13. Memorandum by Dr. Thomas Amlie, Assistant for Technical Systems, Deputy Secretary of the Air Force for Financial Management, to Dr. Probus, OASN, Sept. 14, 1983.
14. Thomas Lawson, "Officer Inflation: Its Cost to the Taxpayer and Military Effectiveness." (Washington, D.C.: Project on Military Procurement, 1983).
15. Air Force Ad Hoc Pricing Review Team report on Pratt & Whitney's thirty-four overpriced spare parts, Fall 1982–Winter 1983.
16. Air Force statement taken from various press accounts and Project on Military Procurement Defense Information Papers, August 1984, p. 24.
17. Navy statement from *Ibid.*, p. 27.
18. The original audit report on the hammer was entitled "An Audit on Contractor Support at Naval Air Station, Whitney Field, Milton, Fla." and was dated May 27, 1983. The audit report that overturned the original audit was from the same base and was dated July 13, 1983. Both documents available upon request. The press conference mentioned took place on Aug. 13, 1983 and Clark Mollenhoff of the *Washington Times* wrote about the incident on Aug. 15, 1984. Boeing stool cap example, Project on Military Procurement, Defense Procurement Issues Papers, August 1984, pp. 28–29.
19. *Ibid.*, pp. 23–29.

6. The Underground

1. Gregg Easterbrook, "DIVAD," *The Atlantic Monthly,* October 1983.
2. Business Executives for National Security, Inc., National Security and the Federal Budget. January 1985, 15 pp.
3. Dina Rasor, ed., *More Bucks, Less Bang.* (Washington, D.C.: Fund for Constitutional Government, 1983), p. 3.
4. Spanton case information taken from an investigation by Donna Martin, outlined in Defense Procurement Information Papers, Project on Military Procurement, August 1984.
5. Rickover quote taken from Ernest Fitzgerald, *The High Priests of Waste* (New York: Norton Press, 1973), p. 398.
6. O'Connor quotation taken from *The Washington Post,* July 17, 1984.
7. *Conservative Digest,* November 1983.

7. The Press

1. *The Wall Street Journal,* Sept. 20, 1982.
2. *Chicago Sun-Times,* Oct. 9, 1982.

8. The Congress

1. Defense Budget figures taken from *Philadelphia Inquirer,* Jan. 29, 1983, story by Frank Greves. Senator Tower's letter and response to it based on news articles, particularly *The New York Times,* March 2, 1983.
2. *Defense Week* had one of the first stories on the C-5B purchase on Jan. 20, 1982.
3. 14 percent of spare parts budget memo sent from General W.H.L. Mullins to Air Force Chief of Staff Lew Allen. Peacetime operations problem letter from Major General Perry M. Smith to James Wade, Deputy Secretary of Defense for Research and Engineering.
4. The Verne Orr briefing is on file at the Project on Military Procurement.
5. The information on Andrew Young is based on Fred Kaplin, "The Flying Lazarus," *The Washington Monthly,* February 1983.
6. *The Washington Post,* June 22, 1982; *Boston Globe,* June 22, 1982; *San Jose Mercury,* June 22, 1982.
7. The schedule slippage documents are on file at the Project on Military Procurement.

8. The law against government agencies lobbying, 18 U.S.C. 1913, reads:

Lobbying with appropriated moneys

No part of the money appropriated by any enactment of Congress shall, in the absence of express authorization by Congress, be used directly or indirectly to pay for any personal service, advertisement, telegram, telephone, letter, printed or written matter, or other device, intended or designed to influence in any manner a Member of Congress, to favor or oppose, by vote or otherwise, any legislation or appropriation by Congress, whether before or after the introduction of any bill or resolution proposing such legislation or appropriation; but this shall not prevent officers or employees of the United States or of its departments or agencies from communicating to Members of Congress on the request of any Member or to Congress, through the proper official channels, requests for legislation or appropriations which they deem necessary for the efficient conduct of the public business.

Whoever, being an officer or employee of the United States or of any department or agency thereof, violates or attempts to violate this section, shall be fined not more than $500 or imprisoned not more than one year, or both; and after notice and hearing by the superior officer vested with the power of removing him, shall be removed from office or employment. (June 25, 1948, ch 645, § 1, 62 Stat. 792.)

9. Kaplin, "The Flying Lazarus," *op. cit.*
10. *St. Louis Post-Dispatch*, Sept. 30, 1982.
11. *Ibid.*, Feb. 28, 1983.
12. Defense Procurement Issue Papers, Project on Military Procurement, prepared by Donna Martin, August 1984.
13. Testimony of Ernest Fitzgerald before Senate Judiciary Subcommittee on Administrative Practices and Procedures, June 29, 1984.
14. *Ibid.*
15. *The Wall Street Journal*, June 30, 1983.
16. These AEGIS numbers are according to a *Wall Street Journal* article on Nov. 4, 1983.
17. Fitzgerald quotation taken from Dina Rasor, ed., *More Bucks, Less Bang* (Washington, D.C.: Fund for Constitutional Government, 1983), p. 310. Dr. James R. Anderson, *Bankrupting America: The*

Tax Burden and Expenditures of the Pentagon by Congressional District. (Lansing, Mich.: Employment Research Associates, 1984 ed.)

9. Beyond the Beltway

1. Weinberger excerpts taken from July 19, 1983 transcript of *Our Times,* by CBS News.
2. Dina Rasor, ed., *More Bucks, Less Bang* (Washington, D.C.: Fund for Constitutional Government, 1983), pp. 8–10.

INDEX

ABC (American Broadcasting
  Company), 9, 50–54, 55, 61, 94,
  194, 284
Adams, Bob, 209, 258, 260
Addabbo, Joseph, 130–31, 238, 245
AEGIS radar-equipped cruiser,
  273–75
Air Force, U.S., 98, 146
  bids handled by, 79–80
  C-5A wing fix and, 62–87, 94, 127,
    233
  C-5B cargo plane preferred by,
    233–60, 263–64
  Contract Management Division
    (CMD), 141, 200–201
  Financial Management Team,
    143, 144
  irresponsibility of, 68–69, 71–72
  Legislative Liaison Office, 241,
    251–52, 254, 257
  lobbying by, 232–33, 236–60
  overcharging of, 188–89, 192–93,
    196
  Zero Overpricing Program, 150, 168
  see also Defense Department, U.S.
Air Force Plant Representative
  Office (AFPRO), 141, 142, 160
Air Force System Command (AFSC),
  254, 268
Allen, Jim, 243
American Legion, 239
American University, 97
Amlie, Thomas, 99, 144, 166, 267
Anderson, Glenn, 245
Anderson, Jack, 70
Anderson, Roy, 256
Andrews, Mark, 125–27
anti-lobbying law, 257–60, 290
APEX engineering report, 68, 70

Army, U.S., 100–101, 115, 120, 134,
  146
  Aviation Development Test
    Activity, 142
  contractors dealing with, 201–5
  Defense Science Board, 142
  design biases of, 36
  information withheld by, 16–18,
    19–20, 25–26
  Logistics Evaluation Agency,
    20–21
  M-1 tank defended by, 3–48, 120,
    131, 209, 213–26
  Safety Center, 144
  see also Defense Department, U.S.
"Assessment C-5N versus KC-10
  versus 747F" (Rasor), 235
Associated Press, 226–27
Associated Press Radio, 51
AWACS plane, 46, 166

B-1 bomber, 143, 161, 238, 262
Badham, Robert E., 246
Baker, Howard, 237, 249
Ball, Duard, 224, 225
Batson, John, 190–91, 193
Battista, Anthony R., 117, 247
Bedell, Berkley, 163
Begin, Menachem, 51
Bell, Steve, 111
Bell Helicopter, 143–44
Bennett, Amanda, 221
Bennett, Charles, 192
Biddle, Wayne, 228–29
Black Congressional Caucus, 240,
  248
Boeing Aircraft, 143, 166, 201,
  234–36, 256
Boodnick, Marvin, 143